Don't Repot That Plant!

And Other Indoor Plant Care Mistakes

Don't Repot That Plant!

And Other Indoor Plant Care Mistakes

Will Creed

Button Street Press
Newfane, Vermont

Published by Button Street Press
PO Box 456, Newfane, Vermont 05345
www.buttonstreetpress.com

ISBN 978-1-939767-16-5

Publisher's Cataloging-In-Publication Data
(Prepared by The Donohue Group, Inc.)

Names: Creed, Will, 1943-
Title: Don't repot that plant! : and other indoor plant care mistakes / Will Creed.
Description: Newfane, Vermont : Button Street Press, [2017] | Includes index.
Identifiers: ISBN 978-1-939767-16-5
Subjects: LCSH: House plants.
Classification: LCC SB419 .C74 2017 | DDC 635.965--dc23

Dedication

This book is dedicated to the thousands of indoor plant owners who have sought my advice over the past 15 years. It is only through their questions that I have identified the most common plant problems and discovered the most common misunderstandings about indoor plant care. By listening to their questions, I have discovered the large gaps in plant information available in existing plant books and on the Internet. I have also learned how misleading and flat-out wrong much of the available information is. Although I cannot possibly anticipate every plant problem that will occur, I have written this book to fill in those gaps of information and to clarify the information obtained elsewhere.

This book is also dedicated to my son, Ben, who at the age of 12 insisted that I had to have a website, which he designed. That website served me well for 10 years and allowed me to reach out to and engage those who needed professional assistance with their plants.

To quote Christopher Kimball in his October 7, 2009 *New York Times* Op-Ed article,

"The world needs fewer opinions and more thoughtful expertise — the kind that comes from real experience, the hard-won blood-on-the-floor kind."

I think my book is consistent with Kimball's observation. Indeed, my first day on the job as a plant professional I managed to cut my finger and actually did leave some blood on the floor!

Contents

Getting Started

It all started badly decades ago when I knew nothing about caring for plants. My then-wife was traveling for a week and asked me to water her houseplants while she was away. Apparently, I had too much time on my hands so I decided to do a little research on how to properly care for houseplants. A popular houseplant book at the time recommended repotting plants every spring. It was spring, so I decided it was time to repot all of the plants. I was quite pleased to discover that as soon as I moved the largest plant into a new pot, I now had a liberated pot to move the next largest plant into. And so on down to the smallest pot. How satisfying it was to find a new home for each plant and to fill each one with fresh potting soil!

My former wife returned after a week and a couple of the plants already looked a bit wilted. "Just adjusting to their new spacious homes!" I proclaimed. After two weeks, more plants were wilted. After three weeks, several plants were clearly dying and most of the others were in decline.

Puzzled, I started searching other sources of plant information. Perhaps it was the light or the watering or the fertilizer or the humidity or maybe the temperature. I searched for evidence of plant pests. Every reliable source seemed to have a different opinion as to what those plants needed and what might be causing their decline. Partial sun or indirect light? Slightly dry or evenly moist? High or low nitrogen? Mist them or use a humidifier? Put them outside in the sun or keep them inside? Fungus or virus?

The more I read, the more confused I became. The plants weren't confused, though. They just continued their decline undeterred and abetted by my constant and ever-changing efforts to understand and revive them. I tried pruning, misting, pesticides, fungicides, and fertilizer. I moved them around from one location to another. Nothing seemed to matter as the plants continued to die and replacements were hastily purchased.

It wasn't until many years later that it finally dawned on me that the reason all my ex-wife's plants had deteriorated under my care was because of my over-zealous repotting. Nothing I had ever read suggested that repotting might not always be a good idea.

1 Read this First: Repotting

I answer thousands of indoor plant questions every year. Here is a typical inquiry that I received:

> Hello Will.
>
> I found your website on a recent article you've written on Allexperts.com.
>
> I love office/home plants and outdoor plants too! I discovered I have a green thumb about 10 years ago. Since then I fell in love with live plants.
>
> However, I just repotted some office plants that hadn't been repotted for years! I got a few from a coworker who passed away with breast cancer, so I took them on. My other coworker asked me to repot her plants too since I was repotting the others. Every plant that hasn't been repotted for years has now started drooping over, leaves falling off, etc. I believe part of the problem is I didn't use new soil (because I ran out), but I added the fertilizer spikes to them.
>
> I'm kind of embarrassed because my coworker who thought I was the "plant queen" in the office, but only to find the plants are starting to wither "after" I repotted them. I had to clip all the dead leaves off one only to hope new bulbs will pop back up soon.
>
> Any advice?
>
> Kathy (Name changed)

Unnecessary and improper repotting is the single most common cause of plant failure — *not* overwatering or poor light or pests or low humidity or lack of nutrients.

Similar inquiries about repotted plants describe the symptoms and speculate that something like overwatering or temperature or low humidity is the cause of the problem. Unlike Kathy, the questioner often fails to make the connection between the repotting and the start of the plant problems. Even in instances where repotting is appropriate, the repotting is usually done improperly.

Why is unnecessary repotting so common with indoor plant owners?

- Plant books, garden center employees, and other experts recommend repotting every spring. That may be a good practice for outdoor potted plants or those in a greenhouse, but not your houseplants.

- Our intuition tells us that if plants come from the earth, then their roots must prefer to have lots of room to grow. Although this seems logical, in fact, root growth and water flow dynamics are different in pots than in the earth.

- If roots look crowded, then we think that can't be good for them. After all, we don't like to be crowded. But plants aren't people and research has demonstrated that moderately crowded roots produce better foliage growth and more flowers. Repotting often deters new growth and flowers.

- If roots wander out of drainage holes, it must be because they are looking for more room. In reality, roots grow in all directions inside a pot and if a root or two grow through the drainage holes, it is just a matter of chance, not necessarily a search by the roots for more space.

- The plant looks too big for its pot or the plant leans or tips over because the plant is too tall. In reality, a plant's root system cannot be judged by the size of the plant. Large plants often have small root systems and vice-versa. A larger pot will rarely stabilize a leaning plant.

- We believe that a larger pot with lots of soil will help a plant grow faster and larger. In fact, soil doesn't determine plant growth. Sun, water, oxygen, and minerals do. Soil is nothing more than the medium that carries and distributes those last three. The volume of soil makes no difference in that equation.

- We think the soil is old and needs to be replenished or replaced. It takes many years for soil to become depleted of nutrients. When that occurs, the addition of small amounts of fertilizer will solve the nutrient deficiency problem far better and more easily than soil replacement or repotting.

- We often believe that our plants need and deserve lots of attention to keep them happy. We over water, over fertilize, mist, and repot our plants so as not to feel guilty about neglecting them. In fact, far more plants are killed by kindness than by neglect!

- The soil that plants are grown in appears cheap and dried out. In most cases, the soil that nursery growers use for your plant is specifically designed for that particular plant. That soil is better for your plant than anything you could replace it with.

- The soil is infested with crawling critters and needs to be replaced. In this case it is better to treat the critters than to replace all the soil. Submerging the pot up to its rim in a tub of water usually forces all critters to abandon ship in search of air. (See section on total soil replacement below.)

- The soil is soaking wet from being overwatered and needs to be replaced. (See section on total soil replacement below.) Again, it is better to let the existing soil dry out on its own. If the pot is not already too large for the plant, then the soil should dry out within a week or so.

- The plastic pot is ugly and needs to be replaced. The solution is to place the plant and its ugly pot inside of a more attractive planter of your choice. (See page 97 on double-potting)

- "And when my plant's are sick and not feeling well, the mother in me wants to comfort them by changing their dirt (or dirty diapers) into new fresh clean soil." Enough said!

- Repotting is fun! The feel and touch of the soil is pleasurable. Repotting gives us a chance to replace ugly plastic pots with more attractive ones. It looks neater and more uniform after we repot. Unfortunately, what satisfy your needs may not be good for your plants.

So resist that urge to repot your plant, especially a newly acquired one that is already under stress from being in a new location. You may want to repot for any or all of the reasons above, but it is important not to. If you do repot, there is a very good chance that your plant will develop problems — maybe not right away, but within a few months.

Why most houseplants rarely need to be repotted

In a nursery or greenhouse where growing conditions are ideal, plant growth is rapid. Just the right amount of light intensity is provided not just from one side but from overhead as well as from all sides. The foliage grows larger and the roots grow similarly. It is common practice for plants in these carefully controlled environments to get "stepped-up" one pot size several times each year in order to accommodate this rapid growth of the root system.

In your home or office, conditions are far

This is a healthy plant in a 4-inch pot with a good root system about ready to be moved to a 5- or 6-inch pot

Extremely potbound Rhapis Palm that is healthy nonetheless

less ideal. The light comes through a window from one direction only. This reduction in light causes the growth rate of indoor plants to decrease slowly but dramatically over the course of several months. Pumping up the plant with fertilizer will not help, as light is the controlling growth factor. The reduction in growth means the roots also stop expanding and even gradually shrink back over the long term. Those roots that seemed to fill the pot when the plant was new, now have plenty of room. There simply is no reason to move this plant into a larger pot, but lots of reasons not to do it.

The Risks of Repotting

How does repotting cause problems? All plant roots need oxygen, as well as water, to survive. Plants that are kept in constantly wet or soggy soil are deprived of oxygen and soon begin to rot. That is why *it is important for potted plants to dry out regularly, every week or so.* That is also why we are warned not to leave potted plants standing in water. This drying out process is all about allowing oxygen back into the soil so the roots can use it. If there is an excess of soil surrounding the roots, then it will take an extra long time for the soil to dry out and the roots may begin to rot as they are deprived of oxygen. At first, this will not be noticeable. However, after several weeks or months, the roots will gradually deteriorate until they are no longer able to absorb water for the plant. Then the plant itself will start to show symptoms of water deprivation. At this point it is usually too late, as the roots have already died.

A plant potted in a pot that is too big is like a plant left standing in water.

Although root rot is the primary risk in repotting unnecessarily, introducing fungus gnats to your plant and home is another common problem that accompanies repotting. Packaged potting mixes are often infested with nearly invisible fungus gnat larvae. Those larvae will soon emerge from the soil as tiny flying gnats and they are not easy to eradicate. (See Chapter 10 on Plant Pests.)

Do you still want to repot? Then, read on…but don't say I didn't warn you!

When to Repot

Sometimes it is good to repot, but much less often than is commonly believed. How can you tell? Here is the easiest and most reliable way to tell — and you won't find this method discussed anywhere else!

If, after a thorough watering, a potted plant dries out sufficiently so that it needs water again in less than three days, then it is okay to move your plant into a pot one size larger.

Yes, it's that simple. You don't even have to take the plant out of its pot to inspect the roots. If you notice your plant needs water every day or two, then it may be ready for more soil to hold water without the risk of rotting the roots — provided you do it properly, as described below.

Plants in small pots (2 to 5 inches) are more likely to need repotting than plants in larger pots (10 to 14 inches). In fact, many houseplants that are purchased in large pots may never need to be repotted. The rule of thumb provided above takes pot size into account automatically.

How to Repot

Note: I am frequently asked how to water, prune, fertilize and treat pests, but almost never how to repot. All of the information that follows assumes that your plant is healthy and has a very extensive root system. If not, you should not repot. Repotting is not as simple as it seems.

1. Repot about 24 hours after watering. That way the roots will be less vulnerable to damage and the soil and rootball will stay together when you take it from its pot. You must have the right size and shape pot to move your plant into. The new pot should be either one or two inches wider and deeper than the old pot. If it is in a shallow pot, then keep it in a shallow pot. And, of course, only use a pot with a drainage hole.

2. You must have a good potting mix available to add to the existing rootball. Try to match the new potting mix to the type that the plant is already planted in. Different soil types include sandy or Cactus soil mixes, porous or succulent mixes, soilless peat-based mixes, and airy epiphytic or Orchid mixes. Avoid changing potting mixes. The nursery grower used the right mix and plants love consistency.

3. Gently loosen the soil and roots around the outside of the rootball. Use your fingers or a fork or a sturdy pointed object to loosen tightly wrapped roots. It's perfectly okay if some of the outer roots get torn or broken — it will not hurt the plant. This loosening of the roots will help them integrate better into the new potting mix that you are adding. Do not remove any soil from the interior of the rootball.

4. Add about an inch of new mix to the bottom of the new pot. Do **not** put a layer of stones or gravel or other drainage material at the bottom of the pot. This is an out-dated practice that has been discredited. Set the plant on top of the new potting mix and see where the top of the rootball is relative to the top edge of the pot. It should be one half to one inch below the rim. If the plant is more than one inch below, then add some soil underneath the rootball. If it is sitting too high, then remove some soil from underneath. *Never adjust soil height by adding soil to the top of the rootball.*

5. Place the plant in the center of the pot and then add soil all around the sides, pressing it firmly as you go. Do **not** add new soil to the top of the rootball even if some roots are partly exposed at the top.

6. Slowly add water all around the surface of the soil. You may notice that some of the new potting mix sinks in and more soil may have to be added to be able to get it up even with the top of the original rootball.

Root Pruning

Root pruning is an alternative to repotting if you are happy with the size of your plant and do not ever want to move it into a larger pot. An example of this would be a spider plant or an asparagus fern that has outgrown its 10-inch hanging pot and it is getting too big and heavy for a larger pot, assuming you can even find one. Another example is a plant that is double-potted inside of a decorative

3 Evaluating Light for Plants

Read this chapter carefully. Nothing is more important for your plants than to put them where they can get the proper amount of light. If the light level is wrong, nothing else will compensate for it.

All plants have a limited range of light intensity that they can tolerate. If the light intensity is outside the plant's tolerance range, it will die; slowly if it is barely outside the range; quickly if it is way outside the range. There is no substitute for light. You can't replace light with plant food or more water or a bigger pot or better humidity. So first and foremost you must provide your plant with the correct light intensity range.

Too Much Light!

Many folks are surprised that their indoor plants can actually get too much light. After all, isn't lots of light good for plants? Well, it depends on the plant species. Most commonly used indoor potted plants grow naturally under the heavily shaded tropical forest canopy so they are adapted to deep shade and suffer when exposed to intense direct sun.

So do a little research before you place your plant on that sunny south windowsill or before you move it outside into the direct sun in the warmer months.

There is lots of confusion about the commonly described light intensity levels. Most plant owners tend to over-estimate the amount of available light, so I will try to shed some light on the subject (pun intended) by explaining these commonly used terms that describe the light intensity ranges:

Direct Sun

This is also called unfiltered light. It is the light that comes in a window on a sunny day; the light that falls directly on the plant's leaves. This light will cast a sharp, clearly defined shadow on a piece of paper. Direct sun is what you get all day long right in front of an unobstructed south-facing window; or what you get in the afternoon in an un-shaded west-facing window; or in the morning in an un-shaded east-facing window. North-facing windows do not get any direct sun in the northern hemisphere. Of course the sun moves and the direct sun rays coming in a window move as well. So many indoor locations receive direct sun for part of the day and indirect for part of the day. Direct sun is what "high light" plants usually require.

Indirect Sunlight

Also called filtered light. This is any natural light that does not include the direct rays of the sun. It refers to locations where the direct sun rays are screened by trees, buildings, porches, roof overhangs, walls, and sheer curtains. Light cast by indirect light yields fuzzy-edged shadows. Indirect light is what you get all day in a north-facing window; or in the morning in a west-facing window; or in the afternoon in an east-facing window. Direct sun can be filtered by using sheer curtains or by placing a plant off to the side of a window and out of the direct rays of the sun. Indirect sun is what all "low light" and many "medium light" plants require.

Plants in very bright indirect light just beyond the direct rays of the sun receive about 90–95% less light than plants in direct sunlight. That's a very big difference!

Bright Light and Low Light

These are variations of indirect light. Bright light is indirect light that is barely outside the range of direct sun. Bright light might include a couple of hours of direct sunlight as the sun moves during the day. Low light is further away from the sun's rays than is bright light and never includes any direct sun. Low light is often the minimum light possible for any plant to survive. A low light rule of thumb: If the light is too dim to comfortably read newsprint throughout the day, then it is too low for long-term survival of any plant. If your "low light" is suitable for a romantic mood, then it is not enough for your plants. So think about low light for plants a little differently than you might otherwise.

Outdoor Light vs. Indoor Light

Because our eyes adjust rapidly and unconsciously to changing light levels, we underestimate how much more intense sunlight is outdoors as compared to sun coming indoors through a window. Outdoor light is not filtered through glass and it comes from all directions, including overhead. Indoors, plants usually receive light from one direction only. You may have noticed that many indoor plants orient their leaves in the direction of the light source, usually the window. This is an indication of the difference in light intensity.

Artificial Light

When it comes to healthy plant growth, artificial light is rarely as good as natural light because only natural sunlight contains light from the full color spectrum. Standard incandescent bulbs produce light in the portion of the light spectrum that is not conducive to good plant growth. Special incandescent grow or plant lights are color corrected for plants, but are prohibitively expensive for most people to operate for the required 8–10 hours per day.

Standard fluorescent bulbs are relatively inexpensive and produce light in the spectral range useful to plants. Many office plants thrive because they receive lots of overhead fluorescent light. The spiral CFL's used in home lamps work moderately well if the plants are within a few feet of the bulbs.

LED's are relatively new on the market and are expensive initially, but have the longest life span and are the most energy efficient. Look for LED's that are color corrected for plant growth.

At best, artificial lights produce adequate light for low to medium light plants and then only if they are on for at least 8 to 10 hours every day and are located close to the plants. In many instances, they are best used as a supplement rather than a substitute for natural light.

Light and Distance

How far away from the window or primary light source a plant is located makes a huge difference. Light intensity drops off dramatically with each foot of distance away from the source. Light intensity drops to half at a distance of a foot; to one-third at 3 feet away; to one-fifth at 4 feet; and one-tenth at a distance of 5 feet. In general, plants should be within 6 feet of a sunny window that gets lots of direct sunlight and within 3 feet of a north-facing window with indirect light.

High, Medium and Low Light Plants

Many people are surprised to learn that more light is not always better for plants. In fact, the most commonly used indoor plants grow in the deep shade of the tropical rainforest. They have adapted over the eons to live in low light and cannot tolerate direct sunlight. Of course, there are other plants that are suited for direct sunlight because that is what they receive in their natural habitat. These sun-loving plants suffer if they are not in a very sunny window indoors. Finally, there are plants whose light requirements are in a middle range between shade and direct sunlight.

All indoor plants can be placed in one of three light intensity groups:

- **High light plants** must have some direct sunlight for at least several hours per day and bright indirect light for the rest of the day. South and west facing windows are the best locations for these plants. No more than a few feet from the window.

- **Medium light plants** must have bright indirect light all day long and can often tolerate a couple of hours of direct sunlight. East and north facing windows are the favored locations for these plants.
- **Low light plants** must be protected from direct sunlight at all times. They thrive in bright indirect light, but will often tolerate minimum light levels. These plants prefer locations close to a north window or away from an east, west, or south-facing window where they are protected from the direct rays of the sun. No more than 6 feet from the window.

You must know which light category your plants belong in so you can locate them properly. Go to http://www.foliagedesign.com/products/live-plants/ for a color photo listing of indoor plants by light category. Many plant problems occur because they are in the wrong light intensity location. If you are having a problem with a plant, then check the light level first.

Symptoms of Inadequate Light: Plants that are not receiving enough light often have a spindly, elongated, stretched looking appearance. The spaces between the nodes (the points where the leaves attach to the stem) on the stem are elongated. The leaves themselves are often small and puny looking. These are *not* signs of inadequate nutrition so do *not* fertilize plants with these symptoms. Prune them back and provide more light for them. That is the only remedy.

Symptoms of Too Much Light: Too much light will cause plant foliage to turn pale green or yellow and in extreme cases brown and dry. Contrary to what some ads suggest, adding plant food will not restore the color to these bleached out leaves. The solution is to protect the plant from the direct rays of the sun by moving the plant. Foliage tissue damaged by excess light will not recover, so trim it off.

Once you have your plants situated in the right light, you have taken a major step toward having a green thumb and maintaining healthy plants. Below are some guidelines that will help you select the right plant plants for various locations in your indoor space.

Low Light

Low light is not *no* light or light so dim you could not read comfortably throughout the day. All plants, other than mushrooms, require at least some light and even the low light plants listed below require more light than most people realize. Low light is bright enough to read newsprint all day long. It is a location within a couple of feet of an uncovered north facing window and within 6 feet of a south facing uncovered window. Keep in mind that sheers, a porch overhang, large tree or tall building outside the window can substantially reduce the intensity of the light.

Heart-leafed philodendron (*Philodendron scandens oxycardium*): is similar to the Pothos but somewhat more fragile. The leaves are a deep shade of green and are thinner. In most cases, a Pothos is a better choice.

Corn plant (*Dracaena fragrans massangeana*): This plant is commonly grown with several thick, bark-covered canes of staggered heights. The foliage grows at the top of each cane. The leaves are broad and long and sometimes variegated with stripes of yellow-green. Overall, this is a tall and slender plant that is good for a corner that receives little light. It is sold in heights from three to eight feet tall. Be careful not to overwater this plant. The corn plant is nearly pest-free.

Janet Craig (*Dracaena deremensis* 'Janet Craig'): is a close relative of the corn plant. It has very dark green, naturally glossy leaves. It is a fuller plant than the corn plant with leaves all along the stems. The leaves are sensitive to the buildup of minerals from fertilizers, hard water, and fluoride as the plant ages. It is a pest-free plant. It is available in heights from three to five feet.

Lisa (*Dracaena deremensis* 'Lisa'): is much like the Janet Craig but it is taller with a more slender profile so it fits well in corner spaces. It holds up much better than almost any other low light plant. It comes in heights of 4.5 to 8 feet. It is an expensive plant, but is a good value. The better quality 'Lisas' are potted in a volcanic cinder mix.

Snake plant (*Sansevieria*): has a reputation as a plant that is tough to kill. If you tend to neglect your plants, then this is the plant for you. As a succulent, it can go for a month without water when kept in low light. It will not need fertilizer or high humidity and will stay in the same pot for years if it is in low light. This plant can adapt more readily than most low light plants to bright light. In good light, the snake plant grows rapidly and puts up new growth with such vigor that it will bend and break its pot! The snake plant comes in a range of sizes from a few inches to 4 feet tall. It is ideal for any location that needs a vertical emphasis. Cuttings root easily in moist soil. Pests are rarely a problem.

Parlor palm (*Chamadorea neanthe bella elegans*): This plant is the Palm of choice for a table that is in low light. It is a quiet, unobtrusive plant that adds just the right touch in many locations. Although it doesn't use much water, it doesn't tolerate dry roots very well. It is also prone to spider mite infestations. This Palm is often included in small dish gardens. It rarely grows taller than three feet.

ZZ Plant (*Zamioculcas Zamifolia*): This is a relatively recent introduction and not one you inherited from your grandmother. It is the closest thing to an easy plant to care for. It is adaptable to almost any light exposure, including low light. It thrives on neglect and can survive a month or more without water. However, if you keep it in its nursery pot it will do better with more frequent watering. As long as you do not unnecessarily repot or overwater this plant, it will do very well for you. It grows slowly and rarely needs repotting.

Lucky Bamboo (*Dracaena sanderiana*): is a very popular plant that is most often sold in a small vase or planter filled with decorative stones and water. It is easy to care for because all it requires is for you to keep the water level above the visible roots or the decorative pebbles. The stems can be cut back and inserted in the water where they will root.

Peace Lily (*Spathiphyllum*): is a very popular low light plant because it will bloom in moderately low light. The flowers are white hood-shaped flowers. It also has beautiful, large, shiny green leaves. There are dozens of hybrid varieties that range in size from 6 inches to nearly 5 feet. The peace lily must stay in moist soil. It collapses pathetically as soon as the soil becomes a bit too dry, but it recovers rapidly when the water is replenished. It is not a good choice for those who prefer to ignore their plants for long stretches. It is relatively pest free, but it is vulnerable to cold temperatures, root diseases, and the buildup of excess minerals in the soil.

Cast iron plant (*Aspidistra*): is well named because of its toughness and adaptability. It has broad, dark green, glossy leaves at the end of short stems. It rarely grows taller than three feet. It tolerates occasional over and under watering better than most plants. Spider mites appear when the air is dry. Its overall look is similar to the peace lily without the flower. This is a slow-growing plant, so it is more expensive than most and you are unlikely to find it at a Big Box store.

5 Full Sun Plants for Indoors Use

It may come as a surprise, but many of the most popular houseplants cannot tolerate full or direct sun. Dracaenas, Philodendrons, Dieffenbachias, Peace Lilies, Chinese evergreens, and Lucky Bamboo are among those plants that need protection from full sun.

But there are many plants that will thrive in direct sun. If you are fortunate enough to have a full sun location for your indoor plants, then this chapter will help you select an appropriate species.

What is Full Sun?

The answer to this question is not as obvious as you might think. Full sun is what you get when the sun's rays come through the window and fall directly on the leaves of a plant for all or most of the daylight hours. This is also called direct sun.

To get full sun in the northern hemisphere, you must have a window that faces mostly south or southwest and the plant must be within 4–6 feet of that window. That window must be unobstructed by window coverings, awnings, overhangs, trees or buildings. So full or direct sun is not commonly available for most houseplants because most folks want some type of protection from the direct sun in their homes. However, many office buildings do provide direct sun, particularly if they are on an upper floor.

What is Partial Sun?

Partial sun is direct sunlight that falls on a plant's leaves for only part of the day. Partial direct sun is provided by an eastern window that provides direct sun in the morning or by a southern window that is covered by blinds that are partly closed.

Partial sun is more commonly available in homes. Check the location for your plant. If it has direct sun coming through the window for about 3-5 hours per day, then it is a partial sun location.

Outdoor Light

Although this book is about indoor plants, I know many folks like to move their plants outside in the warmer months. Low light plants are not good candidates to move outside because the light is too intense for them. Full and partial sun plants can be moved outdoors, but only if you recognize the difference between indoor and outdoor light intensity. Outdoor light can be anywhere from 100 to 1,000 times more intense than indoor light.

A plant that does well in full sun indoors, will burn if put in direct sun outdoors. If you move your plants outside, make sure they are in a shaded location — on a covered porch, under an overhang, on the north side of the house or under a shade tree.

High Light Plants

Indoor plants that require at least several hours of direct sun each day are generally categorized as full sun or high light plants by many retail stores and plant books. What follows is information on the best plant species that require and do well as high light plants.

Hanging Plants for High Light

Spider Plant (*Chlorophytum comosum*): These plants do best when hung in a sunny window with at least several hours of direct sun. Their gracefully arching leaves fill a window space nicely while still allowing a view through the slender leaves. Water thoroughly as soon as the surface of the soil is dry. In good light, these plants quickly outgrow their pots. When they need water every day or two, then it is time to move them up one pot size or to divide the rootball in half.

Asparagus Fern (*Asparagus densiflorus*): This plant is not actually a fern, but is a close relative of the edible Asparagus. It has care requirements very similar to the Spider Plant. Keep it moist and repot or divide it when the tuberous roots fill the pot. Unlike the Spider Plant, the Asparagus Fern is very prone to spider mites, especially in dry winter air. See Chapter 10 on identifying and treating spider mites.

Wax Plant (*Hoya carnosa*): This is an under-appreciated hanging plant that grows slowly and thrives on neglect. However, it will reward you with beautiful clusters of small white flowers with star-shaped red centers. Keep it potbound and allow it to dry deep down into the pot before watering and don't change its location. To enhance flowering, disturb it as little as possible by not relocating or repotting it. Do not use a high nitrogen fertilizer and do not feed it at all during the winter months. Overfeeding causes bud drop. After the flowers are spent, don't remove the flower stalk because that is where new flowers will emerge the following year.

Wandering Jew (*Zebrina pendula*): This once popular houseplant has fallen out of favor and is no longer as readily available. To do well, this plant must have lots of full sun and should be watered well as soon as the soil surface feels dry. It is a fast grower in these conditions and will need regular pruning in order to maintain its shape. Pruning is where most people fall down with this plant because they are reluctant to prune. Failure to prune will lead to a long, stringy plant. See Chapter 11 to learn more about pruning.

Larger Plants for High Light

Ficus species: This includes Weeping Fig (*Ficus benjamina*), Rubber Plant (*Ficus elastica*), Fiddle-leaf Fig (*Ficus lyrata*), and Banana-leaf Fig (*Ficus alii*). These are all excellent choices for locations close to uncovered windows. Although all of them can adapt to very bright indirect light (a north or east window location), they will thrive if given several hours of direct sun every day. Most of these Ficus species are sold in large sizes and will eventually become quite large, so make sure you have room before buying them.

Yucca cane (*Yucca elephantipes*): This plant is often mistaken for the Corn Plant or *Dracaena massangeana* cane because both are potted as multiple, staggered height canes and both have long, strap-like leaves. Unlike the low-light Corn Plant, the Yucca cane thrives in direct sun. In full sun, the leaves and stems grow thick and sturdy whereas in reduced light they tend to be thinner and weaker. Keep your Yucca cane moderately potbound and water it thoroughly when the top inch of soil feels dry to the touch. Fertilize monthly at half strength. This is a pest resistant plant. See page 263 for more detailed information on Yucca care.

Areca Palm (*Chrysalidocarpus lutescens*) and Pygmy Date Palm (*Phoenix roebelenii*): These are two very different looking palms, but they have similar requirements. Both do best with lots of direct sun and soil that is kept moist. Water them as soon as the soil surface is nearly dry. If you wait too long, you will soon see yellowed fronds and spider mites. On the other hand, do not leave these palms sitting in water for more than a few hours. Both palms should be fertilized monthly at half-strength. Lower fronds yellow naturally as new fronds are added on top. Remove then once they start to discolor. See page 221 for more detailed information on Palm care.

Bird of Paradise (*Strelitzia reginae* and *Strelitzia nicolai*): This is a demanding

plant that produces beautiful bird-shaped flowers when grown outdoors in full sun in semi-tropical climates. As an indoor plant, it rarely flowers so it is best selected because of its very large paddle-like leaves, not its flowers. In good conditions this plant grows larger, especially in

width, so make sure you have adequate space. Indoors, it needs a sunny location indoors and should be watered as soon as the surface of the soil is dry. Fertilize it monthly at half-strength. Watch for spider mites, mealybugs and scale insects. See Chapter 10 for information on treating these plant pests.

Drought Resistant Plants for High Light

Cacti: There are hundreds of Cacti species available. Virtually all of them need direct sun if they are to survive for a long time. Cacti are easy to care for when given good light. A thorough watering monthly during the shorter days of winter and every 2 or 3 weeks during the longer, warmer days of summer is about right for most Cacti. They rarely if ever need repotting and require fertilizer only occasionally. These are very low maintenance plants when given lots of direct sun.

Jade Plant (*Crassula argentea*): Jades can survive and do moderately well in bright indirect light, but they thrive in full sun. Direct sun will help this plant develop thick sturdy stems and create a slight reddish tinge on the edges of the leaves. They do best if kept in small, terra cotta pots that do not tip easily. Water thoroughly when the top inch of soil feels dry. Prune it back regularly to keep it from becoming ungainly and to prevent it from tipping over. Repot it rarely, if ever. Fertilize it monthly in the summer at half-strength. Watch for mealybugs and scale insects. See Chapter 10 for information on identifying and treating these plant pests and page 180 for more detailed information on Jade Plant care.

Ponytail Palm (*Beaucarnea recurvata*): This is another plant that will do fine in bright indirect light (a north windowsill), but thrives in full sun. As with many other species, in full sun this plant will grow faster with thicker stems and leaves. Do *not* overwater this plant! The large base bulb can store water during periods of drought, but the roots will rot quickly if the soil is not allowed to regularly dry out deep into the pot. Keep it very potbound and water it only when the soil is dry halfway down into the pot, typically every two weeks or so. See page 244 for more detailed information on Ponytail Palms.

Snake Plant (*Sansevieria trifasciata*): This is a plant that is incorrectly listed in many places as a low light plant. It may survive for a year or so in low light, but soon after that it will suddenly fall apart. In full sun, this plant will grow strong and sturdy and will soon outgrow its pot. Yet, it will thrive on neglect if you forget to water it and never fertilize or repot it. In strong light it is almost indestructible. It is best to allow the soil to become quite dry in between waterings as constantly moist soil will rot the roots. You can fertilize it monthly at half strength and repot it only when it is so potbound that it is bending the shape of the pot. It is tolerant of a wide range of temperatures and is resistant to most plant pests. See page 257 for more detailed information on Snake Plants.

Succulents: This is a broad category of mostly small plants. Many of these species grow in tiny crevices in rocky areas where the soil and moisture is meager and the sun is direct. Other than needing lots of light, they are low maintenance plants that grow slowly and stay small. They rarely need repotting. Water your Sedum only when the soil is completely dry and fertilize it no more than once or twice per year. These plants do not like to be fussed over!

Aloe vera: Bright indirect light is adequate for this plant, but it benefits from several hours of direct sun each day. In good light it produces lots of baby plants (called offsets) that soon fill up the pot and provide ample leaves to cut and squeeze the sap for minor burns and skin irritations. This succulent can withstand drought, but not constantly damp soil. So, keep it in a small pot and allow the soil to dry out halfway down into the pot in between waterings. Fertilize monthly at half strength. Watch for mealybugs and scale. (See Chapter 10 for information on treating plant pests). Breaking off leaves to use for skin irritations will not harm the plant in any way.

Crown of thorns (*Euphorbia milli*): is an unusual looking plant with Cactus like stems, prominent thorns, small green leaves and small red flowers. Surprisingly, it is a relative of the Poinsettia and has white sap that is a skin irritant for some people. It is not a good plant where children and pets are about.

It does best in direct sun, such as a south or west window, but will tolerate lower light. Lower light will discourage flowering. Keep it tightly potted in a sandy or porous potting mix so the roots don't stay wet for too long after watering. Allow the soil to become quite dry in between waterings. Fertilize very sparingly — once or twice per year at half strength. It can withstand temps from 50 to 95°, but it does best in normal room temperatures. Cool temps in the low 60's in the fall and winter when the days are short will help encourage more flowers. Propagate new plants from cuttings that are allowed to dry overnight before they are planted in a porous potting mix.

Colorful Plants for High Light

Croton (*Codiaeum variegatum pictum*): These are very colorful foliage plants. In direct sun and cool temperatures, they have brilliant red, yellow and green leaves that far outshine their rather insignificant flowers. These are not easy plants to care for because they are not forgiving of watering lapses and are very prone to spider mites. They also do best in cool temperatures below 75°, which is hard to maintain because Crotons also like lots of direct sun. For that reason, they often do better in winter than in summer. Always water as soon as the soil surface is dry as they wilt badly and drop leaves if the soil becomes too dry. Keep it potbound and fertilize it monthly at half strength. Poor light and inadequate water will cause extensive lower leaf loss. The only cure for leggy Crotons is to prune them back sharply.

Bromeliads: These brilliantly colored flowering plants are in the Pineapple family. With a couple of hours of direct sun each day their flowers will last up to six months, far longer than any other plant species. They are very easy to care for and very pest resistant. Water the soil (not the cup as is commonly recommended) thoroughly when the surface of the soil feels very dry. Fertilize the soil every month or two at half strength. Bromeliads do not need repotting. Eventually the flower begins to brown and very slowly die. Cut off the flower stem when the flower is no longer attractive. Some people discard the plant at that point because it will not flower again. Others keep it as a foliage plant that sends up baby plants or offsets from the base of the plant. For more information on Bromeliads see page 129.

Purple passion (Gynura aurantiaca): This plant's leaves look and feel like purple velvet. Very fine purple hairs that cover the leaves create this appearance. It does best hanging in a sunny window where the purple color will be more vibrant. In bright indirect light it will develop a greener color and the spaces between the leaves will elongate. Water thoroughly as soon as the surface of the soil feels dry. Keep the foliage dry when watering and don't mist it. Resist the urge to repot it because it grows better when potbound. Fertilize monthly at half strength when it is growing actively. In good conditions it will produce small yellow flowers. Many people find the odor of these flowers objectionable and cut them off before they open. Like most hanging/vining plants, this plant should be pruned back before it looks like it needs to be pruned back. See Chapter 11 for more detailed information on pruning.

Other High Light Plants

Below are some other possibilities for full sun. However, most of these are either hard to find or hard to care for indoors or both.

Banana plant	Citrus trees	Coleus	Datura
Desert Rose	Geranium	Hibiscus	Kalanchoe
Madagascar Palm	Majesty Palm[1]	Mandevilla	Pepper plant
Purple Heart	Senecio (String of beads)		Sweet potato vine

---

1 not recommended

6 How to Water a Potted Plant

The single most important thing you can do for your indoor plants is to put them in the proper light (see Chapter 3). But the most challenging thing to learn about plants is how to water them. Much of the confusion stems from our lack of mutually agreed upon terms to describe soil moisture content. "Evenly moist," "slightly dry," "barely damp," "never dry," "no wet feet": these are all commonly used terms to describe soil moisture levels for plants. In fact, I have seen all of these terms used to describe the preferred moisture level for the same plant. Compounding this terminology problem is the lack of agreement on what these terms mean. If five plant experts stick their fingers into the same pot of soil, they will give you five different verbal expressions to describe the soil moisture level. No wonder so many plant owners are confused about how and when to water.

Don't worry; watering plants properly is not an impossible task that only those born with a sixth sense or a green thumb can divine. However, it will take a little understanding, some observation, and lots of practice. That is the challenge. Meet it and you will be a bona fide green thumb.

A Watering Secret: Properly watering a potted plant is not about really about watering. It is really about allowing the soil to dry out properly.

Roots and Water

All plants must have some water to survive. They obtain that water primarily through their roots. Plant roots also must absorb oxygen for the plant. The oxygen must come from the same place we get it — the air. Just like humans, plants will drown if they are flooded with water and denied the opportunity to receive air. Have you ever seen bubbles percolate to the surface when you water a plant? Those are air bubbles that form when water enters the soil and pushes out the tiny pockets of air around the roots. The bubbles are proof that air is present in the soil when it is dry. As the soil is allowed to dry out the air returns to the soil and fills the spaces around the roots. The cycle of soil watering and drying allows plants to receive both water and oxygen, the two ingredients plant roots must have regularly and consistently.

Soil Structure

Soil structure refers to the size and percentage of air pockets in the potting soil. Most plants prefer a porous soil structure — one that is made up of coarse particles and has many, good-sized air pockets throughout. A dense soil structure has very fine closely packed soil particles that have very tiny air spaces. Porous soil is more efficient at providing oxygen to plant roots; dense soil is better able to retain water for roots. Which is better? Most plants require a soil that can both retain water and also provide air spaces. For plants such as ferns, water retention is more important. For cacti and succulents, porosity is more essential. That is why there are different soil mixes made for different plant groups.

Water: How often? How much?

Once you understand that potting soil is like a sponge that will absorb water, but also contains lots of air pockets, then you will be better able to understand when and how to water.

Professional Secret: The vast majority of commonly used indoor plants have the same watering requirement. If you can master this common requirement, you will not have to make subtle distinctions from one plant to another.

How much water? Plants that are correctly potted should always be watered thoroughly. That means pouring water from the top over the entire surface of the soil and letting it slowly seep into and penetrate the entire rootball. A small amount of water running through the drainage holes as an indication that the soil is totally saturated. Saturation means all of the air pockets in the soil are filled with water. **IMPORTANT NOTE:** Put saucers under all of your plants to catch the excess water that runs through. If you don't have saucers, then you will be tempted to not water thoroughly because you want to avoid water dripping on your furnishings.

How often should you water? After a thorough watering, as described above, all of the air pockets in the soil are filled with water. As the roots slowly absorb this water and as evaporation takes place, these water-filled pockets are gradually emptied and replaced with air. This is important because the roots need not only water, but also oxygen. If the soil is not allowed to dry out adequately, then the roots will rot. So the critical question is: How long does it take for the soil to properly dry out after a thorough watering? Plant care would be so much easier if there was a single answer to that question. Unfortunately, many factors contribute to the time needed for saturated soil to dry out. Pot size, soil porosity, plant species, air temperature and humidity, and available light are some of the more important variables that will affect how fast your plants will dry out. So if someone tells you to water your plants "once per week" or "every other day" or "at every quarter moon phase," don't believe them! There is no formula or schedule that applies to all plants or plant species or even from one environment to another.

How do you tell when the soil is properly dry? If the calendar is of no use in answering this question and you can't see inside the pot, then how do you know when the soil is dry enough to water it again? You have to use your senses and powers of observation. Your most important tool is your finger. If you are new to this, you must stick your finger down an inch or so into the soil every day after you have watered thoroughly. After one day, the soil will probably feel pretty wet. If you pinch some of the wet soil together between your fingers, you will observe that the soil clings together. This means the soil is still too moist to water. Repeat this finger test daily until you notice that the soil feels almost completely dry and powdery and that it no longer holds together when pinched. Now the soil is dry enough for you to give it a thorough watering. Follow this same procedure after the second watering. You will find that it usually takes the same plant about the same amount of time to dry out following each thorough watering. It might be a couple of days or ten days, but now you will know how often to water that particular plant. **IMPORTANT NOTE:** Cacti, succulents (plants with fleshy stems or leaves), epiphytes (Orchids, Anthuriums, and Bromeliads), and Ferns are exceptions to this finger test. Succulents must dry halfway down into the pot. Ferns must be watered as soon as the surface of the soil feels dry.

Some Helpful Watering Guidelines

Here are some general guidelines that help determine how often your plants need water.

- Plants in small pots dry out more quickly than plants in larger pots.
- Potbound plants dry out more quickly than recently repotted plants and are less prone to root rot.
- Plants in high light dry out more quickly than those in low light.
- Dry air dries out soil more quickly than humid air.

- Higher temperatures dry out plants more quickly than lower temperatures.

- Healthy, vigorously growing plants use more water than weak or slow growing plants.

You should be aware of these guidelines each time you relocate or repot your plant and as the seasons change. Thus, watering schedules for plants must change to reflect these environmental changes. Ironically, seasonal changes may cancel themselves out. Take for example, a window plant in the winter: It will receive less light than in summer, but its reduced need for water may be compensated for by an increased need for water as the heat comes on and the humidity drops. The only way to tell is to continue to use the finger test before you water. The more frequently you use your finger, the more sensitive you will become to subtle variations in the soil moisture level.

Limits to the Water/Dry-out Cycle

I reiterate that potted plants should be watered thoroughly and then allowed to dry out to allow oxygen to reenter the air spaces in the soil. I have mentioned the many factors that contribute to the period of time in this wet to dry cycle. Because most plant roots cannot go long periods of time without oxygen, it is important for the soil to become sufficiently dry within two weeks. If your plant still feels quite damp after two weeks, your plant's roots may be slowly rotting. In most cases, the cause for this extended time needed for soil drying is too large a pot with too much soil or inadequate light. Unnecessary repotting often leads to inadvertent overwatering (See Chapter 1) . At the other extreme, a plant that dries out in a day or two following a thorough watering may be ready to go into a larger pot. The extra soil in a slightly bigger pot will act as a sponge that will retain water for a longer period of time.

Moisture Meters

These devices are commonly sold and are seductively simple. You put the soil probe into the soil and a gauge immediately tells you if the soil is wet, dry or somewhere in-between on a numerical scale. In reality, moisture meters do not actually measure moisture content. They measure the degree of electrical conductivity of the soil. Because water is an excellent conductor of electricity, the operating assumption is that the more moisture in the soil, the greater the conductivity which the meter translates into a "wet" reading. All of this is true, but incomplete. Certain minerals are also excellent electrical conductors. For example, a glass of salty water is a much better conductor of electricity than a glass of distilled or mineral-free water. In addition, a highly compacted soil conducts electricity much more than a loose, porous soil with lots of air pockets. Soil with lots of mineral salts from using hard water or fertilizer will also give artificially high moisture meter readings. This means that a moisture meter may mistakenly give a "wet" reading for dry soil that is either compacted or has lots of minerals (excess fertilizer) in it. Conversely, a very porous soil with a low mineral content will read "dry" on the meter when the soil is still damp.

Unfortunately, there is no such thing as a standard potting soil so there is no practical way for you to know about the mineral content or compaction of the soil for any particular plant. Thus, you have no way of knowing if your meter reading is really accurate for any given plant. It is like Russian roulette - more often than not, a meter is reasonably accurate, but periodically it will mislead you badly and you will kill your plant. Moreover, moisture meters appear to be so scientifically accurate that people will ignore their own common sense when it conflicts with their "more scientific" meter reading. That is why I don't recommend their use. I advise people to get used to poking their finger into the soil and understanding that when the surface feels nearly dry, there is still sufficient moisture deeper in the pot. It takes some practice, but in the long run this method is more consistently accurate than the moisture meter.

An Alternative to the Moisture Meter

Perhaps you don't want to break your nails or get your finger dirty by sticking it into the soil. Or maybe you want to know how moist the soil is 4 to 5 inches deep into the pot. A soil probe may be the answer for you. It is a simple mechanical device that probes deep into the pot and removes small samples of soil at different levels. You can then inspect these samples to determine the soil moisture content at each level. There is a simple, plastic soil probe available at www.SoilSleuth. com for about $10. It is one of the few commercial products that I recommend.

Water Temperature

Much is made of the correct temperature of the water you use for your plants. In general, it is best to use water at room temperature. In fact, necessity has taught me that even very cold and very warm water do not have an adverse effect on indoor potted plants. Warm water is absorbed more readily than cold water and is appropriate to use with soil that has become very dried out and almost water resistant.

Some folks like to water their plants by pouring ice cubes on them. I don't recommend this technique, but not because of the cold. The problem is that the ice melts slowly and you don't know how much water has been added to the soil. It is a very imprecise way to water plants.

Watering Summary

Learning to water is the trickiest aspect of good plant care. All plant roots need both water and oxygen to survive. Each plant has its unique water requirements that depends on its size, light, temperature, humidity, root system, and rate of growth. Use your finger as a probe to determine when a plant needs water. Whenever you water, do it thoroughly and then wait until the soil is barely damp before watering again. If you use a moisture meter, be aware of its limitations. Consider using a soil probe instead.

7 Potting Mixes for Indoor Plants

Good quality potting mixes can make a big difference in the way that your plant grows. Poor potting soil can cause a multitude of problems: pests, disease, root rot, and nutrient deficiency. As you know, it is in the potting mix that a plant's roots grow. The root-growing environment is critical to the health of the roots and healthy roots are vital to the health of the plant. Plant roots are like the human circulatory, digestive, and nervous systems all rolled into one.

The good news is that repotting plants is not usually necessary so you won't have to think about potting soil very often. The bad news is that it is not easy to find good quality potting mixes.

Professional Secret: *Do not repot unless it is absolutely necessary.* Nearly all potted plants will grow more vigorously and bloom more profusely if their roots are "tight" in the pot. This means that there are lots of healthy roots growing throughout the interior and around the outside of the rootball. A moderately potbound or rootbound plant usually dries out within 2 to 7 days following a thorough watering and that is a good sign. If your plant can go two days or more without needing water, then your plant does not need to be repotted. Just because a plant "looks too big for its pot," is **not** a good reason to repot. (See Chapter 1 for repotting information).

When is it okay to repot? The short answer is: Infrequently. The negative answer is: Never right after you buy a new plant. The more complete answer is: Repot only when your plant is so rootbound that there is no longer enough soil to absorb and retain water for at least two days. At this point, repotting your plant is an option, but not a necessity. If you don't mind watering your plant every day or two and fertilizing every week or two, then you can keep your rootbound plant in the same pot without any harm to your plant.

However, you may find daily watering more than you care to put up with. Then it is time to repot. Remove the plant from its pot. If it is stuck, bang the sides and bottom of the pot good and hard or slide a long knife along the inside of the pot. You should see lots of healthy roots wrapped completely around the outside of the rootball. In fact, it may be hard to see any soil except at the top. At least 90% of the sides and bottom of the rootball should be covered with roots. If not, then put it back in its pot, give it a good soak and don't repot it.

Finding a Good Potting Mix

Assuming it is appropriate to repot, you will need a good quality potting mix. Unfortunately, there are no quality or ingredient standards for packaged potting mixes. Every nursery seems to have their own blend that they swear by. Bagged potting mixes sold to consumers are just as varied. Miracle Gro seems to dominate the market, but I have received numerous complaints of fungus gnat problems after people have used Miracle Gro and other packaged potting mixes that include soil, humus, compost, bark and other organic materials that tend to harbor fungus gnat larvae. Look carefully for the ingredients list and select potting mixes that include only peat moss, coir, perlite and sand.

It is never a good idea to use garden soil from outside. It has too many insect, bacterial and fungal problems and is too heavy or dense for most potted indoor plants. So what can you do? The first thing to do is learn about soil structure so you will understand what plant roots need from the soil.

Potting Mix Structure and Composition

Soil structure refers to the size and percentage of air pockets in the potting mix. Most potted plants prefer a porous soil structure — one that is made up of coarse particles and has many, good-sized air pockets throughout. A dense soil structure has very fine closely packed particles that have very tiny air spaces. A porous potting mix is more efficient at providing oxygen to plant roots; a dense mix is better able to retain water for roots. Which is better? Most plants require a potting mix that can both retain water and also provide air spaces. For aquatic plants and ferns, water retention is more important. For cacti and succulents, porosity is more essential. That is why there are different soil mixes made for different plant groups.

A porous mix must have large particle material to create air spaces in the soil. Perlite, vermiculite, sand, lava rock, coconut husks (coir) and bark chips are the most commonly used particle materials in potting mixes. Of these, perlite may work the best because it creates air spaces between particles and is also made up of tiny air spaces. Perlite is also very hard and does not decompose or collapse readily. Vermiculite is a soft material that tends to compress and compact over time. Sand is heavy and the particles are not large enough to create large air pockets. If you use sand, make sure it is coarse river sand and never salty beach sand. Volcanic cinder rock works very well, but it is rough on your hands and its water content is hard to assess. Bark chips decompose slowly and are often a food source for fungus gnat larvae.

To make water available to the roots, potting soil needs material that will absorb and hold water. Coir and peat moss perform this function. Peat moss is particularly absorbent, is lightweight, and also retains some air pockets even when wet. Peat moss is also an excellent visual aid to proper watering: When it is wet, peat moss is dark brown and as it dries it becomes a noticeably lighter shade of brown.

Finally, a good potting mix should provide the nutrients that plants need. Every time a potted plant is watered, minute amounts of the nutrients are released and made available to plant roots. Good potting mixes will have nutrients in sufficient quantity to last for several years or longer. That is why the addition of plant food or fertilizer is unnecessary for recently repotted plants.

TO SUM UP: Good potting mixes should have air spaces to hold oxygen, material to retain water, and nutrients to supply the plant. It should be a mix of porous material, peat moss or coir, and a source of nutrients.

> Putting "drainage material" in the bottom of a pot is *not* a substitute for a potting mix that has porous material mixed throughout.

Packaged Potting Soil and Mixes

There are no uniform standards for packaged potting mixes. The labels on these bags make wonderful claims, but the actual composition of the mix is hard to find in the fine print. Some have just garden soil; some add a little peat or bark chips or perlite or sand; some have added fertilizer; others add moisture-retaining chemicals; some are wet and others are dry. Few of them are labeled to give you a complete list of all the additives and their respective quantities.

What to Avoid

Look carefully at the label for any mention of soil, compost, humus, bark chips and moisture controls. All of these substances sound great and they are for outdoor plants. However, for indoor plants these substances often are a source of pest problems, especially fungus gnat larvae. Moisture controls are additives that keep the soil moist longer. Although this seems like a good idea, it ignores the importance of allowing the potting mix to dry out within a week or so following a thorough watering.

Packaged Soilless Potting Mixes

There are peat-based potting mixes available that do not contain any of the substances mentioned above. They are composed primarily of peat moss with vermiculite and perlite added for porosity. Some will also have some fertilizer added to provide nutrients and wetting agents to make it easier to water. Remember, these mixes do not contain soil or other organic sources of nutrients, so fertilizer must be added by the manufacturer or by you. These soilless mixes are usually more expensive than potting soils, but they have many advantages. First, they are sterile and pest and disease free. Second, they are light in weight. Third, they are very clean to handle. Fourth, they are ready to use straight from the bag. If you use these soilless mixes, remember that they should be fertilized with a complete plant food regularly unless the label indicates that fertilizer has been included. (See Chapter 8 regarding fertilizer use.) Also, these mixes should not be used 'as is' for cacti and succulents because they retain too much water for too long.

My favorite potting mix that I have used for years without any problems is Pro-Mix for Potting and Seeding. The label clearly lists the following ingredients: 75–85% sphagnum peat moss, perlite and limestone to adjust the pH to 5.5 to 7.0 range. This pH range is appropriate for nearly all indoor plants. The label also advises that fertilizer should be added regularly because none is included in the mix. This is a good thing because it allows you to control the analysis and quantity of fertilizer used.

A viable and perhaps less expensive alternative is to make your own potting mix as described below.

Making Your Own Basic Potting Mix

This is not hard to do. In fact, it is kind of fun. The recipe for a standard potting mix is simple: 3 or 4 parts peat moss mixed with 1 part Perlite. Mix these ingredients together with some time-released fertilizer pellets and a spoonful of horticultural lime. This will give you a clean, porous, moisture retaining, nutrient filled potting soil.

If you can find coir or coconut husks, when added to your potting mix it will further enhance the desirable qualities of your potting mix.

Cacti and Succulent Potting Mix

Succulents have fine root systems that have evolved in nature to absorb moisture quickly and efficiently move that moisture to the plant for storage. This allows them to withstand drought conditions in their native habitats. Their roots are not adapted to stay in constantly moist soil. Thus, they must be potted in a very porous mix that will not retain water for very long. A good succulent mix will have lots of sand or perlite in proportion to soil or peat moss. You should notice that the water runs through this mix easily and quickly. There are packaged cactus potting mixes available or you can mix your own by adding extra perlite to the basic potting mix.

Fern Potting Mix

Ferns are the opposite of succulents. Ferns grow in areas that are constantly damp for most of the year. So they require a soil mix that has more moisture retaining matter and less porous material. This mix should have little or no perlite in it. The perlite can be replaced with vermiculite. Many people like to add some leaf mold to this mix, as well.

Epiphytic or Orchid Potting Mix

Epiphytes or air plants (Orchids, Bromeliads, Anthuriums) don't grow in the ground like most houseplants. In nature, their roots attach themselves to tree branches. Why is this important? Because many epiphytes cannot be grown in regular potting soil or their roots will rot. They should be grown in a mix of very porous, lumpy material such as sphagnum moss, bark chips, lava rock or vermiculite and perlite. These mixes do not retain water very long so the epiphytic roots will not rot. Epiphytic potting mixes are often available in packages labeled as Orchid Mix.

Conclusion

Unnecessary repotting is one of the most common plant care mistakes made. Plants flourish when their roots are tight and struggle when surrounded with excess soil. Never repot unless absolutely necessary and never repot an ailing or recently acquired plant. On those infrequent occasions that repotting is necessary, move your plant into the next sized pot and use only a good quality, sterilized potting mix. That is the root of the matter.

8 Fertilizer

If you are new to plants, fertilizing should be the least of your concerns. Concentrate on proper light and proper watering of your plants. Nothing is more over-promoted, over-sold, over-used and misunderstood in plant care than the use of fertilizer. Manufacturers promote the use of plant foods as a cure for nearly all plant problems. Retailers push it to increase their profits. Consumers love it because it appears to be a simple cure-all for their plant problems. Just as we look to our physicians to provide us with a medication to solve our health problems, we tend to look for some kind of "healing agent" for our ailing plants.

Fertilizer is neither miraculous nor medicine!

Unfortunately, it is a rare plant problem that can be solved with fertilizer. In fact, too much fertilizing is a much more common cause of plant problems than is under fertilizing. The majority of indoor plants can go for years without fertilizer and never miss it. In 30 years of treating thousands of ailing plants, I have yet to find one that could be solved with the application of fertilizer. So, if your plant is ailing in any way, fertilizer will not help and will only be a distraction from the real problem. Nonetheless, fertilizer does have its benefits in some circumstances. I also know from past experience that many people will use fertilizer even though it is unnecessary. In this chapter, you will learn when and when not to use fertilizer and how to use it properly when it is needed.

Frankly, most of the information in this chapter is not very important to most plant owners. Much of what follows is technical and specifically for those who really want to understand fertilizing. For the rest of you, move on to the next chapter.

The Short Answer to, "When Should I Fertilize?"

Only fertilize healthy plants that are growing vigorously in good light and have not had fresh soil added in at least a year. Recently potted plants, ailing plants, and plants in very low light do not need fertilizer. Plant food is used to enhance the growth of healthy plants. It should not be used to solve plant problems. It is *not* medicine! And it will not do anything miraculous for your plants.

Plants that should *not* be fertilized include:

- Recently purchased plants
- Recently repotted plants
- Sick or dying plants
- Plants in low light
- Plants that are dormant or growing very slowly
- Plants that use very little water

What Is Fertilizer and What Is Its Purpose?

In addition to light, water, and air, all plants require certain mineral elements or nutrients in order to grow healthy new roots, stems, foliage, and flowers. The combination or mixture of these minerals is called fertilizer or plant food. Good quality potting mix already contains these essential minerals. Plants freshly potted in good soil will have at least a one-year supply of these mineral nutrients right in the soil. Each time the plant is watered, the soil releases minute quantities of these nutrients that are then absorbed by the roots.

Although plants can get by for some time with a shortage of nutrients, they cannot be forced to use more than the minute quantities that they need. Excess minerals in the soil are either wasted as they are gradually washed out of the soil or they accumulate in the soil and can burn the roots. Thus, over fertilizing is wasteful at best and damaging to the plant at worst.

The purpose of using fertilizer is to replace the essential soil nutrients that are gradually depleted. A healthy, growing plant that has been in the same pot for more than two years may no longer have an adequate nutrient supply. In addition, plants that are grown in soilless potting mixes also require nutrient supplements or fertilizer. That is because soilless mixes (including most orchid mixes) use primarily inert materials such as peat moss, bark chips, perlite and vermiculite that lack vital plant nutrients. Finally, plants that are grown hydroponically (in water alone) also require the addition of nutrients.

What Is A Good Fertilizer?

Fertilizer brand names are meaningless. The only thing that matters is the components of a fertilizer. All legitimate plant foods and fertilizers list the nutrients on the label. Label listings include the ratio of the three primary nutrient components: Nitrogen (N), phosphorous (P), and potassium (K). The ratio is expressed in an N-P-K format. For example, 15-30-15 indicates that the fertilizer contains 15% nitrogen, 30% phosphorous, and 15% potassium. Plants grow equally well in a 1-1-1 ratio or a 3-1-2 ratio. However because nitrogen is depleted faster than the other nutrients, the latter ratio is more economical and is less likely to cause a buildup of soluble salts. Fertilizers with larger numbers (20-20-20) are more concentrated than those with lower numbers (5-5-5) when mixed according to the label directions.

In addition to nitrogen, phosphorous and potassium, "complete" fertilizers include other essential macro nutrients (calcium, magnesium, and sulfur) and micro or trace elements that all plants also need, but in extremely tiny quantities. These trace elements include iron, zinc, manganese, boron, copper, molybdenum, nickel and chlorine. If you are really serious about fertilizing to the optimum, then be sure you are using a complete fertilizer that lists all of these elements on the label. Foliage Pro by Dyna-Gro is a good example of a complete fertilizer in the right proportions for most foliage plants.

Types of Fertilizers: Liquids, Powders, Spikes, Pellets, and Organics

Adding to the confusion of selecting an appropriate fertilizer are the many different ways to apply fertilizers. Liquid concentrates and powders are diluted with water and then poured into the soil. Fertilizer spikes are stuck directly into the soil. Pellets or timed-release fertilizers are mixed in with the soil before they are added to the pot or sprinkled on top of the soil of an already potted plant.

- Liquids and powders are usually cheaper and are the easiest to store and to apply. You can also easily increase or decrease the strength of these fertilizers by altering the dilution rate. These are usually your best option.

- Fertilizer spikes are not recommended because they are highly concentrated and create nutrient "hot spots" where they are stuck into the soil.

- Timed-Release Pellets have the advantage of lasting for 3 to 6 months without reapplication. They release small quantities of nutrients each time water is applied. Pellets are often a good choice for mixing into soilless potting mixes. Nursery growers often use these pellets. You may notice these gray or yellow pellets in or on the soil of a new plant. The down side to the pellets is that once applied they will continue to release nutrients for 3 to 6 months whether the plant needs them or not. There is a greater risk of over fertilizing with fertilizer pellets.

- Organic fertilizers include all natural products such as fish emulsion, manure, and dried blood (all sources of nitrogen), bone meal (a source of phosphorous), wood ash (a source of potassium), eggshells (a source of calcium), leaf mold, cottonseed meal, compost, and coffee grounds.

The advantages of organic fertilizers are that they are relatively mild and less likely to burn tender roots; they contain important trace elements that not all commercial fertilizers include; they don't leach out of the soil as rapidly; and some will improve soil structure. The disadvantages are that they are harder to find; they are often more expensive; they require larger quantities to get the same result; some have an unpleasant odor; and they must be used in combinations to ensure that all nutrients are included for the plants. As far as the health of the plants is concerned, there is no advantage to using organics or non-organics, as long as they are used appropriately and mixed in the right proportions. Note: Coffee grounds and cottonseed meal increase the acidity of soil, which is not desirable for nearly all indoor plants (see section on soil pH below). Compost should be limited to outdoor use.

Application Rates

Fertilizer and plant food labels provide mixing and application instructions. For example, many labels recommend mixing a teaspoon of liquid or powdered concentrate with a gallon of water for indoor plants and apply monthly. Fertilizer label recommendations are for healthy plants that are growing in optimum conditions, something few of us have in our homes and offices. Thus, in general, it is best to use the recommended label rate at half strength.

> **Rule of thumb:** If your plants really need fertilizer, then cut the application rate in half to account for your less than perfect growing environment.

Many labels suggest more fertilizer in spring and summer and reduced amounts in the cooler months. That is a general rule that may not work for your plants. Plants use more nutrients when they are growing vigorously and little or none when they are not growing, are sick or are dormant. If your plants are pumping out lots of new growth in the dead of winter, then go ahead and fertilize. If your plant is languishing in the summer, then stop fertilizing. In other words, ignore the calendar and pay attention to your plant.

If in doubt, always use less rather than more fertilizer. Adding fertilizer solves few plant problems; too much fertilizer causes a lot more plant problems.

Constant Feed or Fertilizing With Every Watering

If your plants are growing in a soilless potting mix (without fertilizer pellets), then adding fertilizer every time you water may be a good idea. Instead of flooding the soil with lots of nutrients one week and then washing it out with subsequent waterings, it is better to add a small amount with each watering. However, you have to do some math to get the right dilution rate. If the recommended label rate is based on monthly application and you water weekly (4 times per month), then you have to use the recommended amount at one-fourth strength if you apply with weekly watering. If you water twice per week, then use one-eighth strength.

Example: Label recommends 1 tsp. per gallon monthly. Use one-half tsp. per gallon per month because your plants don't have ideal conditions. If you apply fertilizer weekly, then mix one-eighth tsp. per gallon. If you apply fertilizer twice per week, then use one-sixteenth tsp. per gallon.

Fertilizing Orchids and Other Flowering Plants

Most Orchids are potted in media that do not retain or readily provide nutrients — bark chips, sphagnum moss, coir, lava rock, etc. For this reason, it is best to apply a diluted fertilizer with every watering (see Constant Feed above). In general, Orchids need a balanced liquid fertilizer during their foliage growth or non-blooming period. Balanced means the three analysis numbers are similar (20-20-20, for example). Orchids potted in bark chips need more nitrogen, so the first number should be higher than the other two (30-10-10, for example). As the blooming time approaches or when buds begin to form on any flowering plant, it is best to switch to a higher phosphorous content. So you want the middle number to be higher in proportion to the others (15-30-15, for example) to promote flowers.

How Light Affects Fertilizer Application

Plant growth is determined primarily by light. Plants in low light grow more slowly and use less water and need fewer nutrients. Plants in optimal light will grow at optimal rates and need more nutrients. It is important not to put the cart before the horse with plant food by thinking you can promote faster growth with plant food. Light comes first, fertilizer follows, not vice-versa.

How Soil pH Affects Nutrient Availability

Most indoor plants do best if the soil pH is in the 5.5 to 6.5 range. This means that the soil is slightly acidic. (On the pH scale, 1.0 is highly acid, 7.0 is neutral, 14.0 is highly basic or alkaline). It is in this slightly acidic range that essential plant nutrients are more soluble and most available for plants to use. When soil pH is outside of this range, the plant cannot absorb the nutrients. *If a plant shows signs of nutrient deficiency, check the pH first.* In my experience, the classic symptoms of nutrient deficiencies are usually due to improper pH, not lack of nutrients in the soil. If the soil pH is outside the proper range, all the fertilizer supplements in the world will not help.

If the water in your area is hard or has high mineral content, that may gradually affect the pH of your potting soil. Hard water is not good for plants anyway, so it is best to use filtered or distilled water instead.

As soil ages, it tends to become gradually more acidic. For older plants, check the pH periodically. For soil that is too acidic, mix 2 tablespoons of baking soda or one tablespoon of dolomitic lime per gallon of water and water your plant thoroughly. This will raise the soil pH to an acceptable level. The addition of sulfur or iron sulfate will lower soil pH if it is too alkaline.

There are a few commonly used indoor plants that require unusually acidic soil. They include Azalea, Camellia, Gardenia, and Venus Flytrap. Use Miracid or some other fertilizer for acid-loving plants.

If your pets have used your potted plants to urinate, flush the soil with clear water and then add some lime to counteract the odor and acid content of the urine.

The Hazards of Over Fertilizing

Fertilizers are composed of nutrient elements. When these elements become highly concentrated from over application, they can reach levels that are toxic to plants. The buildup of nutrient mineral salts burns tender roots and can cause foliage damage in the form of leaf discoloration or spotting. The problem is exacerbated when the soil dries out because as the moisture level drops, the concentration of mineral salts increases.

Incomplete watering can also lead to the buildup of toxic nutrient salts. It is important to always apply enough water so that it soaks all the way through the rootball. If the water soaks only partially through the soil, soil salts will concentrate at the spot where the water stops. This creates "hot spots" within the rootball. So always water thoroughly and especially when you are adding fertilizer.

If you suspect that there is too much fertilizer in your potted plant or a "hot spot" exists, the remedy is to flush lots of fresh water through the rootball with a hose or faucet. This will help eliminate the excess nutrient deposits. Some plant owners do this routinely with all new plants because greenhouse growers often apply fertilizers at rates that may be suitable for the greenhouse but are excessive for the home or office plant.

How Much Nutrients Do Plants Actually Use?

The amount of nutrients that potted plants actually use is surprisingly small. So small that even I was surprised when I did the math. The recommended label rate is the amount used by a standard healthy foliage plant growing in a greenhouse or nursery.

Plants use nitrogen more than any other nutrient. A liquid fertilizer with a 9-3-6 ratio means that the content of the undiluted fertilizer is 9% of the total liquid. The label calls for a monthly application of that fertilizer at a dilution rate of 1 teaspoon per gallon. That is 1 part fertilizer to 768 parts plain water. But the nitrogen represents only 9% of that. That translates to 1 part nitrogen to 8,533 parts of plain water or 0.0117%!

Plants use the other nutrients in even smaller quantities than nitrogen. So you can see by the numbers that nutrients are a very small part of a plant's diet, compared to sunlight and water. A good quality potting soil contains a supply of nutrients that will take several years or more to be depleted. **BOTTOM LINE:** nutrient deficiency is rarely the source of houseplant problems.

Bagged Potting Soils and Fertilizer Additives

Beware of commercial potting soils that add fertilizer to the soil. Most potting soils are already too high in mineral content. If more is added to the soil, it may be dangerously high for your plants. However, it is appropriate for manufacturers to add fertilizer to soilless, peat-based potting mixes. See Chapter 7 on potting mixes.

Hoaxes, Scams and Marketing Gimmicks

The elements that plants need to grow and thrive are well known. They are listed above (see What Is Good Fertilizer?). Other additives, including B-vitamins and unspecified hormones, are of no proven value to plants. Although these useless additives are unlikely to cause any harm, they are a waste of money and misleading. It is exceedingly rare that a plant problem can be cured by the addition of a nutrient supplement, including fertilizer, to the potting soil. The advertised cures and implied "miracles" play on our hopes for finding an easy solution to our plant problems. For plants, there is no such magic bullet.

Conclusions

Sick indoor plants are unhealthy for a reason, usually improper light or water. Lack of nutrients is almost never the reason. In fact, indoor plants having an abundance of nutrients and excess soil salts is a much more common problem than lack of nutrients. Plants can only absorb a limited quantity of nutrients. Adding more soil salts in the form of fertilizer (organic or otherwise) is at best a waste of fertilizer and at worst will further damage the roots. The only plants that benefit from additional nutrients are those that are growing vigorously and have thereby depleted the level of nutrients in the soil.

Fertilizer is not a medicine or a magic potion that cures plant problems. It merely replaces essential minerals in old soil or in soilless potting mixes. Most fertilizing is unnecessary, but harmless as long as the mineral content does not build up too much. But why take the risk and spend the money?

If you find this all too complicated, then you won't go too far wrong by simply ignoring it and not fertilizing at all or only occasionally with whatever is available.

9 Temperature and Humidity

Best temperatures for indoor plants

Most indoor potted plants or houseplants are tropical in origin. That means they are well-suited for our year-round warm indoor temperatures. It also means that they are easily damaged by exposure to cold. As a general rule, most indoor plants do best in a temperature range of 60 to 80°F (15°C to 27°C). Outside this range some species may experience cold damage to the foliage and stems. Thus, if you are inclined to move your indoor plants outside in late spring, be aware of these temperature limitations. While most tropical plants can survive temperatures down to 50°F. (10°C.), some sensitive plants such as Orchids, cannot.

Semitropical Plants for Cooler Locations

Some plants used indoors are semitropical and can tolerate cooler temperatures than tropical species. They may be a good choice for locations that are cooler than normal household temperatures — near outside doorways or mud rooms, for example. Bear in mind that they cannot withstand freezing temperatures.

Here is a list of cold temperature plants that are safe in temperatures as low as 40°F. (4°C.), except where otherwise noted:

Asparagus fern 45°F. (7°C.)	Aspidistra 35°F. (2°C.)
Azalea	Boston Fern 45°F. (7°C.)
Cactus 45°F. (7°C.)	Holiday Cactus
Camellia	Citrus
Cyclamen 45°F. (7°C.)	Cyperus (Papyrus) 45°F. (7°C.)
Date palm	Dracaena marginata
Fatsia japonica 45°F. (7°C.)	Ficus species
Grape ivy	Hedera ivy
Jade Plant	Jasmine polyanthum
Kentia palm	Maidenhair fern
Norfolk Island Pine	Oxalis (Shamrock)
Passiflora	Peperomia

Purple passion 45°F. (7°C.)	Rhapis palm 30°F. (-1°C.)
Rubber plant	Sedum
Podocarpus	Sago palm
Spider plant	Staghorn fern 45°F. (7°C.)
String of hearts 45°F. (7°C.)	Swedish ivy
Venus flytrap	Wandering Jew 45°F. (7°C.)
White bird 45°F. (7°C.)	Yucca 45°F. (7°C.)

Note: These plants adjust to colder temperatures gradually as the weather dictates. It is not a good idea to suddenly move a plant that has been in warm temps indoors to 40 degree temps outside.

Severe cold damage can occur if a plant is exposed even for a short time to sub-freezing, windy weather. Don't kid yourself that your new plant will be okay for the 3 minutes it takes you to walk to your car in 20°F. weather. On the other hand, brief exposure to temps within 10° of a plant's minimum may only cause minor damage to the plant. So the extent of cold damage depends on just how cold and for how long.

Most folks don't pay much attention to cold exposure until they accidently expose their plant to cold and then notice leaves that have suddenly turned dark and soft. How to assess and treat a cold-damaged plant is addressed on page 98.

Plant Dormancy

Plants native to temperate zones go dormant in winter. They shed their leaves, stop growing and shut down until warmer temps return. Tropical plants, however, are non-seasonal because they grow in regions where it is warm all year round. They do not go into dormancy, except those plants from certain regions where a 2–3 month period of drought is the norm. Some folks starve their indoor houseplants of water in winter because they assume all plants go dormant in winter. Don't do it!

As the heat comes on and the air dries, it is not uncommon for indoor plants to actually need more frequent watering in winter.

Humidity

Low humidity is often cited as the reason that indoor plants do not do well. Symptoms such as brown leaf tips, dying leaves, pest infestations, and general plant malaise are frequently attributed to dry air. Is this true? If so, how can plant owners increase low humidity?

First, a little biology: plants absorb moisture primarily through their roots not their leaves. The moisture is transferred from the roots to the stem and leaf tissues throughout the plant. In dry air, moisture evaporates from the leaves. In humid air, less evaporation occurs. With the notable exception of desert-dwelling plants, the majority of indoor plants originate in tropical regions where high humidity levels are the norm. The assumption is that if plants grow naturally in humid areas, then they must require high humidity to survive as indoor plants. This notion has been reinforced by the luxurious plant growth that occurs in greenhouses where humidity is kept at high levels.

Of course, most homes and offices are very dry in the winter months when heating elements can reduce the humidity to levels that are actually lower than those found in the desert. Our chapped skin and cracked wood furniture are testimony to the dryness of indoor winter air. Yet, most tropical, humidity-loving plants will survive in these low humidity environments. How is this possible?

When we put plants in pots and move them indoors, we are creating an "artificial" environment. Plants do not normally grow indoors in pots. Yet, many plants are adaptable enough to grow quite well in the "artificial" environment of our homes and offices. They are also adaptable enough to adjust to low humidity. When humidity-loving plants are placed in a low humidity environment, they adapt by absorbing more moisture through their roots to replace the added moisture lost to the dry air.

That means indoor plants that are subjected to dry air require more frequent watering than the same plant in high humidity. Because of the low humidity, many indoor plants actually use more water in winter, when sunlight and plant growth is reduced, than they do in summer. In fact, many of the plant symptoms attributed to low humidity are in fact the result of under watering. Many people assume that indoor plants are dormant in winter and need far less water. In fact, they often need more. The resulting brown leaves and leaf tips are really caused by lack of soil moisture, not low humidity.

Note: There are a few plant species that do not adapt well to low humidity. These plants are best grown in terrariums or other enclosed containers that will keep the humidity levels high.

Misting is a False Solution

Plant owners are often told to mist their plants daily in the winter months to counteract the dry air. Although misting never does any harm, misting is *not* effective in raising the humidity. The misted water droplets normally evaporate within 10 to 15 minutes. So, at most, a daily misting raises the humidity for about one-quarter of one hour out of a 24-hour day or about 1%. This simply is not enough to make a significant difference.

Misting does help keep plants clean and is a deterrent to some plant pests such as spider mites but it does not raise the humidity.

How to Increase Humidity

Pebble trays are the simplest and least expensive way to raise humidity around plants. An oversized tray or saucer is filled with a half-inch layer of pebbles or stones. The tray or saucer is then filled with water to the top of the pebbles. The potted plant is then placed on top of the pebbles. The water slowly evaporates into the dry air surrounding the plant. The pebbles keep the plant above the water so the roots do not stay constantly wet. You will need to replenish the water in the pebble trays frequently when the heat is on and the air is very dry. Pebble trays only benefit the plants that are immediately above the trays.

Another technique to raise humidity is to leave open pans of water on top of or close to radiators or other heating devices. This is also only helpful to plants that are close to the evaporating pans.

Room humidifiers are more effective at raising the humidity for an entire room. However, they are more expensive to purchase and operate. Vaporizers and other devices that put water into the air also help increase humidity levels. Note that these devices are only effective while they are operating. They are also notorious for spreading bacteria unless they are thoroughly cleaned daily.

Finally, indoor humidity decreases as the temperature rises. If you keep your thermostat at a toasty 75° in winter, the air will be much drier than if the thermostat is kept at an energy saving 65°. By keeping your home on the cool side you not only save energy, but you also help maintain the humidity for your plants, your furniture and yourself.

Conclusion

If you are having problems with your indoor plants, low humidity is one of the least likely causes. Improper light, water, and soil are the better suspects. So don't knock yourself out trying to raise the humidity to save your plants. Raise the humidity because it will make a difference for your skin, your health, and your furniture. It will also benefit your plants marginally.

10 Indoor Pests and Diseases

If you are very lucky, you have never had any pests on your indoor plants. But the chances are that if you haven't seen plant critters already, you will be before long. Plant pests are not a sign of poor hygiene; they are just part of nature. There is a lot you can do to prevent plant pests and even more you can do to treat them successfully. This chapter will help you prevent plant pests and also treat them successfully without the use of toxic chemical pesticides.

"Where did they come from?!"

There is no simple answer to the question "How did my plants get these bugs?" Plant pests can spread from one plant to other nearby plants. They can also be transported via clothing and gardening tools and even through the air. In most instances, they are already on the plant at the time of purchase, but in such low numbers that they are virtually invisible to the naked eye. They can stay that way for years and then suddenly start reproducing madly when the environment is favorable for them. A plant under stress (improper light, water, humidity) is much more vulnerable to plant pests. To prevent pests, keep your plants healthy and check them regularly for early signs of their presence. Plant pests are much easier to eradicate when caught in the early stages.

The spreading of plant pests from one plant to another is often exaggerated. It can and does happen, but not nearly as easily or as often as is commonly believed. Isolating a new plant for a period of time does not guarantee protection.

Here is what I suggest that you do with new plants. Spray the new plant very thoroughly with soapy water until all stem and leaf surfaces are dripping wet. This will probably take care of any existing pest problems and it will be safe to put your plant among other plants.

More importantly, you should always inspect your plants regularly for signs of plant pests. Just because they do not have pests now does not mean they never will. If you discover plant pests early, they are much easier to treat and you will be able to correct the underlying source of stress sooner. So look at the undersides of the leaves for tiny spider mites and check the nooks and crannies for mealybugs and you can save yourself a lot of aggravation.

Why did my pest treatment fail?

People tell me that they tried a number of remedies, including pesticides, for their plant pest problems and none of them worked. The reason is lack of complete and thorough coverage. Many remedies rely on direct contact with each pest. A normal spraying will allow many of the minute critters to go untouched in between the tiny spray droplets. If even a few survive, they will reproduce and the problem will return in a few months. No matter which of the many remedies you use, you must spray until all leaf and stem surfaces are dripping wet. Yes, this is a messy proposition and may best be done outside where drip run-off is not an issue. However, it is worth the effort because if you are thorough a single treatment is often sufficient to eradicate the pests.

How to identify the most common plant pests

Although there are many varieties of pests that may feed on your indoor plants, you don't need to be an entomologist to recognize them.

Spider mites are very tiny (a half dozen will fit on the head of a pin!) and difficult to spot with the naked eye until they are well established on a plant. Look for them on the undersides of leaves in good light. They appear as tiny specks of dust, but dust does not collect on the bottoms of leaves. As the spider mite infestation advances, the mites begin to make very tiny webs. Misting will cause water droplets to adhere to the webs and make the webs easier to spot. By the time the webs become noticeable, the spider mite infestation is fairly well advanced. Spider mites use needle-like projections to extract fluids from plant foliage. In time, they will leave the foliage with a permanently mottled appearance as they remove little pinpricks of chlorophyll from the leaves. Favored hosts for spider mites include Palms, Crotons, *Dracaena marginatas*, Scheffleras, Ivies, Dieffenbachias, and Norfolk Island pines.

Scale insects are hard to identify because they don't look like bugs and don't appear to move. They are oval, slightly raised bumps about an eighth of an inch long and are usually found along leaf stems or on the undersides of leaves. In the juvenile or crawler stage, scales are translucent and take on the color of the leaf or stem surface. As they mature, scales develop a hard, dark brown shell that is more visible. These scales are easily scraped off the plant tissue with a fingernail. As the infestation increases, these sucking insects will secrete a sticky substance called honeydew that falls onto leaves, furniture and floors. This stickiness is the most obvious sign of scale and the one that most people notice first. Favored hosts include Ficus, Spider Plants, Ferns, Scheffleras, and Aralias.

Mealybugs are actually a distinct type of scale insect. I list them separately because they look very different than other types of scales. Mealybugs develop a soft, white outer coating as they mature. This gives the appearance of tiny bits of white cotton found in nooks and crannies where leaves join stems. For this reason, they are more noticeable than other scale insects. Favored hosts for mealybug include Chinese evergreen, Pothos, Philodendron, Jade, and China doll.

Fungus gnats usually go unnoticed until they reach the adult stage. As adults, they have wings and they fly about and look like tiny black gnats. Before they mature, their larvae live in the upper surface of a plant's potting soil. In good light, the larvae can be seen as minute worm-like things with dark heads swimming on the surface of the soil following the application of water. These gnats can emerge from the soil of any plant; particularly those that are high in organic matter and are kept constantly moist.

Aphids commonly appear as clusters of tiny insects (less than an eighth of an inch) on tender new growth. Look for them on the ends of plant stems and on newly formed leaves. Ivies are among the favored hosts of aphids.

White flies are aptly named. They are tiny, white flying insects. They are usually in clusters that fly about in "white clouds" when disturbed. White flies are found on Hibiscus and Poinsettias, but are relatively uncommon on houseplants.

Pest Prevention

In most instances of houseplant pest infestations, the pests are on the plant at the time of purchase. However, they are there in such small numbers and in nearly invisible juvenile stages, so that they go undetected. If the plant is healthy, it will have a greater ability to fight off the infestation of the bugs and so it may be several years before the bugs reach a critical (visible) mass. Plants growing in unfavorable conditions (poor light, improper water, etc.) have little resistance to pests that will then reproduce rapidly and soon overwhelm the plant. Plant pests can also be introduced by other plants, by hitching a ride on clothing, or by coming in from outside when the temperatures are warm. If you repot or add fresh soil, there is a good chance the packaged potting soil will introduce fungus gnats larvae.

> **There is no absolute way to keep critters out of your home. The best defense is to keep your plants healthy and inspect all of your plants regularly for early signs of these pests.**

Pest treatment: Pesticides aren't the answer

I am not an advocate of pesticide use because pesticides are not only hazardous to people and the environment, but are also toxic to certain plants, especially if they are applied without proper dilution or in direct sunlight. In addition, there is increasing evidence that these toxic pesticides are harmful to humans, animals and drinking water. Pesticides are hazardous because few have been adequately tested by independent agencies. U.S. government standards on the testing of pesticides are notoriously lax. Many people have allergic reactions to certain pesticides. Pesticides are rarely tested as carcinogens, so the long-term effects are unknown. Finally, most pesticides have damaging effects on other wildlife, including beneficial insects (honeybees and lady bugs, for example), birds and fish, and on the water supply. There is no question that pesticides can be very effective in treating plant pests, but there are many questions about their safety. Although occasional use may not pose much of a threat to an individual, why risk it when there are alternatives that are safe to use and effective in eliminating indoor plant pests. Many nurseries are now using bio-controls or natural predators to fight unwanted pests. Pesticides are a risk to the environment and collectively we need to start moving away from their use for the sake of future generations.

Pest treatment: Safe solutions

Silicon, soap, alcohol, hot pepper, and oil sprays all work by either smothering or dehydrating the plant pests. They all kill on contact with the pest. They are not toxic to humans, pets or the environment. They do not have any residual effect, as toxic pesticides do. (A residual effect means that poison stays on the plant tissue long after it has been applied and any pest survivors that come in contact with it will get zapped.) The non-toxic sprays mentioned above kill only by direct contact. So if you miss getting the spray on some of the crafty critters that are hidden from view, they will reproduce and the infestation will re-occur. Thus, the effectiveness of the contact sprays is limited to the applicator's expertise in getting complete coverage. Be sure to spray both the tops and bottoms of all leaf surfaces *until they are dripping wet.*

Soap sprays: A solution of liquid dish soap and water will smother plant pests that it covers. Soap is effective against spider mites and aphids, but not very effective against other plant pests. It can be applied via a hand sprayer or mister. Smaller plants can be turned upside down (hold one hand over the plant so that it doesn't fall out of the pot) and swished around in a sink filled with soapy water. This method guarantees complete coverage of all leaf and stem surfaces. Insecticidal Soaps are formulated to have a stronger drying effect than ordinary soaps. However, they can also cause some plants to develop yellow leaves and some people to have allergic skin reactions. Liquid dish soap can be just as effective if applied thoroughly.

Alcohol solutions: Ordinary rubbing or isopropyl alcohol (surgical spirits in the UK) is effective at breaking through the protective coatings on scale insects and mealybug. It can be mixed as one part alcohol with 5 parts water. A squirt of liquid soap makes it a bit more effective. For more delicate plants, such as ferns, the alcohol can be applied with a Q-tip directly on each scale insect.

Oil sprays: Oils will clog the breathing apparatus and smother most plant pests. They are effective against scale and mealybug. Oils are usually applied as sprays mixed with water. It is best to use horticultural grade oils, such as Sun Spray Ultra Fine. Neem oil comes from the oil of the neem tree. Allegedly, it has anti-feedant properties that cause pests to avoid any plant that has been sprayed with it. It is moderately expensive and it has a strong burnt onion odor. Mixing in a bit of Pine Sol lemon scented cleaner can mask the odor.

Pepper sprays: Solutions containing cayenne pepper will kill most small plant pests on contact. It is especially effective in treating spider mites. A commercial solution called Hot Pepper Wax is now available in many garden and plant centers. Wax has been added to the hot pepper so that the solution adheres to the plant foliage. It works best against spider mites, mealybugs and aphids. Hot Pepper Wax needs to be mixed with warm water to be effective. There is an information website for it at http://www.hotpepperwax.com/.

Silicon sprays: The hands-down best weapon against mealybug and scale insects is Brand X Foliage Cleaner. It is particularly effective because it contains silicon, which has an unusual penetrating ability that allows it to get into tiny crevices and places that other remedies do not reach. It is available through Southwest Plantscape Products in California. You can read about and order it at www.buybrandx.com. Brand X is also a very good leaf shine that dries quickly to a non-oily, glossy finish with no wiping necessary. **One caution:** Avoid getting it on floors because it will make them very slippery.

Sand and diatomaceous earth: These two substances are effective remedies of limited effectiveness alone for fungus gnat larvae and other soil-borne pests. The sharp edges of these materials slice through the larvae as they attempt to emerge from the soil. Sprinkle enough sand or diatomaceous earth to cover the top layer of the potting soil.

Other home remedies: There are a variety of other home remedies that act as deterrents to plant pests. Some are more effective than others. Always test them to be sure that they will not damage your plant. These natural remedies also work by direct contact, so thorough coverage is essential.

Some helpful precautions

- Always read label directions carefully and follow all directions for safe use.

- Do not use liquid sprays on fuzzy-leafed plants.

- It is always a good idea to apply the spray to a single leaf as a test and wait a few days to see if the plant is sensitive to that particular spray.

- None of these sprays should be applied to plants in direct sun or in high temperatures.

- If you use them as preventives, dilute them by at least one half and don't apply them more than once every couple of months. This is because the oils and soaps and waxes can build up if used too frequently or applied too heavily.

Biological Pest Controls

For serious pest infestations that don't seem to respond to any of the non-pesticidal remedies mentioned above, consider using biological controls as an alternative to chemical pesticides. Bio controls often rely on natural predators to keep plant pest in check. These natural predators are beneficial insects that are usually very tiny and not noticeable. Ladybugs and praying mantids are the most commonly recognized natural predators, but they don't work with indoor plants. For a complete description of the bio controls available for your indoor plants go to http://greenmethods.com/site/. This is a highly detailed and informative site and also a source to purchase bio controls. Another very useful site for information on biocontrols is: http://www.bugladyconsulting.com.

Treating Mealybugs and Scale Insects

The key to successfully eradicating these creatures is to also spray the ones that are out of sight. That means that whatever treatment you select, you must get complete coverage, to the drip point, of all leaf and stem surfaces. If you miss a few, they will live to breed another day.

The best non-toxic treatment for mealybug and scale insects is Brand X Foliage Cleaner, available only through Southwest Plantscape Products in California. Read all about it and order it at www.buybrandx.com. It is a silicon-based product so it is very slippery. Its ability to penetrate is probably the key to its effectiveness because it gets into the tiny crevices that other sprays miss.

You may want to try spraying with rubbing (isopropyl) alcohol. Mix 1 part alcohol with 5 parts of water and add a squirt of liquid soap. Be sure to spray all leaf and stem surfaces thoroughly. The common practice of applying alcohol with a Q-tip is not effective because it misses the ones you can't see. It is also best if you repeat this treatment again in 5 to 7 days to catch any crawlers that you missed the first time. After that, you should check your plant weekly to see if they return.

Sun Spray Ultra Fine horticultural oil is also mixed with water and effectively smothers the scale. Complete coverage is important.

Mealy Bugs

Another effective non-toxic spray is Hot Pepper Wax. Its main ingredient is hot cayenne pepper that overheats the plant pests. There is an information website for it at www.hotpepperwax.com.

Finally neem oil works similarly to horticultural oil. It should be diluted with water and Pine Sol to counteract the onion-like odor.

Horticultural oils, Hot Pepper Wax and neem oil are all available nationwide at plant and garden centers and also by mail order.

IMPORTANT: None of these should be applied to plants in direct sun or in high temps.

Treating Spider Mites and Aphids

Plain soap and water, insecticidal soap, and Hot Pepper Wax can all be used safely to treat spider mites. The key to all of these products is to get 100% coverage of all leaf and stem surfaces — top and bottom. If you miss a few of the mites, which is easy to do because they are small enough to reside between spray droplets, then they will start to reproduce and you will have another infestation again in a few weeks. Try to spray in a location where you can thoroughly drench all leaf surfaces without worrying about all the run-off. Run your fingers along the leaf and stem surfaces to help get complete surface coverage. Use rubber or latex gloves to avoid skin irritation. It is also advisable to re-spray again about 5 days later to get any mites that you may have missed the first time.

The best mite prevention is vigilance. Any mite-prone plants, such as palms, should be checked every week for early signs of mites — look for "dust" particles on the undersides of leaves. Treat the mites at the very first sighting. They are much easier to eliminate in the early stages.

Spider mites often are introduced on newly acquired plants or by plants that have been outside in the summer. You may want to spray such plants before you bring them inside. Spider mites also prey on plants that are under stress. Thus, it is important to keep your plants healthy by providing good light and proper water.

Spider mites can reproduce in the 54°F to 110°F range, with the optimum range of 85°F to 90°F. In unfavorable conditions (cooler temps, shorter day length, reduced plant vigor) they go into diapause when they hibernate (don't feed or lay eggs). Pesticides are ineffective during diapause because the mites are not feeding. When favorable conditions return, the mite population can explode and give the appearance of coming out of nowhere. Nitrogen fertilizers encourage tender new growth, which is very attractive to mites. Mites suck the chloroplasts out of green cells and leave a telltale mottled appearance on the foliage. Mites use webs to travel from one feeding spot to another. Lots of visible webs mean an extensive infestation that has been there for quite some time.

Treating fungus gnats

Adult fungus gnats fly around and are an annoyance, but they are not harmful to people. Each gnat lives for about 5 days. The trick is to get rid of the next generation — the gnat larvae that live in the top layer of the soil. The larvae feed on decaying organic matter. Decaying pine bark in potting mixes and decaying plant roots feed the larvae.

Try to keep the soil as dry as possible. Remove all loose soil from the top surface of the rootball that is not in immediate contact with roots. This will eliminate many of the larvae that live close to the soil surface and it will allow the soil to dry out sooner and deprive the larvae of essential moisture. Keep the soil as dry as possible between waterings for the same reason. You can put a light layer of coarse coir (coconut husk) or sand or diatomaceous earth on the soil surface, but this is not essential. These substances have sharp edges that carve up the larvae.

Replacing the soil to eliminate the gnats may cure the problem, but it will also kill the plant. Don't do it!

Another safe technique is to place ½ inch slices of raw potato on the surface of the soil. After a day or so, discard the slices along with the larvae inside. Repeat this until there are no more larvae in the potato.

For more serious infestations try Gnatrol to treat fungus gnats. It is a biological product that is safe to use and kills the gnat larvae in the soil. It is available online for about $30.

Detection trick: Add a little water to the soil and then look very closely for tiny fungus gnat larvae swimming in the water as it pools on the surface. You need good light and good eyes to see them. If you don't, then your plant is probably gnat free.

Prevention is often the best remedy. Gnat infestations often follow repotting because the potting soil used is contaminated with gnat larvae. Use sterile potting mixes that are free of compost, soil and bark chips. The potting mix should have ample drainage material, such as perlite so that it drains well and allows the soil to dry out frequently. (See Chapter 7 for information on selecting a potting mix.) Fungus gnats can nearly always be traced back to over-potting, overwatering and/or poor soil quality.

Treating Whitefly

Whiteflies are not a common indoor plant pest problem. They are mostly found on herbs, Hibiscus, Geranium, Poinsettia and plants that are usually grown outdoors. Whitefly eggs are found on the undersides of plant leaves where they are barely noticeable. If possible, take the infested plants outside (if temps are above freezing) and spray the undersides of the leaves with a moderately strong hose spray. Be thorough so as to get all of the eggs. In the process, most of the adult (winged) whiteflies will also fly off. Doing this outside will also keep the whiteflies from flying about in your house. Those that leave your Hibiscus will not survive long in the cold outdoors. Those that stay on the plant will be killed by direct contact with the soap spray. That is why this should be done outside.

If you cannot treat your plant outside, then whiteflies are best treated at night when they are less inclined to fly about when disturbed. If you have a hand vacuum, use that first to vacuum the winged adults that are on the leaves. Then use a solution of soapy water (use liquid dish soap) in a spray bottle and thoroughly spray all leaf and stem surfaces until they are dripping wet. If you are really thorough with your spray treatment, it should not be necessary to re-spray. However, do be vigilant for signs of live whiteflies. Dead carcasses may fall from the leaves onto surfaces below, but as long as they are not flying, you are okay.

It is important to treat all of the infested plants at the same time so that they don't re-infest each other. Inspect your plants carefully each week and at the first sign of any new whiteflies, treat that plant again as described above

Thrips

Ficus trees, most of which are grown in Florida, sometimes experience a major infestation of thrips. Quality growers treat their trees so that this is not a problem. Big box stores often do not purchase their trees from quality growers.

I suggest you start your treatment by removing as many of the infested leaves and stems as possible. Because most of the thrips are in new growth and new growth is always at the ends of stems, simply trimming off the last several inches of all stems will probably remove most of the critters.

If you don't mind using pesticides, Malathion is effective in treating thrips.

Alternatively, you can use a fine horticultural oil spray. With both products, it is important to spray in a well-ventilated area and to get complete coverage of all leaf and stem surfaces.

Powdery mildew

This is not an insect pest, but a fungus growth. Powdery mildew appears as irregularly shaped patches of white on the leaf and stem surfaces of some plants, such as African violets and grape ivies. This fungus wipes off leaves, but brownish leaf spots are left behind. Powdery mildew often attacks the tender new growth and destroys it. Once established on a plant, powdery mildew is hard to eradicate because the microscopic spores float invisibly through the air and onto other areas of the plant.

Unless your infected plant is of great personal value, you may want to consider discarding the plant because the success rate in treating powdery mildew is not high.

The first step in treating powdery mildew is to cut off the infected tissue, usually the entire leaf or stem. Next you can try spraying all leaf surfaces and stem surfaces and also the surface of the soil with a solution of 1 tsp. baking soda to a quart of water. The sulfur in garlic is also effective, so you can spray with a solution of garlic and water. Safer's makes a non-toxic sulfur spray for mildew. It is reasonably effective but will leave a strong sulfur odor on your hands, so use rubber gloves. Neem oil and horticultural oil sprays are also effective treatments for powdery mildew. Repeat the spray treatments again in about a week.

NOTE: Be sure to test any of these sprays on a single leaf before spraying the entire plant to be sure that it does not damage the plant.

Powdery mildew thrives in locations that are warm, humid and lacking good air circulation. Installing a fan nearby can help deter powdery mildew.

Mushrooms or soil mold

These unwanted plant growths come from fungus spores in the soil. They thrive in cool, damp conditions. They are not harmful to plants. Fungal molds usually only occur if you do one or more of the following:

- Use unsterilized potting soil, garden soil or compost
- Use a soil mix that is compact and doesn't drain well
- Add food substances to the soil, such as soda or coffee
- Keep your plants constantly wet and/or in low light

The use of a peat-based, soilless potting mix usually prevents the problem. If you repotted your plant prior to seeing mushroom growth, then there is a very good chance that the soil that you used is contaminated with fungus spores. You may not want to use it again. See Chapter 7 for information on potting soils.

First, try scraping off excess loose soil and the mold from the surface of the rootball. You may notice some whitish substance just below the surface of the soil. This is the equivalent of fungi roots and is called mycelia. Try to scrape as much of this out as possible. The application of a light spray of diluted alcohol sometimes helps. Then let the soil dry out as much as possible without damaging the plant. It is usually necessary to repeat this process each time you see new mushrooms pop up. With persistence, you will eventually get it under control. A warmer, sunnier location will also help deter the mold. In extreme cases, a systemic fungicide can be applied as a soil drench.

ONE OTHER THOUGHT: Sometimes excess minerals in the soil accumulate as a white deposit on the surface of the soil. These mineral deposits are sometimes mistaken for fungus or mold. If this is what you have, scrape off the deposits, flush the soil thoroughly with clear water, stop fertilizing and don't water from the bottom.

Critters in the Soil

A common problem is the appearance of crawling insects in the soil. Usually, these critters are some type of centipede or, perhaps, ants. These critters are unlikely to damage the plant, but no one wants them in the house. Here is the best way to treat them.

Take the plant and plunge the pot up to its rim in a tub filled with plain water. Leave it for 30 to 45 minutes. This flooding of the soil will drive the critters to the surface in search of air. You can then sweep them off the soil surface and dispose of them. Remove the pot from the water and let the soil drip-dry. One treatment usually does the trick, although occasionally a second treatment is necessary.

11 Why You Don't Prune — But Should

If repotting is the most overdone plant care practice (see Chapter 1), then pruning is the most neglected plant care practice. Often, the difference between a mediocre looking but healthy plant and a terrific looking plant is pruning. Regular pruning keeps your plants looking young, full, compact and shapely. Pruning is usually the only remedy for spindly, leggy, overgrown plants.

So why is pruning so often neglected? Because plant owners are afraid — afraid that pruning is like amputation and will cause the plant pain; afraid that pruning is as complicated as surgery; afraid that they will damage or traumatize their plants; afraid they will do it at the wrong time of year; afraid they will do it incorrectly and kill the plant. There are also many folks who believe that Mother Nature intended plants to grow as large as possible and that bigger is better.

First, let's deal with the amputation fear. If we surgically remove someone's finger or limb, it will not grow back. Human amputation is pretty drastic and not something we ever want to face. Pruning off a tree limb or plant stem, however, will result in a new limb growing back. Keep this in mind the next time you feel squeamish about pruning a plant.

With a few exceptions (see below), pruning does not stress or damage a plant. Nor will pruning cause the plant to bleed to death or to cry out in pain. To use a better analogy, pruning is like getting a haircut — it won't affect health or cause pain; it will only alter appearance.

As with haircuts, the hardest part of pruning is deciding what you want the plant to look like when you are done. Sometimes a trim is in order. Other times, you may want a radical new look. Part of this process is knowing how the new growth will come in after pruning. More on that later.

Another consideration that keeps folks from pruning regularly is the popular idea that "bigger is better." Although that may sometimes be true, especially with starter plants, in most cases that maxim overlooks the fact that a plant's proportions change considerably if allowed to grow unpruned. From a design perspective, a plant's proportions are far more important than its overall size. After all, we are not growing Redwood trees!

Bonsai is the best example of proportions being more important than size. Bonsais are trees that have been pruned constantly so that the end result is a miniature tree often less than a foot tall, but perfectly proportioned. It is the proportions of the Bonsai that we respond to. So think again when you decide not to prune because you want a larger plant. Judicious pruning will allow your plant to grow larger, but more slowly and with better proportions.

Nearly all common houseplants are non-seasonal, meaning they can be pruned at any time of the year without injury. Outdoor temperate zone plants and trees do have pruning seasons, but not indoor tropical plants. So don't let the time of year deter you from pruning.

What happens if you don't prune regularly? If you are reading this chapter, you probably already know. Most unpruned plants will eventually become over-grown with long, leggy stems that are too tall or too wide and have lost most of their lower foliage. They often require stakes and walls to prop them up. You can neglect pruning a plant for just so long before it becomes unruly looking, takes over the room or pushes against the ceiling. If you wait that long, you have wait-ed too long. Pruning a badly overgrown plant is much more complicated and will require a radical and prolonged adjustment following the pruning. So start pruning your plants now even if they don't look like they need it yet.

Now take a deep breath, grab your pruners and plunge in without fear!

Some Plants Cannot Be Pruned

Before you prune, you must be sure that your plant is a species that can be pruned. If your plant has multiple stems or branches, then it probably can be pruned. If it has a single growing point and no visible stem, then it probably cannot be pruned. Here are some examples of plants that cannot be pruned: African violet, Alocasia, Aloe, Amaryllis, Anthurium, Bird of Paradise, Bird's Nest Fern, Bromeliad, Clivia, Cyclamen, Date Palm, Moth Orchid, Oxalis (Shamrock), Peace lily, Ponytail palm, Sago palm (Cycad), Snake plant, Spider plant, and ZZ Plant.

Nearly all Palm species should not be pruned unless there are multiple stems in the pot that you want to eliminate. Examples of Palms that should not be pruned are Majesty, Areca, Parlor and Kentia. Pruning individual stems back to the soil line can thin Bamboo palms and Rhapis palms, if there are multiple stems in the pot.

Below are some plant species that can be pruned, but only under special cir-cumstances:

Norfolk Island Pine: Once the top growing tip is removed or damaged, new growth will cease and the plant will very slowly die after several years. There is nothing much you can do about a NIP that outgrows its space.

Cane type plants, such as Massangeana cane and Yucca cane: The thick, bark-covered canes cannot be cut back, but the smaller stems that grow out of the tops of these canes can be pruned back.

African violets, Anthuriums and Philodendron selloums may develop tall, leggy stems after many years. If so, the main stem can be pruned back and the top section rooted in damp potting mix.

Boston ferns and Asparagus ferns generally do not need pruning. However, if they get very sparse, they can be rejuvenated by giving them crew-cuts right back to the soil-line. New growth will then emerge from below the soil.

Lucky Bamboos are cuttings rooted in water. The thin stems that grow out of the thick, rooted stems can be cut back, but the thick stems cannot.

How to Prune

Now that I have convinced you to prune your plants, I had better explain how to do it! Although I can provide some general guidelines, it is hard to be very specific because pruning techniques vary from species to species and because each individual plant is unique.

How you prune also depends on what your ultimate goal is. For example, I have a beautiful Ming Aralia that I grew from several small cuttings 30 years ago. It could easily be 6 feet tall by now. However, the only space I have for it in my small apartment is on a windowsill that will not accommodate a pot larger than 7 inches. So my Aralia stays in its 7-inch pot and I keep it pruned to a height of 24 inches. I never allow it to get larger than that because it has to fit its space. So space is a valid consideration in deciding how you prune.

My 24" tall Ming Aralia

Where to Prune

Always make your pruning cut just above a node. What's a node?! A node is a tiny swelling on a stem where a leaf or leaf stem is or was attached. It is out of this node that new growth will emerge. If you cut just beyond the node, then you will not leave an unsightly bare stub at the end.

Because plant stems often have many nodes, you have just as many choices as to where you make your pruning cut. The node you select is a judgment that only you can make. Try to visualize how the plant will look if you cut at various nodes on a stem. Also remember that new growth will emerge and grow out and up from the node where you make the cut. It is this visualization that is the key to successful pruning. Visualization gets easier with experience. Just remember that pruning in the "wrong" place will not damage the plant. At worst it will simply create a temporary look to your plant that does not satisfy you. But, like a bad haircut, it will grow back in. With pruning, there are second chances!

Pruning Vining Plants

Vining or trailing or hanging plants are the easiest plants to prune and they yield abundant cuttings that can be used to propagate new plants (see Chapter 12). Vining plants stems can be cut at any point along the stems. After pruning, new growth will emerge at the node just below where you made the cut. In other words new growth will be at the new end of the cut stem.

You can prune off the last inch or two of a stem, but within a month or so you will have to do it all over again after it has grown back. This technique is called trimming and requires regular attention.

A better technique for pruning vining plants is to select a few of the longest stems and cut back each one to a length of 1–3 inches. This technique will create new growth on those cut stems close to the base of the plant where older plants tend to get sparse. Pruning stems way back to the base is the only way to get new growth at the base. Very few plants push up new growth from below the soil. So every month or two, prune back a few of the longest stems. This will maintain a full and compact plant that never goes bare in the center.

Pruning Very Tall Plants

Because many folks fail to prune at all, they are often faced with a plant that is pushing up against the ceiling with no place to go. Although it is best to prune long before a plant starts touching the ceiling, I realize that this is a problem that must be addressed.

Plant species that often outgrow their spaces are Dieffenbachias, Corn plants, Dracaena marginatas, Yuccas, Dracaena reflexas, Ficus trees, Rubber Plants, Norfolk pines, Bamboo palms, Ming aralias, and many others.

Norfolk Pines cannot be pruned (see above). Overgrown Bamboo palm stems should be pruned off at the base. Ficus trees should be pruned back evenly all around.

Dieffenbachias are rapid growers that outgrow their space and end up propped more than any other common houseplant. If yours is badly overgrown (close to the ceiling or leaning severely), then cut it back to a height of 2-feet or less. The top section can be rooted in soil.

The other plants have to be pruned back by cutting through the stems that are too tall. If the stem has lost most of its lower leaves, that often means cutting below all of the leaves on that stem, leaving a leafless stem. That leafless stem will not die, but will produce new growth starting just below the pruning cut and grow up from there. Keep this in mind when you choose a place on the stem to make a pruning cut. In other words, prune back to the point where you would like to see new growth emerge even if that is 6 inches above the pot.

Note: most of these taller species don't have clearly defined nodes mentioned previously, so you can make your pruning cut just about anywhere on the stem.

Miscellaneous Pruning Questions

What is the proper angle to make a pruning cut? It really doesn't matter. Just make a clean cut with a sharp cutting tool at any angle that makes the cut stem look less noticeable.

Do I need to seal the pruning wound? No, this is an obsolete practice that is no longer recommended, even with outdoor trees. A plant's natural healing ability is more effective than any artificial sealants. I should note here that some plant species (Ficus, Poinsettia, Euphorbias) bleed a white, sticky sap. You may want to put some absorbent tissue or paper towel on the cut ends of these plants to keep the sap from dripping on furnishings. The bleeding will stop on its own within a few minutes.

Can I prune back a stem so far that there are no leaves remaining? Yes, you can as long as the stem is healthy and there is at least one node remaining on the stem after pruning. A plant needs only one healthy node to continue to grow. Badly overgrown plants with long, nearly bare stems will require pruning back well below the lowest remaining leaves on those leggy stems. After pruning such an overgrown plant, you may be left with a rather unattractive collection of short, leafless stems. However, patience will be rewarded after a few months when new growth has had a chance to grow in. Again the best way to avoid this temporary state of bareness is to prune proactively — before it looks obvious that the plant needs to be pruned.

Can the pruned off pieces be used to get new plants? Yes, most pruned off sections, especially from vining plants, can be used to propagate new plants by rooting them in soil or water. For more information on this topic see Chapter 12.

12 Propagating Your Plants

Most items that we purchase have a finite life span. They eventually wear out and we have to pay to have them repaired or replaced. Electronic devices are often obsolete after a couple of years. One of the great joys of owning plants is that we can make more plants from the ones that we already have. In fact, some plants are so easy to propagate that we can pot-up lots of new plants and give them away to friends and loved ones as gifts. Plant propagation is also a wonderful learning opportunity for children. It is simple, direct, and visual.

There are three primary types of propagation: Cuttings (including air-layering), division, and seeds. You can propagate some houseplants using all three methods. With other plants, only one or two of these methods will work.

Propagation by Cuttings and Air-layering

Taking cuttings is the easiest and most common way to get new plants from old plants. This technique is appropriate for most common houseplants. It is a form of cloning and it will produce new plants that are identical to the parent plants. Air-layering is a special method of getting propagated cuttings from woody-stemmed plants and other plants that do not root easily from cuttings.

Pruning: When you take a cutting from a plant you are also pruning that plant. Most indoor plants respond well to periodic pruning because it keeps plants from developing long, leafless branches and stems. Do not view taking a cutting as damaging your plant. (See Chapter 11 on pruning.) Remember, you are helping your plant stay full and bushy. A pruned stem or branch on a healthy plant will produce new growth just below the point of the cut. Decide where you would like to see new growth and prune back to that point.

The best cuttings for propagation are small tip cuttings taken from the ends of stems or branches. Tip cuttings usually have no more than two sets of leaves and just enough bare stem to fit into a small pot. These cuttings are more viable because the tissue is younger and more vigorous.

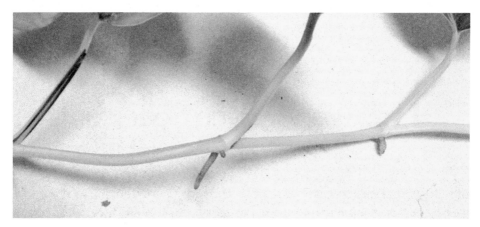

Pothos nodes

For roots to develop on a cutting, one or more nodes must be in contact with water or moist potting soil. A node is a place on a stem where a leaf attaches to it. On some plants the nodes appear as small bumps.

When inserting cuttings into soil there should be as little stem showing above the soil as possible. This will create a less leggy, more compact look.

In general, plants that root from cuttings can be rooted in either water or moist soil.

Water: Rooting cuttings in water is pretty easy. All you do is change the water every week or so. Wait until you have one-inch roots before moving the cutting to a small pot filled with a porous potting mix. Remember, the roots on cuttings are very fragile initially and cannot withstand the stress of under and over watering as well as an established plant can.

Soil: When you place unrooted cuttings or already rooted cuttings in soil, it is important to have a good soil medium that retains water, but also drains well. A mix of peat moss and perlite is excellent for this. You must keep this potting mix damp, but not constantly wet. Rooting powder might help a bit, but it is not essential.

When cuttings are first moved into potting soil, they often fail because their undeveloped roots cannot supply moisture as fast as moisture evaporates from the leaves.

You can prevent this by doing the following:

- Put the pot and cuttings in a clear plastic bag.
- Blow it up with your personal carbon dioxide supply and seal it closed.
- Set the whole thing in indirect light and away from any direct sun.

You now have your cuttings rooting in their own mini greenhouse eco-system. Wait about two weeks, then gradually open the bag and remove it over the course of a week. Keep the potting mix moderately damp at all times. Gradually increase the light.

Air-layering

Air-layering is a method of propagating woody stem cuttings that are difficult to root in water or soil. It is a technique that allows the roots to develop on the cuttings before they are completely severed. Here is how to do it:

1. Pick the place that you want to cut the stem back to. At this point, take a sharp knife and cut a V-shaped notch one third of the way through the stem. This is where the new roots will develop and grow. Alternatively, remove the bark and outer layer of the stem in a one-inch band around the stem.

2. If you have rooting hormone, put it into the notch or on the exposed area. If you don't have it, don't worry about it.

3. Wrap a handful of damp sphagnum moss in a ball completely covering and surrounding the wound. The roots will grow into this moist sphagnum moss.

4. Place clear plastic wrap around the wad of moss covering the wound. Seal the plastic wrap tightly with tape or rubber bands. This must be airtight so the moss cannot dry out.

5. Wait patiently for roots to develop and grow into the moss. This usually takes a month or more. If you can't see anything after a month or so, carefully remove the plastic wrap and check for roots and to make sure the moss has not dried out.

6. When you have a healthy batch of roots growing in the moss, completely sever the stem just below the developing roots. Remove the plastic and pot your rooted cutting into a small pot. Do not remove the moss in which the roots are now growing.

Here are some other things you should know about rooting cuttings:

It often takes a couple of months for roots to start to develop and another several months to become well established. In the interim, it is not uncommon for some lower leaves to yellow and die. Until your cutting has fully functioning roots, it cannot support a full set of leaves. Be patient and never let the soil get too dry or stay soggy for long because the new roots are still fragile and vulnerable to improper watering.

For most indoor plants, it is best to put lots of cuttings together into the smallest pot that they will fit into. This allows the roots to fill the pot more quickly and then start growing "up top" more vigorously. They can always be moved to a larger pot later on. Multiple plants in a single pot will also create a fuller looking plant.

While the cuttings are rooting, keep them out of direct sunlight. This is especially important for cuttings rooting inside a clear plastic bag.

Long hanging indoor plants almost always end up deteriorating after they reach a certain length. You end up with 10-foot vines with five feet of bare stem and no foliage at the base of the plant. The best way to prevent this is to prune back long stems before they start to lose leaves close to the base of the plant.

When rooted cuttings are moved from water to soil, the roots must go through some structural changes as they adapt from water to soil. That takes some time. The cuttings will also use most of their energy to develop new roots throughout the soil. That also takes time. During this "waiting time" it is important to keep the soil moderately moist. The newly developing roots are fragile and easily damaged if the soil is allowed to get too dry or kept wet for too long. Even though your cuttings may not be putting out visible new growth, do not worry. As long as the cuttings are not withering, then you can be sure that everything is okay.

Propagating Succulents

Succulents are plants that come from arid regions and have thick stems that store water during dry periods. They include Cactus species, Jade Plants, Snake Plants, Sedum, Crown of Thorns, Aloe veras, Agave and Kalanchoes. They have a special requirement when propagating them by taking stem cuttings. Allow the cutting to dry in the open air for 24 hours before inserting the cut end in a damp, porous succulent potting mix.

Propagation by Division

Plants that have multiple stems or shoots in a single pot can be divided into one or more separate potted plants. This method will not work for plants that have only a single stem or trunk emerging from the pot. Before you divide multiple plants into individual plants, consider the likely results first. It is quite common for nurseries to put several plants into the same pot because that will produce a larger, fuller looking plant overall. If you separate these plants and pot them up individually, each pot is destined to have only one plant that will grow taller, but not much wider. Consider if this is what you want before you make the division. Note: Some plants, such as Sanseverias, produce lots of new shoots from below the soil. These plants will fill out any pot following division and are an exception to the previous point.

Division is a fairly simple, but a risky and messy process. You can either pull the roots apart gently or you can cut through the rootball with a sharp knife. In general, it is better to use the former technique for smaller plants or those with tender roots. You will find that you can pull the roots apart fairly easily with these plants. For larger plants and plants that have coarse roots that have massed in the rootball, a large, sharp knife is the only way to separate the roots.

The pulling and the cutting will inevitably damage some of the roots. However, as long as you are working with a healthy root system, then the limited number of damaged roots will not adversely affect your plant. Damaged roots will heal, but they are more susceptible to bacterial, fungal, and viral infections. Thus, it is important to use clean cutting tools and pots and sterile soil when you divide the roots.

After you have divided the roots and separated the plants, put each division into a pot that is just large enough for the roots to fit into comfortably, but snugly. If you use too large a pot, you greatly increase the risk of overwatering. Your newly potted plant will need a period of time to recover from the shock of the root division. It will also need time to produce new roots that will fill the pot before it will resume active foliage growth. A very large pot will prolong this recovery time.

Root division can be traumatic to the plant. You may lose all of the divisions if it is not done properly. Proceed with caution!

Propagation from Seeds

Most houseplants do not produce seeds. When they do, they are often infertile. In addition, many seeds have unique temperature, moisture, soil, and light requirements that must be met before they are ready for germination. If you are interested in growing plants from seeds, I recommend that you purchase the seeds from a seed supplier. The seeds will be ready for germination when you receive them and the supplier will provide you with the unique requirements for those particular seeds.

Leaving the unique requirements aside, here is some general information that applies to most seed propagation:

- Use a sterile potting mix with lots of peat moss and perlite to germinate your seeds. Seedlings are very vulnerable to a disease known as "damping off" that attacks tender stems right at the soil line. Unsterilized garden soil increases the chances of this happening.

- If you are germinating many seeds at one time, spread them out over a broad surface. If they are too close to one another, you will have a difficult time separating them later.

- Most houseplants are tropical in origin. Their seeds will germinate more quickly if you can provide warm temperatures and high humidity. Placing your germination container on top of a warm appliance may provide the gentle heat required. Do not place the germinating seeds directly on a heater. A plastic cover over the top of the container will help retain the soil and air moisture.

- After the first set of leaves emerge, gradually remove the plastic cover and acclimate the seedlings to lower humidity over the course of several days.

- Most seedlings require lots of bright indirect light for 10 to 12 hours each day. Lack of light will produce leggy plants. Fluorescent lights placed right above the seedlings are an excellent source of light for seedlings.

- The best time to separate multiple seedlings is just after the second set of leaves (the first set of true leaves, so called because these leaves are the first to have the same shape as the mature leaves) have emerged. Before this time the roots are not adequately developed. After this time the roots begin to entwine and are difficult to separate.

- Separating seedling roots is a delicate procedure that requires the gentle and steady hands of a surgeon. Do not be alarmed if some of the roots tear or the stems break during this process.

- Pot your seedlings into small 2-inch or 3-inch pots and keep them there until the roots have spread throughout the rootball. Resist the urge to make them grow faster by putting them into larger pots before they are ready.

Conclusion

So there you have the basics of plant propagation. If you haven't experienced the joy of successfully propagating plants, then now is the time to start. It is one of the more fulfilling aspects of plant care. A plant that you have propagated is a plant that is truly your own.

A final caveat: Propagation leads to ever more plants in your collection, which in turn produce more cuttings and divisions. Family members should not be asked to move out of the house in order to accommodate your propagation skills!

13 Roots

The roots of a potted plant are often neglected because they are out of sight. We know they are there, but we never see what or how they are doing. Yet, roots are probably the most important part of any plant. The roots are a plant's alimentary, circulatory and respiratory system all in one. A plant's above ground portion may be completely damaged but if the plant's roots are healthy, new growth may soon emerge. But if a plant's roots die, the plant is lost.

What Roots Do

Roots have three major functions. They spread out and help stabilize and support a plant so it doesn't fall over. They absorb water, nutrients and oxygen. They move the water, nutrients and oxygen into the rest of the plant where those elements are used by plant foliage to photosynthesize them (in the presence of light) into healthy new growth. The entire plant is dependent on the ability of roots to perform these tasks as nature intended. That is why it is so very important that we keep the roots healthy even though they are out of sight. Remember, your heart and lungs are not visible to you, but their health is of critical importance to you.

Healthy Roots

The appearance of roots varies from one species to another. This is because different root structures have evolved over the eons so that different species can take advantage of local environmental conditions. The roots of some plant species have to survive in wet, swampy areas while others must adapt to very dry desert climates. Some plants develop root structures that are bulb-like and help to store water and nutrients during dry spells. Other plants are adapted to go into periods of dormancy during drought or very cold temperatures. These

This is a healthy root system

and many other environmental conditions determine the appearance of root structures.

In general, healthy plant roots should be firm. Most indoor potted plants are tropical in origin. The roots of these plants are generally light-colored and slightly fleshy. Roots that are soft and mushy or have a strong odor are not healthy. Likewise, roots that are dry and brittle are not healthy, unless a plant is in its dormant period.

Don't be afraid to unpot your new or healthy plant and examine the roots — without removing the soil. Once you know what healthy roots look like, it will be easier for you to tell later on if they are still healthy.

Root Hairs

Root hairs are very thin hairs that grow out of the larger, thicker roots. The root hairs are very fine and easy to overlook. Yet, it is the root hairs that do most of the work — absorbing water, oxygen and nutrients. If these root hairs are damaged, it will affect the overall health of the plant.

Anytime we repot a plant, some of those roots and root hairs are damaged. Fortunately, there are enough roots and root hairs that damage to some of them will not be a problem. However, there is a common practice — that *I do not recommend* — that can severely compromise most of the vital root hairs. That practice is washing all or most of the soil away from the roots. Some folks mistakenly believe that "replacing" old soil with fresh soil is good for the plant. Other plant owners wash away soil in order to remove soil pests or diseases. In either case, the removal of the soil damages most of the root hairs and puts the plant under enormous stress until it is able to slowly grow new root hairs. In most instances, the plant cannot survive while it is without the vital root hairs. Diseases or plant pests are then mistakenly blamed for the demise of the plant. In fact, it was the soil replacement and the damage to the root hairs that was the real cause.

How Do the Roots Work?

Good quality soil has lots of tiny spaces between the soil particles. This is referred to as *soil porosity*. Granular, gritty material, such as perlite, sand, and ground bark chips provide the air pockets that good soil should have. These pockets or spaces within the soil are very important because they will fill up and retain water for the roots, but they will also dry out and hold air for the roots. Plants need both water and air and roots must must have access to both.

Dry soil is soil that has no water in the tiny air pockets. Wet soil is soil that has no air in those pockets. Right after a plant is watered thoroughly, the water displaces the air in the pockets and you see the air bubbling up to the surface and out of the soil. The roots then absorb the water and the nutrients that have dissolved into the water. However, if the soil is not allowed to dry out for an extended period of time, then the roots will be deprived of oxygen and will begin to rot. That is why it is so important to allow the soil to dry out sufficiently in between waterings. Constantly wet soil deprives the plant roots of oxygen. On the other hand, soil that is kept too dry deprives the roots of necessary water and the roots will eventually die of dehydration.

Root System and Rootball

The root system refers to all of the roots collectively that belong to a plant. The root system along with the surrounding soil held together by the root system is referred to as the rootball. A properly potted plant with a healthy root system will have a rootball that is filled with roots and covered on the outside with a web of roots. When you pull a plant with a healthy root system out of its pot, the rootball should stay intact because the web of roots and root hairs will hold it all together. Many folks think that this means the plant is rootbound and in need of a larger pot. In fact, this is rarely the case. See Chapter 1 on repotting to determine just when a plant needs a larger pot.

If your plant is ailing and you are not sure why, gently remove it from its pot and inspect its root system.

- If large clumps of soil fall loosely from the rootball, then that means the pot is too big or the roots have shrunk back and may be dying. Remove loose excess soil not held in place by the root system. Move the plant into a smaller pot just large enough to accommodate the root system.

- If roots look soft and mushy, trim them off, as they will not recover. If there are no healthy remaining roots, take the cuttings and discard the plant.

- If the root system is wrapped around the rootball and the roots appear healthy, then return the plant to its pot and be confident that your pot size, soil quality, and watering routine are all okay.

- If the roots are so wrapped around the entire rootball that almost no soil is visible, then repotting *may* be in order. See Chapter 1 on Repotting for further information.

Stray Roots

It is quite common for healthy roots to poke through a drainage hole in the bottom of the pot. It is commonly assumed that this is a sign that the roots are crying out for a larger pot. Not so! There may still be plenty of room for the roots to grow in the pot, but a few roots may simply have grown out of the hole because roots just grow in all directions, not because they have run out of room in the pot.

However, stray roots may dry out because they are no longer in contact with moist soil. Although such drying out will not seriously harm the plant, it may cause a few leaves to develop discolored spots. So stray roots can be cut off where they emerge from the drainage hole. This will prevent further foliage damage.

Sometimes stray roots are an indication that there is a mass of roots growing at the bottom of the rootball. If you find this to be the case, simply slice off these roots along with the bottom half inch of the rootball. Put a half-inch of fresh soil in the bottom of the pot and put the plant back into its pot.

Root Pruning: Maintaining a Plant in the Same Pot Indefinitely

Suppose you have a healthy plant that is growing vigorously, is terribly potbound and needs a larger pot, but you don't have room in your home for a larger pot. The solution is to prune the roots. Remove the plant from its pot. Use a long sharp knife to slice off about a half-inch of soil and roots all around the sides and bottom of the rootball. This will not damage the plant because a severely pot-bound plant will have lots of healthy roots and roothairs throughout the rootball to support the plant.

Add a half-inch of fresh soil to the bottom of the same pot. Center the pruned rootball in the pot and fill in the side with fresh soil. The root system will now have fresh soil to grow into and the plant will still be in the same pot. You can do this any number of times over an indefinite period of time. I have kept a Ming Aralia on my small windowsill in the same 7" pot for over 30 years by root pruning it every 3 or 4 years.

By the way, root pruning is at the heart of the technique used to create bonsai plants. Bonsais are plants or trees that are miniaturized by regular pruning of both top growth and roots over the course of many decades. So root pruning is a safe and effective technique for maintaining plants at the size you prefer.

Root Diseases

There are a number of fungal, bacterial and viral diseases that can affect roots. Knowing the cause of plant failure is very important for professional nursery growers because their livelihood is invested in their plant crops. Soil and tissue analysis is done in a lab to identify the specific culprit. For the layperson, however, knowing if your plant roots are infected with a specific bacterial or fungal infection doesn't much matter. By the time you suspect your roots may be diseased, it may already be too late.

Nearly all root diseases, including root rot, can be prevented by taking the following precautions:

- Always use sterile packaged potting mixes. Garden soils and compost may be organic and loaded with nutrients, but they may also be contaminated with bacteria and fungus. The word organic on the label does not mean disease-free.

- Never re-use soil that has come from another plant, especially one that has died. That old potting soil is best used outside in your flowerbeds.

- Make sure your potting mix is properly porous so that it will dry out quickly between waterings. Add perlite if it needs more porosity.

- Do not over-pot. Using a pot that is too big is the single most common cause of root rot. See Chapter 1 on Repotting.

- Always allow the soil to dry out sufficiently in between waterings so that the roots can get necessary oxygen. See Chapter 6 on Watering Your Plants.

Although there are many commercial products sold that are supposed to cure various root diseases, I don't recommend them unless you have had a soil and root tissue analysis done by a lab. Otherwise, you won't know what disease you are trying to cure and what product to use. By the way, fertilizer will not cure *any* root disease so resist the miraculous claims made or implied by fertilizer manufacturers.

Conclusion

Pay attention to your potted plant's roots. Look at them when the plant is healthy and check them again if your plant starts to fare poorly. If the condition of the roots has changed, then you can be sure that your plant will only recover after you have determined why the roots have deteriorated. The chances are that one or more of the precautions listed above have not been taken. As usual, prevention is the best remedy for root problems.

14 Root Rot Caused by Repotting

Your plant is suffering from root rot? When you repotted unnecessarily, you made the very common and classic mistake of fixing something that was not broken. Nearly all potted indoor plants do best when they are kept moderately potbound, as yours was prior to the repotting.

How Repotting Can Cause Root Rot

Here is what happens when a plant is moved to a pot that is too big. All the excess soil that you add acts like a giant sponge, absorbing water and holding onto it for a long time. The roots are then surrounded by the wet/damp soil and slowly begin to rot. Roots need oxygen as well as water and when wet soil deprives them of oxygen for an extended period of time, the roots begin to rot, but you won't see this happening.

Repotting Properly is Important

I am quite sure your plant did not need a larger pot, but even if it had, repotting has to be done properly (see Chapters 1 and 7). It should have been moved into a pot no more than one size larger. You need to use a good quality, peat-based, soilless potting mix. Miracle-Gro potting mix contains material that retains moisture for a long time (moisture control) and lacks porosity throughout which is what creates good drainage. Pro-Mix is a good potting mix if you can find it. Otherwise, mix up 4 parts of peat moss with 1 part of perlite. Perlite mixed into a potting mix is the best way to increase drainage. Adding drainage material as a bottom layer is an out-dated and discredited practice that does not help.

When you repotted, you probably made the common mistake of adding soil to the top surface. That added soil prevents evaporation and it also prevents you from accurately assessing how dry the soil is in the root zone where it matters.

What to Do Now

The root rot has already started, but let's hope it has not damaged too many of the roots. To remedy the situation, carefully un-pot your plant, removing all of the soil that you added around the original rootball. Try to keep the original rootball intact. Then, put that rootball back into its original or similarly sized pot with drainage holes. It should fit snugly and you may need to add just a small amount of a porous potting mix to fill in any spaces left from portions of the original rootball that may have loosened and fallen off.

Changing the pot size in itself will not save your plant. Root rot takes place gradually, so it takes a while before a plant starts to show symptoms. By moving the plant back to a smaller pot, you remove excess soil that is like a sponge and retains moisture around the roots for too long and prevents oxygen from returning to the root zone. Removing excess soil will help prevent further root rot.

After downsizing the pot, the plant will continue to struggle for a month or so until the roots have a chance to dry out properly and to regenerate roots that have already been damaged. It is a process that takes time and for which there is no immediate cure. Allow the soil to dry properly and be patient.

The goal here is to get things back to where they were prior to repotting. That way the soil surrounding the roots will dry out regularly and allow oxygen back into the root zone. Recovery will take time, so expect continued leaf loss for a while. Look for healthy new growth as a sign of recovery.

Proper Watering to Avoid Root Rot

Every plant is different and none can be watered on a pre-determined schedule. Keep all your plants quite potbound and then learn to water them just before they start to wilt. That is different for different species. Some plant species such as Peace Lily and Croton should be watered as soon as the surface of the soil feels almost dry. Other plants, such as Cacti and most succulents, must be allowed to dry halfway deep into the pot before watering. Most other common houseplants should be watered when the top quarter of the soil is dry to the touch. After a while you will see a pattern for when each plant seems to need water.

However, as soon as you move plants into pots that are too large, these rules of thumb no longer apply and the risk of root rot is very high for any plant species. So think twice before you repot your plants.

15 Plant Cosmetics:
Making Your Plants Look Their Best

No, this is not about using plants to manufacture products to enhance facial appearance. It is about helping your plants look their best. Besides keeping their plants healthy, what do the professionals do to enhance the appearance of their plants? They trim off yellow and brown leaves and leaf edges. They remove unruly growth. They remove dust. They keep leaves clean and glossy. They put top dressing over the soil. They use attractive planters. Although none of these practices do much for the health and longevity of the plants, they do make the plants look more attractive.

If you are only concerned with the health of your plants, you can skip this chapter. But if you also care about how your plants look, then this is the chapter for you.

The Meaning of Discolored Leaves

For many different reasons, all or parts of green leaves may turn yellow or brown. Usually this discoloration starts at the leaf tip, but sometimes it starts at a leaf edge. It may eventually discolor the entire leaf or just a small portion of it. Leaf discoloration is often a symptom of a plant care problem — improper watering, inadequate light, poor water quality, plant pests, etc. See Chapter 16 for information on using symptoms to diagnose plant problems. It is important to eliminate the cause of the leaf discoloration. If you don't determine the cause, the discoloration will continue and the plant will decline in appearance and health. Removing the discolored leaves will not solve any underlying problems; it will simply improve the appearance of the plant temporarily.

On the other hand, even after you have corrected the underlying problem, the already discolored foliage will remain. There is no way to restore a healthy green color to leaf tissue that has turned yellow or brown. Although leaving the discoloration in place will not damage the plants, it will continue to spoil the appearance of the plant. As an added benefit, removing discolored leaf tissue will make it easier to determine if the discoloration is decreasing or getting worse.

That is why plant professionals trim and remove discolored leaves immediately. You may be surprised to discover how much healthier your plants look after you remove discolored leaves.

I have found that many plant owners are reluctant to remove discolored or damaged foliage because they don't know how. They are ferarful of causing further damage if they don't do it properly. It is important to make a distinction here between trimming off discolored foliage and pruning healthy plant stems. Pruning does require some specific understandings and those are covered in Chapter 11. Trimming, however, requires no special techniques. The only understanding required is that removing damaged foliage never does any harm to the plant. If you see a leaf that has turned yellow or brown, then remove the entire leaf, including the leaf stem. It's that simple. Trimming can be done at any time of year.

How to Trim Properly

There is a technique to trimming an individual leaf that goes beyond just cutting off the discolored portions. The key is to maintain the original contour or shape of the leaf that you are trimming. If a pointed leaf has a brown tip, cut into the green portion just enough so that the point is maintained after you have removed the brown tip. Likewise, an oval shaped leaf should be trimmed to maintain that oval shape. After you have trimmed a plant, it should not be apparent that you have done any cutting. Blunt cuts are a giveaway that you have had to remove an unsightly problem. Even if that is true, why announce it?! Cosmetic techniques are designed to create an illusion — to make things look better without being obvious about it.

When trimming, use long, sharp scissors to help you do a better job.

Trimming Leaf Tips and Edges

If it is just an edge or a tip of a leaf that is discolored and the discoloration does not progress further, then it may be appropriate to trim off only the discolored edges and tips. Plants with long, slender leaves, such as Spider Plants, Ponytail Palms and Dragon Trees, often develop dry, brown leaf tips. There is not much you can do to prevent this, but trimming off these tips when they are noticeable will improve the appearance of the plant. Use long, sharp scissors to cut the leaves at a sharp angle so as to preserve the pointed end of the leaf.

With broader leaves, such as those of a Corn Plant, discoloration may develop along the edges as well as the tips of the leaves. These discolored edges can be trimmed off in the same manner so as to preserve the original shape of the leaf. This may mean cutting off some healthy, green portions along with the brown or yellow, but that is okay.

You may observe that after you trim off a leaf tip or edge that a thin brown line or edge develops along the trim line. This cannot be avoided, but it is far less visible than the larger discolored portion that you removed. And this is all about cosmetics or appearance.

Removing Discolored Leaves

Sometimes all or most of a leaf becomes discolored or unhealthy looking. A green leaf that starts to turn a pale green will gradually lose more of its color and fall off. There is no remedy for saving it. If it is a lower leaf, then it is probably just part of the normal aging process. If it is new growth that is discolored, then that is often symptomatic of a more serious problem, usually root related (see Chapter 16).

Sometimes you have to choose between trimming off the dead portion of a leaf and removing the entire leaf. A good rule of thumb is that if more than half of the leaf is discolored, then complete removal of that leaf is usually the way to go. If it is apparent that the discoloration is progressing — getting more extensive — then it is probably best to remove the entire leaf. Removing discolored leaves never damages a plant so don't hesitate.

A mostly discolored leaf should be removed entirely by detaching it where it is attached to a green branch or stem.

Disposing of Dead Leaves

A common practice is to leave dead leaves and trimmings on top of the soil at the base of the plant. The assumption is that this "mulch" will add nutrients to the soil. In fact, composting only works outdoors so there is no added benefit to this practice with your indoor plants. On the downside, this dead plant material looks unattractive and may attract pests and plant diseases.

Pruning

Pruning is another way to enhance the appearance of your plants. Cosmetically, pruning is a way to dramatically reshape a plant's overall size and appearance. Unlike trimming, pruning involves the deliberate removal of large portions of healthy plant tissue. Because pruning is a bit more complicated than trimming, I have devoted a separate chapter (Chapter 11) to this topic.

Spent Flowers

There are so many different kinds of flowers that it is hard to generalize about them. Some flowers are tiny and last only a day while other flowers are spectacularly large and may last for several months or more.

In any case, don't expect your plant's flowers to last as long as the plant. A dying flower does not mean a dying plant. As soon as a flower starts to wilt or fade in color, then you can be sure it is on its way out. No one wants to look at dying flowers, so remove them as soon as they start to fade. The flower stem should be removed as well. However, if there are multiple flowers on a stem, wait until all of the flowers are spent before removing the stem.

The Hoya or Wax Plant flower stem (called a spike) should never be removed because that is where future flowers will emerge.

The popular Peace Lily is notorious for producing white pollen that falls onto the dark leaves below long before the flower dies. This white pollen dust is often mistaken for mold or a plant pest. It is harmless and it dusts off quite easily.

Some plants such as the Corn Plant and Snake Plant produce very sticky flowers that can be quite messy. If you don't want to deal with the sticky mess, it's okay to cut off these flowers as soon as they appear.

Dust Removal

Some locations are dustier than others. Some offices and homes that do not have windows that open are largely dust-free. But most of us experience some degree of dust in our living spaces and that dust accumulates on plant leaves as well as furniture. When excessive on plant leaf surfaces, dust can block out needed light and affect the health of the plant. Otherwise, it is probably best to dust when you notice the dust. Just as some folks may dust several times a week while others may go months, this is more a matter of personal taste than plant health.

Small plants can be rinsed with plain water in the sink. Larger plants can be hosed off outside or rinsed in a shower. Broad leafed plants can be wiped with a damp sponge or cloth. However, if you have a lot of dusty plants that are not easy to move around or too much to hand wipe, then some type of duster is in order. Ostrich feather dusters are very effective at removing and holding onto dust, not just sending it back into the air. They can be washed in soap and water periodically. Swiffers and similar dusting devices can also be used to efficiently remove dust from many plants.

Misting may help wash away some dust, but if there are minerals in your tap water (hard water), then those minerals will leave a white residue when the water evaporates. Filtered or distilled water will work better.

Removing Surface Leaf Spots

Sometimes new plants have a coating of whitish spots that don't wipe off easily. Theses spots may be the residue from pesticides sprayed on the foliage in the nursery. White leaf spots also result from misting or spraying leaves with hard water.

To remove these pesticide and hard water spots, elbow grease is the best ingredient. A solution of mostly water with a bit of liquid soap and white vinegar may help loosen stubborn stains, but it may still require some vigorous rubbing on your part. Vinegar works because it is mildly acidic and it cuts through the alkaline mineral salt residue from hard water. There is no special ratio of vinegar to water. Start with 4 or 5 parts of water to 1 part vinegar and see if that is effective in rubbing off the spots. If they don't come off, increase the proportion of vinegar. Do keep the vinegar out of the soil as the roots could be damaged by the acid in the vinegar.

There are commercial cleaning products available, but they are best reserved for professionals who have hundreds of plants to clean.

Leaf Shine

This is a bit of a controversial topic. Part of the controversy is personal preference for shiny vs. natural looking leaves. Even plant professionals have their own preferences in this regard. Again, this is about appearance, so do what looks good to you.

Most leaf shines and some leaf cleaners have some type of oil as a primary ingredient. Oil-based products do leave a shiny appearance on the leaves, but they can also leave the foliage feeling sticky if applied too heavily. In addition, these oil-based products leave a film on the leaves that tends to attract and hold onto dust. If dust is a problem for you, then avoid any oily leaf cleaning products. If you want to make your own leaf shine, plain mineral oil diluted with water and applied lightly with a soft cloth works quite well.

Note: Leaf shine products can block essential, breathing pores on the undersides of leaves so be sure to apply these products only to the top surfaces of leaves.

There are other leaf shine products that are not oil based. They are sprayed on and they dry to a hard shine that does not hold onto dust. Brand X Foliage Cleaner is my personal favorite for certain plants. It is silicon-based and has the side benefit of being able to penetrate tiny crevices and the outer coverings of many plant pests. It is a plant cleaner, not a pesticide. It is only available at www. buybrandx.com.

Whatever product you choose, it should be one that can be diluted with water so that you can mix it to the strength that you prefer. This allows you to control the degree of shininess to suit your personal taste. There is no need to slavishly follow the label dilution instructions with these plant cleaners that are diluted with water. Do heed warnings not to spray in direct sunlight or unusually warm temperatures.

There are a variety of home remedies that are often used to shine plant foliage. Most of these "natural" leaf shines use food products such as milk, mayonnaise, and cooking oils. I don't recommend them because they sometimes have odors and may attract ants and other pests. However, they are not likely to harm your plants.

Some plant leaves are naturally shinier than others. The ZZ Plant and The Dracaena 'Janet Craig' are two plants with naturally shiny foliage. Usually, keeping them dust-free is all that is required. At the other extreme, plants with fuzzy leaves, such as African Violets and Gesneriads will never shine. In fact, it is best to avoid spraying such plants altogether. Dust particles may be removed from fuzzy plants by blowing on them vigorously.

Aerosol sprays should be avoided. The chemicals used to make aerosols work can damage the foliage of some tender plant species. Only use commercial cleaners and shines that have pump sprays.

Top Dressing

A nice finishing and professional-looking touch is provided by adding a top dressing over the surface of the soil and pot. Although a top dressing may slightly reduce evaporation of soil moisture into the air, it generally does nothing more than make plants look nicer. Top dressings are not the same as mulch which is used on outdoor plants. Top dressings are particularly effective when a plant growing in a nursery pot is double-potted inside of a second decorative planter. The top dressing covers the unattractive inner nursery pot.

There are many top dressing choices. Bark chips were once popular, but many professionals no longer use them because of their tendency to decay and harbor fungus gnats. Green sheet moss is used by many florists to dress up flowering plants, such as Orchids. Green moss tends to last only a month or so before it dries and turns yellow-brown, so it must be replaced frequently. Spanish moss is light and airy so it allows for good air circulation around the soil and roots. It has a natural gray color that it retains even after it has dried and been in use for a long time. Spanish moss sometimes harbors spider mites, but I have found that to be a relatively rare problem.

For a more modern look, polished stones and river rocks of various hues can be used. These stones are quite heavy, so faux stones made of polyresins are a good alternative. Small pieces of recycled cork and rubber that have been dyed to various colors are also lightweight alternative to stones.

All of these materials can be spread over the surface of the soil and will provide a nice finished look to your plants. But, again, I must stress that the only purpose of these top dressings is to improve the appearance, not the health of plants.

Unattractive Pots

Most plants are grown in inexpensive, unattractive black or white plastic pots, called grow or nursery pots. This creates the impulse to immediately repot the plant into something more attractive. That's fine, **but** you probably won't do it correctly.

It is important to disturb plant roots as little as possible. In addition, unnecessary repotting is the most common cause of plant problems. Read Chapter 1 before attempting any repotting.

The best way to deal with this dilemma is to double-pot or cache-pot. Select a decorative pot or planter of your choice, but make sure it is large enough for you to put the plant **and** its nursery pot inside of it. With this technique, the unattractive pot is hidden, repotting is unnecessary, and the roots remain undisturbed.

If for some reason you do not want to double pot, then the next best alternative is to get a decorative planter that is exactly the same size as the grow pot and also has drainage holes. After watering the plant, the rootball should remain intact as you remove it from its grow pot and slide it into the new decorative pot. Little or no soil should be added to the repotted plant.

Summary

Often the difference between an average and a great looking plant is a result of good cosmetic work. If the appearance of your plants matters to you, then get out your scissors, dusters and leaf shine and dress them up. But remember, all the cosmetics in the world will not make your plants any healthier.

16 Diagnosing Plant Problems

"My plant is dying! What should I do to save it?!" This is a common question that I receive. When I ask what symptoms they are observing, I may be told yellow leaves or brown leaf tips. That information is never adequate for me to make a proper diagnosis. In many cases, I will have a dozen more questions about available light, watering routine, repotting, etc. before I can properly diagnose the problem. Of course, if a plant is really dying, then it cannot be saved. Many plant owners believe that once they see yellow or wilted leaves that means the end is near. Fortunately, that is usually not the case. A few yellow leaves now and then is normal and not a cause for concern and may warrant nothing more than removing the offending leaves. At the other extreme, some plant owners wait until nearly all the leaves have died before seeking help. In that instance, it is probably too late and indeed the plant is dying and nothing short of a miracle will bring it back.

This chapter is intended to help you recognize relevant symptoms of plant problems on a timely basis, understand the causes, and treat the plant appropriately.

Diagnosing Symptoms

Yellow leaves mean a plant is not getting enough water. *Wrong!*

Wilting leaves mean under watering. *Wrong!*

Diagnosing plant problems would be easy if a specific symptom was always associated with a specific problem. Unfortunately, that is not the case. I am often asked to diagnose a plant problem based on a single symptom. It can't be done. Anyone that tells you otherwise is misinformed. And beware of those neat charts that list a specific cause for each specific symptom because they are only correct some of the time.

Most common plant symptoms — yellow leaves, brown leaf tips, wilted leaves, etc. — are generic symptoms, each with several possible causes. In this chapter I will first outline a strategy for determining the most likely cause. Then, I will discuss various plant symptoms and explain how you can use these symptoms as a guide for helping you provide better care for your indoor plants.

If the deterioration of your plant is sudden — literally overnight — then you can assume that some sudden change in the ***physical environment*** of the plant has caused this sudden damage. Exposure to cold temperatures or extreme heat (in a closed vehicle); exposure to strong outdoor sunlight after being inside; foreign chemical substances added to the soil, including pet urine and swimming pool water; and exposure to unusually bad air pollution, such as smoke from a fire, paint fumes or manufacturing pollutants. If any of these apply, you must remove the plant immediately from the physical environment that is causing the problem. Trim off damaged foliage and flush the soil with clear water if a foreign substance is in it. Unless the roots were severely damaged, the plant should gradually recover after the cause has been eliminated.

If your plant is languishing and getting more discolored leaves than you think it should and you don't know why, then follow the steps below. They are guidelines listed in order of probability. Start at the top and work your way down the list.

First: Check the pot size. Have you recently moved your plant into a larger pot or added new soil? If so, this is the most likely cause of your plant's problems. Unnecessary repotting and over potting are the most common cause of plant problems, yet the most overlooked. See Chapter 1 for information on repotting problems.

Second: Consider the available light. Every plant has a range of acceptable light intensity. If the available light is outside that range (either too little or too much), then your plant will gradually decline. Fertilizer, humidity and changing the watering frequency will not correct light deficiencies. You must match your plants with their light requirements. See Chapter 3 to help you evaluate light intensity.

Third: If the pot size is okay and the light intensity is acceptable, then improper watering is the next most likely cause of plant problems. Most potted plants do best when the top quarter of the soil is allowed to dry before watering thoroughly. However, some plants (succulents) must dry out more than that between waterings while others (Peace Lilies, Ferns) must be watered as soon as the surface of the soil feels dry. See Chapter 6 on watering properly.

Fourth: If leaf tips and edges are discolored, evaluate your water quality and fertilizing routine. Excess mineral salts cause leaf tip damage. These excess mineral salts come from using hard local tap water for your plants and from using too much fertilizer. The solution is to use distilled or filtered water or to stop fertilizing.

Fifth: Examine your plant for signs of insect pests. Spider mites appear as dust-like particles on the undersides of leaves and make tiny webs. Mealybugs appear as tiny specks of white, cotton-like material where leaf stems join trunks or branches. Scale insects look like small raised freckles along leaf stems and on leaf surfaces. They also leave a trail of sticky "honeydew" under the infested plant. Fungus gnats show up as tiny flying gnats. Aphids are oval, slightly raised bumps on tender newly emerged growth. White flies are aptly named and swarm about when a plant is disturbed. Make a habit of checking your plants regularly (at least monthly) for early signs of plant pests. They are much easier to eradicate when you treat them before they infest the entire plant. See Chapter 10 on identifying and treating indoor plant pests.

Sixth: Check the pH of your soil. Soil that is too acid (below 6.0 pH) or too alkaline (above 6.8 pH) prevents soil nutrients from being absorbed by plant roots.

Seventh: Consider temperature extremes. Most houseplants are from tropical regions where temperatures are in the 55°F to 90°F range. Temperatures outside this range can cause damage to plant leaves and stems and to plant roots if the exposure is for an extended period of time. See Chapter 9.

Next to last: Very dry air can be a problem for a very limited number of exotic houseplants. Contrary to popular belief, most houseplants can do just fine in low humidity, as long as the soil is watered properly. Plant symptoms are often attributed to, but are rarely the result of low humidity. Misting helps keep plants clean, but does not effectively raise humidity levels. If you have a humidity-sensitive plant such as some ferns, some Orchids and terrarium plants, then increase the humidity by using a humidifier or a pebble tray. See Chapter 9.

Last: Nutrient deficiencies are often assumed to be the cause of plant ailments and fertilizer is assumed to be the cure. Nutrient deficiencies are, in fact, the least common cause of all plant problems. Indoor plants use minute quantities of nutrients and they cannot be force-fed. Most potting soils have several years' worth of nutrients. If your plant has been in the same pot and soil for several years or more and is growing well, then it may benefit from diluted fertilizer. Ailing plants are poor candidates for increased nutrient supply. If you suspect nutrient deficiency, check the soil pH first. See Chapter 8 on using fertilizer.

Specific Symptoms

Below are some specific symptoms and some of their possible causes. Note that there is no single cause associated with any of these symptoms.

Wilted Leaves

Let's start by looking at wilted or droopy leaves as an example of a common plant symptom. Wilting does mean that a plant is not getting enough water. So presumably the solution is to water it more frequently. That might be true, but consider this. A plant that has been overwatered develops rotted roots that can no longer absorb water for the plant. So what happens? The overwatered plant wilts because there is no water available through the rotted roots to go to the stems and leaves. So wilted leaves can mean either too little or too much water. If you guess wrong, then you will aggravate the problem further.

If the soil is moist or if you water the plant and it does not perk up within a half day, then you can correctly assume that the roots are not absorbing water and that is probably because the roots have rotted. There is rarely a solution for root rot, although sometimes a plant will slowly recover once you adjust your watering to allow the soil to dry out properly between waterings. Replacing the soil is not a solution.

If the soil is bone dry deep into the pot and the water you add seems to run right out the drainage hole, then the wilting is caused by excessive dryness. After the soil is saturated once again, then the plant should perk up within a half-day although some leaves may yellow and not recover. Note that soil that is extremely dry does not absorb water readily so it may be necessary to leave the pot standing in water for several hours in order to re-wet it properly.

Brown Leaf Tips

Brown leaf tips or edges are another common symptom. Possible causes include using hard water, too much fertilizer, improper soil pH, low humidity, inadequate light, and either under watering or overwatering. You can tell from this list that the cause of brown leaf tips is not so easy to sort out!

First, understand that some plants, especially those with long pointed leaves (Spider Plants, Ponytail Palms and Dracaena marginatas, for example) quite normally get some browning of the last inch of their leaf tips. So don't worry about that.

Excess minerals in the soil are a common cause of more extensive leaf tip burn or browning. Excess minerals come from hard water and plant fertilizers. If your local tap water is on the hard side, then use distilled or filtered or rainwater for your plants. If you are fertilizing regularly, then stop. Contrary to popular opinion and fertilizer manufacturer ads, your indoor plants rarely if ever need fertilizer.

Soil pH refers to how acidic the potting soil is. This is not a problem for most potted plants when they are purchased. However, using hard water for your plants can gradually change the soil pH and cause brown tips and other problems. In addition, if you use homemade soil mixes, including garden soil and compost, then there is a good chance that the soil may become too acidic. The use of coffee grounds in your potting soil is a likely cause of making the soil too acidic.

Most common houseplants manage to do just fine in the low humidity of our artificially heated homes and offices. However, there are a few sensitive species that do not do well in low humidity and one of the first symptoms they exhibit is brown leaf tips. Many fern species, aquatic plants and the Nerve Plant (Fittonia) are examples of plants that require high humidity. But these plants are exceptions.

For a plant that is not getting enough light, the first symptom is often brown leaf tips. In Chapter 3, I discuss how to determine if your plant is getting proper light.

Finally, either over or under watering can cause leaf tips to turn brown in much the same way as improper watering causes wilting (see above).

Yellow Leaves

Every plant will get some yellow leaves from time to time. Sometimes this is just a normal part of the plant's growth process. As it adds healthy new growth on top, it quite naturally loses some older leaves at the bottom. However, a sudden increase in yellow leaves or an excessive amount of leaf yellowing can signal a problem that needs correcting. Unfortunately, just about any condition that stresses a plant will cause an increase in yellow leaves.

If your plant has an abundance of yellow leaves, don't assume anything! If you do, there is a very good chance your assumption will be wrong. The best approach is to methodically go through the list of possible causes and try to narrow it down to one or two likely causes.

- Is it getting enough light?
- Did you recently repot?
- Are you watering properly?
- Is your tap water hard?
- Are you using too much fertilizer?
- Is the light too strong?
- Is the humidity too low?

Symptoms of Plant Pests

Plant pests typically leave very specific symptoms. Tiny bits of soft cotton-like material are a sure sign of mealybugs. Fine, tiny webs and a mottled appearance on leaves mean a spider mite infestation. Stickiness found on leaf surfaces and surfaces underneath the plant are a good indication of scale insects or mealybugs. Small, slightly raised brown or translucent bumps on leaves and stems are also indicative of scale. Tiny flying gnats around or near your plants are a sure sign of fungus gnat larvae living in the soil of one or more of your plants. White powdery dust on leaves and soil surfaces are caused by a fungus disease known as powdery mildew. (Don't confuse powdery mildew with the white pollen that falls from Peace Lily flowers.) Clusters of light-colored bumps around tender new shoots are aphids.

Each of these plant pests can be treated safely and effectively without pesticides. For further information on these pests and how to treat them see Chapter 10.

IMPORTANT NOTE: Plant pests are very often a sign of a plant under stress for other reasons. A plant that is not watered properly, gets improper light or is otherwise unhealthy is much more likely to become a target for insect pests. So treating the pests may not be enough. Finding plant pests is a warning that your plant may be stressed for other reasons and you need to investigate that as well as treat the pests.

Unhealthy New Growth

The discoloration and loss of lower leaves is usually not a serious problem and can be easily corrected. However, when new shoots and buds are discolored or stunted, this indicates a more serious problem. A stressed plant will sacrifice older (lower) leaves in order to produce healthy new growth. When the new growth is unhealthy, the plant is in serious trouble and may not recover. Seriously compromised roots are the most common cause of distorted new growth and root rot is usually the source of the problem. As I have mentioned elsewhere, there is usually no cure for root rot, especially after new growth has already been affected. All you can do is allow the soil to dry properly, water less frequently and hope for the best.

Other Plant Symptoms

Pale green or bleached leaves: Too much direct sunlight; improper soil pH; chilling damage

Spindly new growth: Inadequate light

Long spaces between leaves: Inadequate light

Newer leaves are very small: Inadequate light

Leaves are dull colored, and soft with water spots: Exposure to cold temperatures

Stems are rotting close to the soil: Soil is too moist and roots have started to rot

Bad odor: Root rot from over watering; pet urine; food or beverages added to the soil

Soft, dark roots: Root rot caused by soil staying too moist for too long

A Holistic Approach to Diagnosing Plant Problems

In general, any particular plant symptom has multiple possible causes. If something seems wrong with your plant, you should try to take into account everything you know about that plant and its requirements. Is it getting proper light and water? Is it in the right sized pot? How is your water quality? Has it been exposed to a sudden temperature change? Has the plant's environment changed recently (new location, new pot)? On what part of the plant have you observed the symptoms?

A symptom is a signal that something is wrong, but it is up to you to be a detective and determine what the cause or causes are likely to be. Remember also that sometimes there is more than a single cause. Often a plant that is not getting adequate light is also developing root rot because the soil is staying too moist. In this instance the plant needs not only more light, but also needs to be watered less frequently. The root rot may also be accompanied by fungus gnats that will have to be treated.

Okay, Sherlock, now you have the tools to observe your plants, watch for their warning signs and treat them accordingly.

17 Undoing the Damage: How to Fix Plant Problems

Accidents happen. Sometimes through no fault of our own, our plants get over or under watered. They lean and topple over. They get exposed to cold temperatures, sunburn and cat urine. No one plans these things, but they happen and they are not among the common issues addressed in most plant books. Sometimes we are the unintended victims of bad information or advice. Other times, we simply are not able to provide the right care for a particular plant.

Here are some of the answers to questions that have come my way over many years of answering plant questions.

How to fix a leaning plant

Many potted plants put out new growth only at the top ends of stems. This means they tend to grow ever-taller. After a while, the plant becomes top-heavy and gravity starts to take over. The result is a leaning plant. Out come the broom sticks, and wires and string and tape to prop up these plants. To me there is nothing more unsightly than an overgrown plant supported by a variety of artificial devices.

These props are entirely unnecessary and a larger pot is **not** the answer. Proactive pruning is the best way to keep plants from becoming too tall in the first place. But you probably wouldn't be reading this if you knew that. It is difficult to provide general rules for dealing with a leaning plant as each plant species is different, but I will try.

If the plant looks too tall for its space or its pot, then it will have to be pruned back. See Chapter 11 on pruning to learn more about how to go about doing this.

If your plant is not overgrown, but leans precariously to one side, then repositioning the plant in the pot is usually the best solution. Moving the plant to a larger pot is rarely the answer, although that is what many folks try first. Instead of repotting, try to firmly push the main stem in the direction opposite to the lean while holding the pot steady. If you can push it slightly past the vertical, then you can press the soil down tight around the stem to hold it in place. This surprisingly simple solution that requires no special equipment or supports or horticultural knowledge is often all that is required. This will not damage the roots.

In some cases, the stem resists any attempt to push it to a vertical position. This is usually because it is quite potbound. But that doesn't mean a bigger pot is the answer. Instead, pull the rootball (soil and roots) up from the pot and settle it back in again at an angle sufficient to put the stem in a vertical position. That means the top of the rootball will now be at a slightly tipped angle when put back into the pot. You may need to add a little soil to one side of the rootball in order to maintain its new position in the pot. Press the soil down tight from the top until it is steady in the pot.

If the plant really is in need of a larger pot, then a variation of the above technique should be used to straighten the leaning plant. When repotting, the rootball should be set into the larger pot at an angle so that the stem is straight up. Adding a bit more soil on one side of the bottom of the pot will help support the rootball in this slightly skewed position. Likewise, fill in the sides of the pot as you observe that one side of the pot will need more soil than the other because the rootball is set in at an angle. When you are finished, add just enough soil to the surface of the rootball to make the surface even again.

How to fix a toppled plant

Sometimes a plant becomes so top heavy that it just topples over and you find it on the floor half out of its pot. That's a very distressing sight in part because it is always unexpected.

Carefully lift the toppled plant up and see if you can place it back into its pot, disturbing the roots as little as possible. It is not a good idea to replace the soil or to move the plant into a larger pot. Do try to get it firmly positioned back into its original pot. You may need to add some additional soil to replace any that spilled out. If the plant is still unstable after you have done this, then read the next section on dealing with tippy pots.

Inspect the plant for any damaged stems or leaves resulting from the fall. Any stems or leaves that have snapped or been creased by the fall are not likely to recover, so it is best to prune them off.

Next you have to determine what caused your plant to topple over so it doesn't happen again. If it is top-heavy, pruning may be the answer. If it is leaning, then straightening it in its pot is the answer. If the pot, as well as the plant, seems unstable, then read the next section.

How to fix a tippy pot

Sometime a plant becomes so top heavy that the pot and plant become unstable and are in danger of tipping over. The obvious solution is a larger pot, but don't assume that is the best solution.

If a plant is badly potbound and needs water three or more times per week, then a larger pot is probably best for the plant. (See Chapter 1 on when and how to repot.) Remember to use a pot one size larger even if that is not large enough to keep the pot from tipping over. In that case, read on.

If the plant is the right-sized pot for the roots and your pot is still in danger of tipping over, then there is another solution. Take the pot and plant and insert them both into a larger, heavier planter. Ceramic or terra cotta planters are good choices. This outer planter should be big enough and heavy enough to accommodate the plant and its pot and to keep them from tipping over. If you need still more weight to prevent tipping, then fill the space between the inner pot and the outer planter with decorative stones or some other heavy material. The goal here is to create more ballast (weight at the bottom) to counteract the weight of the top-heavy plant without disturbing the roots by putting them directly into a pot that is too large for them.

How to fix damaged foliage

Did the leaves on your favorite plant get shredded by your favorite pet or toddler? Damaged leaves don't repair themselves, so generally you should remove them by cutting them off entirely. However, if more than half of any leaf is intact, then trim off the damaged portion in such a way that the original contour of the leaf is maintained. If the leaf was pointed, keep it pointed. If it was rounded, make a round cut. This will help disguise the fact that the foliage was damaged and had to be trimmed back.

Leaves that are chewed or shredded will have no effect on the overall health of the plant, so no need to be concerned about that.

How to fix a broken stem or branch

If a stem or branch is broken more than halfway through its thickness, then it will not heal and should be cut off just below the break. If the stem has just a partial tear, then sometimes wrapping tape around the stem to hold it in place will enable the stem to heal over and the tape can later be removed.

How to fix an over-potted plant

Fixing any plant that has been over-potted for a long time is risky. Gently remove the plant from its pot when the soil is moderately dry, maybe just before you would ordinarily water it. Much of the outer soil will fall away because there are few if any roots to hold the soil in place. Look for healthy roots that are firm and light in color. If you find healthy roots, leave the soil in place that is in direct contact with these roots. Use a pot that is barely large enough to hold these healthy roots along with just enough soil to surround those roots. The less soil used the better as that will allow the soil and roots to dry out sooner between waterings.

If you do not find any healthy roots, then the plant cannot be saved.

How to fix a dried out plant

Suppose you go away for an extended period and have not made proper plans to have your plants watered. Or suppose you come upon a discarded plant that has not been watered in a very long time. Forgot to water a plant and it has wilted badly? Sooner or later it happens to every plant owner. You want to nurse the drought-stricken plants back to health.

Some plants withstand drought better than others. Cacti, for example, are adapted to periodic drought in their native desert climates so they withstand drought just fine. That is also true for most succulents. On the other hand, aquatic plants and those that are native to constantly damp climates do not tolerate drought very well at all. Azaleas and Peace Lilies are unlikely to recover from soil that becomes completely dried out. If all the leaves on your drought-stricken plant are dry and crispy and the stems are shriveled, then it is not likely to recover and it is best discarded. However, if there are still some signs of life in your dried out plant, here are some things you can do.

When soil gets completely dried out, it often becomes water repellent, just like a hard, dry sponge. You may also notice that the soil has shrunk away from the inner sides of the pot, creating a space between the outside of the rootball and the inside of the pot. So the water that you add resists being absorbed by the dry soil and runs around the outside of the rootball and out the drainage holes of the pot. Little of the water gets absorbed and the soil and roots remain dry.

To prevent this, you have to break up the hard surface soil with a fork or knife. Then press the soil in tight in the space along the inner wall of the pot. If you do this right, then water will have a better chance of getting absorbed by the soil. **NOTE:** Warm water is more readily absorbed than cold water.

Sometimes it is easier to re-wet hard, dry soil by sitting the pot in a large saucer or tub that is kept filled with a couple of inches of water for about an hour. The water will slowly wick up by capillary action from the saucer and throughout the rootball to the top of the rootball.

Once you have successfully re-wetted the soil, it should not ever be necessary to water this way again — unless you let the plant get that dry again. Normal watering can be resumed after this initial re-wetting.

Plants that suffer from drought end up with dry shriveled leaves. These discolored leaves will never recover, so remove them completely. After proper watering is resumed, healthy new growth should emerge within a month. If that does not happen, it is because the roots became so dry that they have died and the plant cannot be salvaged.

Now you can concentrate on removing the damaged leaves and stems. Completely or mostly dried or discolored leaves should be removed. Partially discolored leaves can be trimmed so that only green remains and the original contour of the leaf is maintained. Dry, brittle stems and branches are dead and will not recover so prune them off. Leggy stems or vines that have lost many leaves should be pruned back to eliminate the legginess.

Do **not** fertilize a desiccated plant because that will just aggravate the problem. Do provide appropriate light and be sure not to let the plant get so dried out again. On the other hand, don't try to make up for the drought by flooding your plant and keeping it constantly wet.

How to fix an overwatered plant

Many folks panic when they suddenly realize they (or someone else!) have over watered their plant. More often than not, the panic reaction is to replace all the soggy soil with fresh soil that is drier. But more often than not, this soil replacement only aggravates the problem and merely hastens the demise of the plant.

It is important to understand that an overwatered plant is not one that was given too much water at one time. It is a plant that has not been allowed to dry out sufficiently between many waterings. In other words, an overwatered plant is one that has been watered too often and too soon. If the soil and roots are kept too wet for an extended period of time, then the roots will rot and die. Once most of the roots have started to rot, the plant is destined to die no matter what you do. However, if you realize the overwatering problem before the roots have badly rotted, then you may be able to save the plant.

Let the soil dry out. It's that simple. An overwatered plant simply needs to dry out in between waterings. Providing some extra warmth and light and reduced humidity will help hasten the drying out process. Improved air circulation from a fan will also help it dry. Other than that, there is nothing you can do.

Replacing wet soil with drier soil will damage most of the fragile root hairs, so that is not a good solution. However, sometimes a plant gets overwatered because it is in a pot that is too large. An overly large pot has extra soil that stays wet for a long time after watering. That is what causes the roots to rot. In this case, it is best to take the plant from its pot and remove the extra soil that was added to the outside of the original rootball. Then put the slimmed-down rootball into a smaller pot that is just large enough for the smaller rootball. Removing the extra soil and down-sizing the pot will help the soil dry out sooner in the future. **NOTE:** This does not require replacing the soil. It is removing excess soil only. See How to fix an over-potted plant above and in Chapter 14.

How to fix a plant potted without a drainage hole

For a variety of reasons, many plants end up potted in planters or pots that do not have any drainage holes. In such a setup, the excess water, which has no place to drain, may accumulate in the bottom of the pot and rot the roots. You are flirting with disaster if you leave your plant in a pot without drainage holes.

Adding drainage material to the bottom of the pot is *not* the answer. That just prolongs the inevitable.

There are two remedies — use a nursery pot with drainage holes or find a decorative planter with drainage holes. In both instances, the new pot has to be the same size as the existing rootball so no new soil is added.

Remove the plant from its existing pot that has no drain holes. Move it into a pot that is just large enough to accommodate the plant's rootball without adding any soil. Size matters!

How to treat root rot

Root rot is often fatal after it reaches the point where the foliage symptoms are obvious. Thus, the best treatment is prevention. Root pruning rotted roots and replacing soil are false solutions. They suggest that the rotted roots and the soil are infected with a disease that will spread to the other roots unless they are removed. In fact, roots rot because the presence of constantly damp soil deprives the roots of oxygen and causes the roots to slowly die, some sooner than others. Theoretically, removing dead roots will do no harm, but often the process of removing them is traumatic to the remaining healthy roots and tiny roothairs. Replacing the soil also invariably damages the vital root hairs. I don't recommend doing either. The only solution is to allow the soil to dry out properly around the roots so that oxygen can return to the root zone.

How to get rid of that ugly plastic pot

Plants are usually grown in black plastic pots called nursery pots. They are not very attractive, so the impulse is to buy a more attractive pot and repot into it. Because repotting is fraught with potential problems (See Chapter 1), I don't recommend doing this. The best solution is to double-pot, putting the nursery pot inside of a slightly larger, more attractive planter.

If the existing pot is an ugly plastic nursery pot that you hate, then do as follows. Get a decorative planter of your choice that is large enough for you to hold the nursery pot inside. This is double-potting and its purpose is to use the inner pot to allow excess water to drain away from the soil and roots and the outer pot to hide the inner pot. When you double pot, the outer planter does not have to have a drainage hole. However, you do need to monitor the space between the two pots to make sure that no water is accumulating at the bottom. If water does accumulate, then lift the inner pot out and pour the accumulated water out of the outer pot before re-installing the inner pot.

Spread a little Spanish moss over the top to disguise the double-potting and the nursery pot will no longer be visible. At the same time, the plant will be much happier remaining in the nursery pot.

How to fix a cold-damaged plant

Exposing a tropical houseplant (most houseplants are tropical in origin) to cold temperatures will cause the foliage to quickly turn soft and dark-colored. Such damaged foliage cannot be repaired so it is best to prune off the affected foliage and stems right away, as painful as that may be. A few additional leaves may also be affected for a day or two after you move your plant to warmer temperatures.

The roots are insulated by the soil and the pot so that they are not affected by cold as quickly as the exposed foliage is. So it is possible that although much of a plant's foliage is cold-damaged, the roots may still be okay. If that is the case, then the roots will help the plant produce healthy new growth in the future and your plant will slowly recover.

Other than providing warm temperatures and removing damaged foliage, there is nothing more you can do. Replacing the soil, flooding the soil with hot water, and using a hair dryer on the leaves are **not** recommended. Fertilizer will not help. Be patient and watch for signs of healthy new growth. If, after a month, there is none, then you can assume the roots were also damaged by the cold and the plant will not recover.

How to fix a sunburned plant

It happens every year. On that first warm day of spring, some folks move their sunlight-starved plants outside into the sun. The sudden change from reduced indoor light to outdoor direct sun is like a resident of a northern climate going to a tropical beach in mid-winter without any sun protection. There is no sunblock for plants, so it is best to avoid this scenario if you can. But assuming you didn't know this and you have a sun damaged plant, here is what you can do.

Sun damaged foliage is unusually pale in color. Dark green leaves may become pale green. Light green leaves may become bleached almost white or pale yellow. In any case, the leaves will not look healthy. Unfortunately, sun damaged leaves do not recover their healthy color, so it is best to remove them entirely, painful though that may be. As long as the plant is protected from exposure to strong outdoor light, the new growth should be fine when it emerges.

For trees with long stems and branches, it is best to prune back the stems by about a third. This is because new growth emerges at the ends of stems and pruning will help eliminate the leggy look of stems that have lost lower leaves due to sun damage. See Chapter 11 for information on pruning.

How to care for a plant that doesn't get enough light

Maybe you purchased or were given a plant without realizing you don't have enough light for it. If exchanging the plant for a lower light plant is not an option, then there are a few things you can do to get the most out of your plant. I must admit that I am sometimes surprised to see plants living moderately well in light that would appear to be inadequate for those particular plants. So there is (almost) always hope.

First: make sure you are doing everything possible to enhance the available light for your plant. Keep the nearest window uncovered as much as possible during the daylight hours. Move the plant as close as possible to the light source. Use a fluorescent light or grow light to supplement whatever light you already have. If your plant is in an office, move it closer to a window on the weekends.

Second: never repot your plant. Plants in reduced light grow very slowly at best and their roots tend to shrink back. Repotting will simply aggravate the stress it is already experiencing from poor light. If the pot it is in is unattractive, then leave it in that pot, but put that pot inside of another more attractive pot. But leave the roots alone.

Third: reduce your watering. Plants in low light do not use much water and are quite prone to root rot. Allow the soil to dry out a bit deeper into the pot. When you do water, try to add just enough so that the soil is appropriately dry again in about a week.

Fourth: skip the fertilizer and other nutrients. Slow-growing plants in low light use very few nutrients and there are more than enough nutrients in the existing soil. Excess fertilizer will lead to the buildup of mineral salts in the soil and that will damage the tender roots.

Fifth: keep your plant a bit warmer than usual. Warm temperatures promote faster growth and help the soil dry out sooner. Plants that are short on light and that are also in cool locations really struggle.

Sixth: in low light, many plants tend to get leggy over time. Their stems are thin and their leaves are sparse as a result of not getting enough light. For many plant species, you can keep such a plant looking better by pruning back leggy stems. (See Chapter 11 on Pruning.)

Seventh: be especially vigilant for plant pests. Plants under stress are much more vulnerable and attractive to plant pests. Plants that are not getting enough light are under stress and more likely to attract pests.

In general, it is best to do less rather than more with plants that are not getting as much light as they should — less repotting, less water, less fertilizer, less fussing. And keep your expectations low as plants in low light grow very slowly.

How to care for plants that have to be moved indoors for winter

There are some flowering plants that generally do better outside, but they are tropical or semi-tropical in origin and cannot withstand winters where temperatures drop below freezing. Citrus, Hibiscus, Azalea, Desert Rose, and some Bonsai species are in this category. These plants often have a hard time adjusting when they are moved inside after a long spring, summer and fall outside. The reduction in light and increase in temperatures are the two biggest issues for these plants.

Indoor light is not nearly as intense as outdoor light. So even a plant that has spent the warmer months in light shade still must adapt to reduced light when it is moved indoors. You can ease this light reduction adjustment by gradually decreasing the light for 3 or 4 weeks prior to moving it indoors. Once indoors, move the plant to your sunniest available location.

With the reduction in light comes a reduction in plant growth and that means a reduction in water usage. After plants are moved indoors for the winter, be careful to adjust your watering routine so that the interval between waterings is extended. This is a gradual process that takes place over the course of a month or so before stabilizing at a reduced rate of needing water. Allow your indoor winter plants to dry gradually deeper into the soil before watering.

As with water, reduce your fertilizing during the winter months. For most plants, that means not fertilizing at all until vigorous new growth returns in the spring.

Most of these plants prefer cool temperatures in winter, although not freezing temperatures. Do some research on each individual species to learn just how much cold each can tolerate so you will know when to move them indoors in your area. Once indoors, try to provide a cool location for these plants. An unheated room with a sunny window is ideal for them in winter. Most homes have a room that tends to stay cooler than the other rooms. As long as that room can provide adequate light, then that is probably the best location. Trying to provide both good light and cool temperatures is not easy and that is why many of these plants languish in winter.

Finally, low humidity in our heated winter homes can sometimes be a problem for these plants. However, low humidity is not nearly as big a problem as reduced light and warm temperatures. Putting a plant in a bathroom with little light in order to gain some additional humidity is not a good idea. Getting a humidifier or using humidity trays is a better solution.

In some cases, you may only be able to barely keep the plant alive in your winter environment. The plant may look pretty bad by the end of winter, but as long as it is still alive by the time it is warm enough to move it outside, then consider it a success. Keep these plants pruned to eliminate legginess. Just before moving your plants back outside when the warm weather returns, prune them back sharply to make the transition to better light easier and to eliminate the winter legginess.

How to deodorize a stinky plant

If you use poor quality soil or a foreign substance gets poured into your potted plants, the soil may start giving off an unpleasant odor. It is the soil, not the plant that is the source of the odor. If the smell is suddenly so bad you can't stand it, then it is probably best to discard the plant. Otherwise there are some remedies to try.

First, try to determine and eliminate the cause. If someone has been feeding your plant coffee or soda or any other food substance, have them stop. If you use compost or outdoor garden soil for your indoor plants, use packaged peat-based potting mixes instead. If your local tap water is very hard, switch to filtered or distilled water for your plants. If you keep your plants too wet, causing the roots to rot and smell, then let your plants dry out more.

Flush lots of clear water through the soil. This will wash out many odor causing substances. Add a little horticultural lime to the surface of the soil to help neutralize any remaining odor.

Resist the natural impulse to wash all of the soil off the roots and replace that soil. This may eliminate the odor but it is extremely traumatic to plants because it invariably damages the vital tiny root hairs. I liken this to having all of your blood replaced to get rid of a cold! However, if all else fails, I suppose it is worth a try — but only as a last resort.

How to fix a urine-soaked plant

It happens! You discover one day that your kitty has been using your plant as a litter box. Yuck! I cannot tell you how to train your cat to stop doing this — ask your vet — but I can help you fix the urine-soaked plant.

Don't assume that replacing the soil is the only solution. In fact, that is the last resort because it will probably kill the plant. Here is what you can do.

Flush lots of fresh warm water continuously through the soil and into the sink. This is usually sufficient to remove most of the toxic residue and odor from the soil. Then add some horticultural lime to the surface of the soil. This will counteract the acidity of the urine and ameliorate the odor.

Now about that cat…!

How to move plants long distance

People relocate to new homes, sometimes in locations far away. They want to take their plants with them. I am often asked how to go about that.

The first consideration is temperature. If your plants are likely to be exposed to very warm (above 80°F) or very cold (below 50°F) temperatures, then you will have to find a way to protect them. Inside a moving van or any other vehicle that is not temperature controlled, temperatures can easily drop below freezing in cold weather and soar to over 100°F in warm weather. Tropical houseplants can be protected from chilly, but not freezing, temperatures by wrapping them in heavy brown Kraft paper sleeves. But they cannot be protected from cold for very long (more than a few hours) or from very warm temperatures. Try to arrange your move at a time when temperature extremes are unlikely. Or make sure they are moved in a vehicle that is temperature controlled.

Commercial moving companies usually hate to move plants because they are perishable and easily damaged. If you are using a commercial hauler, discuss your plants with them in advance and find out if they charge extra and what their liability limits are. Plants have to be secured so they don't fall over in transit. It is best if they are loaded last on and first off.

If you move your plants yourself, then small plants can be placed together in a shallow cardboard container that will hold them in place. Taller plants will have to be secured to prevent toppling. In some cases, tall plants can be carefully laid on their sides, but they still must be secured so they don't roll or slide. You may be able to nestle your plants in between softer items that are part of the move.

Water your plants the day before they are to be moved. That way they will have several day's water supply without still being wet when they are loaded.

Most plants will do okay for several days without any light in the back of a vehicle. If your move takes longer than that, then you will have to find a way to get them several hours of light each day along the way.

After your plants arrive at their new location, check first to see if they need water. Then, try to locate them in places that match as closely as possible the light they received in their old location. The greater the change in light, the more difficulty the plant will have adapting to its new environment.

How to move a plant a short distance

Sometimes people want to move a plant from their home to their workplace or to a friend or relative's home not far away. You don't necessarily have to wait until warm weather to do this. Even if the outside temperatures are below freezing, you can safely move your plant a short distance.

Wrap the plant in heavy brown paper or heavy plastic and close it up as best you can to keep any cold air out. For small plants, a plastic shopping bag is adequate. Warm up your vehicle in advance and then take the wrapped plant quickly to the heated vehicle. Try to park close to your destination and then move the plant quickly from your car to its new indoor home.

Of course, in warm weather, all of these precautions are unnecessary. However, in warm weather you do need to protect your plants from wind damage. Foliage can get pretty beat up when a plant is placed in the back of a pickup or in a car with the top or windows rolled down.

How to deal with hard water

In many parts of the world, tap water is very hard. Not only does it taste bad and make it difficult to get soap to lather, it is also not healthy for most plants. Hard water has a high concentration of mineral salts. These mineral salts can be toxic to plants if they are allowed to accumulate around plant roots.

Ironically, water softeners also add chemicals to the water that are not good for plants, so don't use softened water either.

If your local tap water is on the hard side, use filtered, distilled or rain water for your plants.

How to remove white mineral deposits on terra cotta pots

Crusty, powdery white deposits often build up on the rims and the outsides of terra cotta pots. These white deposits are the residue of excess mineral salts that have built up in the soil and have gradually leached through the porous terra cotta. The source of the problem is usually using hard water for your plants or using too much fertilizer.

Scrape off the loose deposits with steel wool. Then wipe the remainder with a sponge or cloth soaked in white vinegar. The acid in the vinegar will neutralize the alkaline quality of the mineral deposits and restore the normal color to the terra cotta.

How to get small plants to grow large

Getting a cutting or start to grow into an 8-foot specimen plant is not something you can do in your home. Very large specimen plants are taken from special plant stock and grown in environmentally controlled greenhouse conditions. That said, there are some things you can do to maximize the growth potential of your smaller plants or starts.

Try to provide optimum light. Optimum light varies from one plant species to another, so you need to know what the optimum light is for each plant. For most indoor plants, even low light plants, optimum light is very bright indirect light. However, some plants require as much direct indoor sunlight as possible. In any case, light is the key factor in plant growth and there is no substitute for light. Pumping up a plant in low light with fertilizer or plant food will not work and will eventually damage your plant.

Keep the pot small. Yes, contrary to your intuition and conventional wisdom, a large pot will not make a plant grow larger any more than big shoes will help a child grow taller. Plants grow best when they are moderately potbound with lots of roots visible on the outside of the rootball. A very potbound plant that requires water every couple of days will benefit from a pot one size larger. But a plant that is moved prematurely into a larger pot or is moved into a pot that is too large will tend to put most of its energy into filling the pot with roots at the expense of the top growth that you prefer. So step your plants up slowly from one size to the next and only when necessary.

Make sure you understand your plant's water requirements and meet them diligently. More water does not automatically mean faster growth. Most plant species need to dry out some in between waterings and some need to dry out a lot. Getting a good handle on your plant's water needs will help it grow faster and stronger.

If your plant has been in the same pot for at least a year, then it may need a fertilizer to supplement the nutrients that have been depleted. But don't overdo this. Use half the recommended label strength.

How to save money with your plants

Okay, your plants will not actually produce income or savings for you, but you can save a little money if you follow some of these tips.

It is rare that plants need to be repotted. So you can save money on pots and soil by not repotting unless absolutely necessary. As a side benefit, your plants will do better when kept moderately potbound and are less likely to rot. Not having to replace plants will save you money.

Don't bother with fertilizer, plant food, hormones, vitamins and other supplements that are often expensive and rarely necessary.

Instead of using an expensive humidifier for your plants, try pebble trays as an alternative.

Skip the moisture meters. They are notoriously inaccurate and cost up to $20. If you really want to know what's going on inside the rootball, get a Soil Sleuth for about $10 (www.soilsleuth.com).

Skip the commercial pesticides. They are often expensive and no more effective than the safer alternatives I describe in my chapter on treating plant pests.

How to give a gift plant

The short answer is, "Don't!" Unless the recipient is experienced and knowledgeable and has expressed a desire for a particular plant species, it is probably best to find another gift.

Plants are fragile and perishable when not given proper care. When you gift someone with a plant you are giving them a responsibility that they may not want or be ready for or able to meet. If you give someone a plant that requires a lot of light and the recipient doesn't have much available light, the plant will gradually die no matter how diligent the care. If you give someone a beautiful plant such as an Orchid and they have no prior experience with Orchids, it will probably die. If you give someone a plant before they go on a three-week vacation, the plant may die due to neglect. If you buy an expensive Bonsai houseplant for someone, you and the recipient probably won't understand that it may require cold winter temperatures without which it dies.

A gift should be a source of pleasure, not an obligation. I cannot tell you how many times I receive desperate pleas for help with dying gift plants. The desperation is brought on by an imminent visit from the gift-giver who will undoubtedly want to see how their gift plant is faring. The desperate recipient is distraught because the plant is dying and doesn't want the gift-giver to think the recipient is ungrateful or uncaring. Usually when I get these calls, it is already too late.

Giving a gift plant to someone who is grieving is also not usually a good idea. Although plants are often viewed as an affirmation of life, unless they are properly cared for, they will quickly become a reminder of dying — the last thing a grieving person needs. In addition, people who are grieving do not need the additional responsibility of caring for a plant when they are having trouble coping with their routine daily responsibilities.

Unless you really know what you are doing, find another gift. Cut flowers that are expected to be discarded after a week or so make a better gift than a potted plant that is expected to live.

18 The Health Benefits of Indoor Plants

Health issues are of increasing concern for most people. Many folks are seeking natural or alternative ways to stay healthy. In that context, questions about the health benefits of indoor plants are on the rise. In this chapter, I address the most common questions and misunderstandings about the health benefits of plants.

Oxygen

A persistent myth about potted plants is that they steal oxygen at night and should not be used in bedrooms or sick rooms. While most plants do use a bit more oxygen than they produce after dark, they also produce more oxygen during the daylight hours than they use at night. So for any 24-hour period, indoor plants will help increase the oxygen supply while also decreasing the carbon dioxide in the surrounding air.

Although plants do not produce oxygen at night, enough oxygen is produced during the daylight hours to more than compensate for the oxygen debt that occurs at night. Even if you were to fill a room with plants, the amount of oxygen used by the plants at night would be too small to have any ill effect on people in that room. Whatever oxygen debt occurs at night is paid back with interest during the day. The notion that plants steal oxygen and are harmful is completely false. In fact, plants provide at least a small benefit in oxygen production.

Clean Air

NASA scientist B.C. Wolverton and others have conducted many studies that demonstrate that potted plants are effective at removing various pollutants from the air. Unfortunately, these studies have been condensed and misunderstood and a lot of unsubstantiated claims about the air cleaning abilities of specific plants are rampant on the Internet and in the media.

The NASA studies were limited to a few plant species in controlled lab environments that don't duplicate the typical home environment. Regrettably, lists have been published claiming that certain plant species are better than others at removing air pollutants. Consequently, folks have been purchasing specific plants based on their alleged superiority as air cleaners.

Unquestionably, indoor plants do help filter the air and that is reason enough to have houseplants if you enjoy them and are willing to care for them. However, potted plants are not a panacea for bad air and are not likely to make much difference to folks who suffer from air-born allergies. If you have serious air pollution problems in your home, don't substitute a couple of plants for a good HEPA air cleaner. If you smoke tobacco or live with a smoker, don't rely on plants to clear the air.

Selecting a particular plant species because of its air cleaning abilities is also not a good idea. A plant that is healthy, growing vigorously and has lots of leaf surface will be an effective air cleaner — regardless of its species. So choose a plant based on its light requirements and your ability to keep it healthy and growing vigorously, not because it showed up on someone's list of the 10 best plants for air cleaning. See Chapter 2 on Selecting a Plant.

Psychological Benefits

Most people enjoy plants because they are alive, because they are green and colorful, because they make us think of the outdoors and because they have pleasing shapes and contours. In addition, plants help soften an environment filled with hard surfaces and objects.

Numerous scientific studies have demonstrated that people are more relaxed, more productive and friendlier when plants are part of their environment. This is true even for people who are not particularly aware that plants are in their environment. It seems that plants are good for our mood even when we are not aware of their presence.

Of course, this does not mean that someone with serious anger management issues will become a puppy dog in a plant-filled room! But it does establish that plants do make most people feel and respond better in subtle ways.

Want Proof?

According to *Consumer Reports On Health* (May 2009, p.3), a study has shown that recovering surgery patients who had plants in their hospital rooms needed fewer pain killers, had less anxiety, lower blood pressure and heart rates.

According to *Consumer Reports On Health* (September 2008, p.3), researchers compared office workers in windowless offices who had plants with office workers who had windows but no plants. They found that the workers with plants but no window reported better job satisfaction and that they got along better with their co-workers.

Here are links to several research studies that document the health benefits of indoor plants:

http://www.eurekalert.org/pub_releases/2008-05/asfh-gom051908.php

http://krex.k-state.edu/dspace/handle/2097/227

http://greenplantsforgreenbuildings.org/resources/benefits-of-green-plants/

Can Plants Be Unhealthy?

Some people do have allergies to pollen and mold. For them, a potted plant could be a health problem. Certainly, flowering plants are not a good choice for someone with severe pollen allergies. But most foliage plants should not be an issue.

Likewise, not all plants and soil mixes are sources of mold. In fact, healthy plants potted in soilless potting mixes should be mold free if properly cared for. In addition, bright light, good air circulation and soil that is allowed to dry out properly all create an environment that is inhospitable to the growth of mold.

Indoor plants are susceptible to certain plant pests. While these plant pests can affect the health of the plant, they are not hazardous to people or pets. Plant pests — spider mites, aphids, mealybugs, scale, whitefly, and fungus gnats — all require either live plant material or decaying organic matter to survive. Unlike mosquitoes and other noxious outdoor pests, these plant pests are not interested in people or animals and are not a health hazard.

It is the treating of the plant pests with pesticides that is a potential hazard to people and pets. There are a wide variety of pesticides available to the consumer to treat plant pests. Presumably the government regulates and does not allow unsafe pesticides on the market. However, all pesticides are potentially hazardous if they are not used properly and few people bother to read the fine print label instructions on proper use of these pesticides. Fortunately, there are non-toxic, non-pesticide treatments for all indoor plant pests that will not expose people or pets to hazardous substances. Liquid dish soap, rubbing alcohol, mineral oil and cayenne pepper are among the safe but effective ingredients that can be used to safely treat plant pests. (See Chapter 10 for information on safely treating plant pests.)

Conclusion

With the possible exceptions of unusual allergies and the misuse of pesticides, there is no downside to having potted plants in your home or office. And although the benefits have sometimes been overstated, indoor plants do provide both physical and psychological benefits that are subtle but undeniable.

If you are seeking health benefits from your plants, make sure you keep the plants healthy. After all, an ailing or dying plant is going to depress you more than raise your spirits and its ability to produce oxygen and filter the air is very limited. So be judicious in selecting an appropriate plant for your environment and learn what you need to know to care for it properly.

Happy and healthy growing!

19 Plant Terminology

Years ago I had a professor of physics who blanched every time we loosely used words such as force, acceleration and speed. "Define your terms!" he would yell. His point was that the vocabulary of science is very precise so that there can be a common understanding as to what words mean. I subsequently learned that even beyond the realm of science, there is a great deal of disagreement and misunderstanding that is a direct result of people having different ideas as to the meaning of words and language. I have found that this applies to the language of plant care, as well.

This is not a scientific text and it is written in plain English without technical words with technical definitions. However, there are some common terms that are used and misused by plant owners. Below is a mini-glossary to help clarify some misunderstandings that occur over the poor choice of certain words. These are not scientific definitions, but they are descriptions that will help you better understand what is written here and in other publications and will help you to describe your plant problems to others when you are seeking help.

For ease of use I have grouped the terms by category: Plant Type, Plant Structure, Propagation, and Miscellaneous Terms then alphabetized them within each category.

Plant Type

Bamboo: This refers to a plant genus in the grass family. It does not include a popular plant sold as Lucky Bamboo, which is actually a Dracaena sanderiana. This misnaming causes considerable confusion. True Bamboos do not make good indoor plants because they require so much light.

Bonsai: This is a technique used to miniaturize plants that ordinarily grow very large. Bonsai is not a type of plant or plant species. It is a technique or method of growing a plant so that it can be kept in a small shallow dish. Not all Bonsais have the same care requirements. If you acquire a Bonsai, you need to know what plant species it is, just as you do with any other plant.

Botanical name: This is the scientific name given to each species of plant. A plant may have several common (non-scientific) names, but it will have only one botanical name. Common names are easier to remember, but they are often a source of confusion because the same common name may refer to several very different plant species. Whenever possible, find out and use the botanical name to avoid confusion.

Epiphyte: This refers to a type of plant that does not grow in the ground as terrestrials do. Epiphytes usually grow in damp areas with frequent rainfalls. They attach their roots to the outside of moist bark on trees, above the ground. An epiphytic plant (most Orchids and Bromeliads and some ferns) has roots that usually rot if covered with soil.

Hybrid: This refers to a plant that has mixed parentage. The purpose of hybridizing is to emphasize certain plant characteristics — more flowers, better color, darker leaves, etc. Often hybrids sacrifice other qualities such as durability and longevity.

Orchid: This is the name of the largest plant family with over 30,000 different species. As with Palms, different Orchid species have very different cultural requirements so you must find out just which species of Orchid you have. Phalaenopsis is the most commonly used indoor Orchid species.

Palm: Technically this is the name applied to a large family of many plant species. As with the Orchid family, the Palm family includes a wide range of Palm species that have a wide range of cultural requirements. It does not include plants that we think look like Palms — *Dracaena marginatas* and the misnamed Ponytail Palm, for example. It is not enough to know that you have a Palm. You must know *which* Palm species you have.

Succulent: This refers to any plant that has fleshy leaves or stems and can withstand drought better than most non-succulents. Most require lots of sunlight and suffer badly when over potted and overwatered. Cacti and Jade Plants are two examples of succulents.

Tropical plant: This is any plant whose native habitat is a warm region of the world where temperatures are mild year round. Most indoor plants are tropical or semi-tropical in origin. Tropical plants are well suited to indoor use because we keep our living spaces warm year-round. Most tropical plants do not tolerate temperatures below 50°F.

Plant Structure

Aerial or air roots: These are roots that grow from the base of a plant potted in soil out into the air rather than down into the soil. In nature, these roots may absorb moisture from humid air or attach themselves to damp soil or tree bark. For plants potted in soil, aerial roots serve no necessary purpose so you can cut them off without damaging the plant. However, epiphytes such as Orchids and some Ferns also put out roots that extend into the air. These epiphytic roots should not be cut off.

Branches: This refers to smaller, thinner stems that branch off of the main stems that grow out of the soil.

Cane: This refers to a thick, bark-covered stem section that has been cut down and rooted in soil. Smaller stems with foliage then grow out of the top of the cane. Many Corn plants and Yuccas are grown from "cane' cuttings.

Gall: This is an abnormal growth that occurs usually on a plant's stem or branch. Galls are caused by many organisms living on plants, including insects, mites, fungi and bacteria. They are relatively rare on indoor plants and there is no practical way to treat them without knowing the cause. In most cases, they can be left untreated.

Heads: This refers to the stems and foliage that emerge from the tops of canes.

Leaf Stem: This is the slender portion of a plant that connects a leaf to a branch or main plant stem. Its scientific name is petiole.

Rhizome: This is a sturdy root stock that grows under or above ground. When above ground, a rhizome will put down smaller roots when the rhizome comes in contact with moist soil. The "feet" of a rabbit's foot fern are rhizomes. They do not have to be covered by or in contact with soil.

Rootball: This refers to a plant's roots and all of the soil encased by the roots. With a healthy, properly potted plant this is what you have when you remove a plant from its pot.

Spike: This is an elongated flower stem that emerges from the base of the plant and produces flowers high above the rest of the plant. Many Orchid species have flowers at the ends of tall flower spikes.

Stalks or Stocks: These are common terms used to describe stems, branches and canes. Because these two words are used to describe very different things and do not distinguish between them, it is best not to use either term in describing parts of your plant.

Stem: This refers to the part of the plant that emerges from the soil. A stem has roots at one end and leaves or branches on its aboveground portion. Not all plants have stems.

Propagation

Air Layering: This is propagating technique. It is a method that wounds a plant's stem just enough to trigger it to produce roots before it is actually completely severed.

Cuttings, Clippings, Starts, Slips: These are sections of the plant that you get when you cut off the ends of plant stems. These stem sections include at least a few leaves and are used to propagate new plants by inserting them in water or moist soil. Shorter tip cuttings root more readily than longer cuttings.

Division: This is a method of propagating plants. It is usually done by slicing through a section of the rootball and taking that divided section that includes roots, soil and foliage and moving it into its own small pot.

Offsets: This term describes baby plants that grow above the ground or just below the soil surface of the "mother plant." They develop while attached to the main plant and can usually be separated from the main plant when they are several inches in size. They are commonly found on Bromeliads, Ponytail Palms, Aloes and Africa Violets.

Miscellaneous Terms

Acclimatize: This is a plant's way to adapt to a changing environment, most often a change in light. Various plant species have a variety of ways to acclimate, some more effectively than others. Acclimatization takes time and plants cannot acclimate to extreme change in light, temperature and water. Plants can adapt, but they prefer a constant environment.

Capillary action: This refers to the process by which water that is wicked up from bottom to top through soil or via fabric wicks. Bottom watering and most self-watering pots are based on the principle of capillary action.

Direct sunlight: This refers to a location where the rays of the sun fall directly onto a plant placed in that location. The sun moves during the day so few indoor locations receive direct sun all day long. A south window receives the most direct sun and a north window receives the least.

Dormant: This term refers to a plant that requires a rest period during the course of the calendar year. Temperate zone plants often shed their leaves and stop growing during winter freezes. Some tropical plants have a dormant period triggered by drought during which their leaves die back. However, most of our indoor potted plants do not have a dormant period and grow all year round.

Gray water: This is water previously used to wash dishes or clothing, for example. It can be used for watering indoor plants, but it is not preferred because various substances in the gray water may accumulate and negatively affect the plant over time. Gray water is best used to water outdoor plants planted in the ground.

Growth habit: This refers to the manner in which a plant species naturally grows. Some species tend to produce many stems and branches, while others have only a single, upward growing tip. Some species are naturally full and compact while others grow lanky and tall. Some species are very slow growers and others are rampant in their growth. We can manipulate the growth and appearance of a plant, but only within the limitation of that particular species' growth habit.

Guttation: You have probably never heard this word, but it is the only term used to describe the process in which small droplets of water are produced at the ends of new leaves of some plants. It is not a problem and does not require any treatment. It occurs most frequently with Pothos and other Aroid family member species.

Hard water: Hard water contains an excess of minerals that build up in the soil of plants over time. These minerals affect the pH or soil acidity range that makes essential nutrients insoluble and unavailable for plant roots to absorb. Use filtered or distilled or rainwater for your plants if your tap water is hard.

Hardiness Zone: Every plant species has a hardiness zone that identifies the temperature ranges that species will tolerate. Higher numbered zones are tropical regions where frost never occurs. Low numbered zones are cold climates with hard winter freezes. Knowing the hardiness zone of a plant will help you determine if and when you can place or plant it outside.

Indirect light: This refers to a location where natural sunlight falls nearby but not directly onto the plant. It is a bright location but does not experience very much direct sunlight throughout the day.

Leggy: A plant that has long stems or vines with large spaces between the leaves is called leggy. A leggy plant is usually unattractive and is best corrected by proper pruning.

Low light: This refers to the minimum intensity of light that a selected few plant species need to survive. A low light location receives no direct sun during the day, but it is close enough to a window (usually within 5–6 feet) that it provides excellent reading light all day long. Overhead fluorescent and plant lights can provide low light for plants. Dim light in corners or in spaces where there are window coverings do not provide the minimum light required for any plant to survive.

Overwatering: This refers to keeping soil so moist that the soil does not have a chance to dry out and the roots do not have a chance to absorb oxygen. Typically, overwatering results from watering too frequently, not from adding too much water at one time.

pH: This is a scientific measure of the acidity/alkalinity spectrum. Most indoor plants prefer a soil pH in the 5.8 to 6.8 range. If your soil or water is much outside of this range then the nutrients the plant needs do not dissolve properly and cannot be absorbed by the roots. Most nutrient deficiencies in potted plants occur because the pH is outside the proper range, not because there are nutrient deficiencies in the soil.

Plant Food: This refers to plant fertilizers used to supplement nutrients that may be depleted from the soil of potted plants.

The Most Popular Indoor Plants

In this section, you will find very specific care instructions on the most commonly used indoor plants. They are listed in alphabetical order.

The detailed information you will find on each of the plants listed in this section is more comprehensive than the standard information commonly available on these species. Because of the detail, space requires that the species listed are limited to the most popular plants used. Some other plant species not included in this section can be found in Chapter 5 Full Sun Plants. More unusual and exotic species will require you to do additional research. However, if you have read the first part of this book on the principles of plant care, you should be able to extrapolate from that how to care for species not listed in this section.

Anthurium

Anthurium

Anthuriums are popular flowering plants because they flower more readily than most potted flowering plants. The flowers are showy and usually brilliant red, although they also come in pink, orange and white. The flowers look like smaller, more colorful versions of Peace Lily flowers.

They are low maintenance as long as you can provide lots of bright indirect light. They rarely need repotting and are not excessively fussy about watering. One weakness is that they bloom only sporadically after the first flowering cycle. Another is a tendency to develop brown spots on the foliage. There is not a lot you can do about either of these tendencies because they are part of the genetic structure. Of course, poor care will aggravate both of these problems. So do your best to follow the guidelines below and hope for the best.

Buying an Anthurium: Close inspection of the foliage on an Anthurium can tell you a lot about how it was grown and what its light requirements will be. If the leaves are dark green that tells you that it has been grown in moderate light conditions and will do well on a north windowsill. If the foliage is a lighter shade of green, it was grown in brighter light and will need to be kept on an east or west windowsill where there is more sunlight available.

Light: Anthuriums do not do well in low light. Be sure you keep yours on a windowsill or close to an uncovered window. If light is inadequate, flowering will be infrequent and the flowers will be undersized.

Repotting: Most Anthuriums are grown in 6-inch plastic pots and can stay in those pots indefinitely. They are epiphytes with fine root systems that need to dry out moderately about every week or so. They also do best in a porous potting mix to prevent root rot.

If you find the plastic nursery pot unattractive, then purchase a decorative planter that is large enough for you to put the nursery pot inside. This double-potting (cachepot) is much easier and better for the plant than repotting directly into another planter.

Water: If your Anthurium is properly potted and left in its nursery pot and provided good light, then a thorough watering once per week will be just about right. Never leave the pot sitting in water for more than half a day and never re-pot into a pot that has no drainage holes. It is better to err on the side of dryness with this plant.

Temperature & Humidity: Anthuriums prefer warm temperatures above 60°F. Normal home temperatures are fine for an Anthurium, although it should be protected from very cold drafts coming through open doors and windows in winter. They are reasonably tolerant of low humidity, but may benefit from additional humidity provided by a pebble tray when the air is artificially heated in winter. If you summer your Anthurium outdoors when temps are in the 60°F to 80°F range, be sure to keep it in the shade at all times.

Fertilizer: Even in good light, Anthuriums are relatively slow growers. Fertilize monthly at half the recommended label strength as long as the plant is putting out new growth. Fertilizer is not medicine and should not be used to treat Anthurium problems. Nor should it be used to force faster growth.

Pests: The leathery leaves of Anthuriums make them unattractive to most plant pests. Chapter 10 provides detailed information on identifying and treating indoor plant pests if you have reason to think this is a problem for your Anthurium.

Discolored leaves: Cut off flower stems as the flowers start to fade. Trimming leaves with brown spots is optional. Sometimes discolored edges can be trimmed off without adversely affecting the overall appearance of the leaf. Central leaf spots are more problematic and can only be removed by trimming off the entire leaf. This trimming is simply a matter of your making the plant look the best that you can.

Flowering: Although Anthuriums can bloom throughout the year, giving them a 6-week period of cool temps in the 55°F to 60°F range will help promote flowering. This is hard to do in most homes, but can be done in early fall if you have a good outdoor location for your Anthurium.

Dormancy: Anthuriums are tropical in origin so they do not have a dormant period. They often grow just as well in winter as in summer.

Propagation: Anthuriums do not propagate easily. If there are multiple plants in the pot, they can be divided, but I don't recommend doing it.

Azalea, Gardenia and Camellia

These three flowering plants are popular gifts and are often sold at holiday times. The Gardenia and Camellia are noted for their lovely scents and the Azalea is noted for its brilliant hues. What's not to like about these gorgeous plants? Their difficulty as indoor plants is what is not to like about them. Ordinarily, I would not include these flowering plants in my book because they are not plants I recommend for indoor use. However, I do recognize that they are popular gifts and folks do want to know what to do with them. The shortest and most direct answer to that question is to discard them after they finish flowering. If you can bring yourself to do that, then that is what I recommend and you need not read any further. For the rest of you, read on…but don't say I didn't warn you!

Why these plants do not do well indoors

- Like most flowering plants, these three species need lots of direct sunlight if they are to thrive. No direct sun, no flowers. Without a sunny window, they have no chance.

- These three plants also must have cool temperatures, good air circulation and air that is not too dry. Most of us live in warm homes with little air flow and desert-dry air in winter.

- None of these plants are forgiving of watering lapses. Even a single episode of delayed water can disrupt the flowering cycle and may lead to heavy foliage loss.

- Plant pests love these three plants even more than you do. Spider mites, scale insects, mealybugs and aphids are all prepared to do battle with you over rights to these three flowering plants.

Have I discouraged you, yet? If not, then you have some challenging plants to care for and you should read on to learn the specifics. Good luck!

Azalea
Rhododendron

Azaleas are part of the *Rhododendron* genus that includes over 800 species and countless hybrids. Unless you purchase your Azalea from a high-end nursery that provides good labels, there is no practical way for you to determine just which species or hybrid you have. However, if you acquire an Azalea sold as a houseplant the chances are very good that it is a hybrid. Unfortunately, hybrids are usually genetically determined to produce a flourish of spectacular blooms at the time of sale, but tend to be rather weak subsequently. For that reason, most people discard these plants after they have finished flowering.

Water: All Azaleas have a mass of fine roots that easily rot from too much water or die easily from drought. Thus *it is imperative that you monitor the watering carefully* as a single lapse in watering can cause flowers, buds and leaves to shrivel overnight. Shriveled flowers and leaves do not recover. Allow the surface of the soil to get almost dry to the touch. Then, water thoroughly making sure not to leave the pot sitting in excess water. If your local tap water is on the hard side, then use distilled or filtered water.

Repotting: Don't disturb your Azaleas fragile root system by repotting. Repotting disrupts the flowering cycle and tends to result in inadvertent over watering and root rot. If keeping your Azaleas soil properly moist (see above) means watering every day or so, then do that rather than moving it to a larger pot

Light: Azalea flowers will hold up longer if they are given lots of natural sunlight. Your sunniest windowsill is the best location. Inadequate light — even bright indirect light — will shorten the life span of the flowers and the plant itself.

Temperature: Azaleas are not tropical in origin so they do not adapt to our overheated dry homes as well as other houseplants. If you have an unheated or cool room in your home that also has good sunlight, then that is the best location for your Azalea. Increasing the humidity in winter by using a humidifier or a pebble tray is recommended.

Fertilizer: If you plan to discard your Azalea after it finished flowering, then fertilizer is not necessary. After it flowers and is putting out new green growth, use an acidic fertilizer such as Miracid at half strength monthly.

Flowers: Most potted Azaleas are brought into bloom in the spring. Indoors, the flowers may last for up to a month if the light is good and the soil is kept constantly damp. It is unlikely to flower again for another year. You should always prune back new stem growth after your Azalea has finished blooming. This will help maintain its shape and promote new flowers next year. If you delay pruning you may prune off new buds that form during the summer.

If you want to try to get your Azalea to re-flower the following spring, move it outside to light shade for the summer. Fertilize it monthly with an acidic fertilizer. The flower buds are formed in the summer and are much larger than leaf buds.

In the fall, keep it outside until temps fall close to freezing. This cold fall period will help the plant set buds for the following spring. Bring the plant inside before the first frost and give it a sunny, but cool indoor location below 60°F for another month or so. Look for buds to start to open as the days lengthen in early spring.

These are difficult conditions to meet. If you cannot, it may be best to discard your Azalea.

Gardenia
Gardenia jasminoides

Gardenias produce lush, white flowers with a magnificent scent. They are an irresistible plant, but are one of the more difficult plants to grow and bloom indoors successfully, so much so that they may best be used as a seasonal plant and discarded after they have finished flowering. Gardenias are not easy to bloom indoors because they have rather strict temperature requirements.

Buying a Gardenia: Never buy a Gardenia that is not already in flower because the chances of you successfully getting a Gardenia to flower are very slim. Likewise, it is best not to buy a Gardenia that has mostly unopened buds because these buds are very temperature sensitive and will blast or fall off if temperatures between 55 and 65 are not strictly maintained. If you are confident that you can provide these constant cool temperatures, then you can consider purchasing a Gardenia with lots of buds that will open and extend the flowering period of your Gardenia. Be sure to disturb the in-bud Gardenia as little as possible. *Do not repot or fertilize it.* Provide bright, but indirect sun. Keep the soil moist by watering as soon as the surface soil starts to feel dry.

Otherwise, it is best to buy a Gardenia with lots of open flowers. Flowers are initially white and become a pale yellow as they mature. Individual flowers last 4 to 7 days and turn brown on the edges if handled too much. Enjoy the flowers while they last and then discard the plant unless you have an environment where you can attempt to meet the challenging requirements described below.

Re-blooming: Gardenias are extremely difficult to get to re-bloom successfully. Unless you are experienced with plants, I think you should put your time and energy someplace else more rewarding. When the flowers are finished, you can move your Gardenia to a sunny window and no longer worry about warm temperatures. 6–8 hours per day of direct sunlight, high humidity, and acidic soil (5.0 pH) are also important for maintaining Gardenias long term. The soil must be kept evenly moist at all times, but not wet. Water whenever the surface of the soil feels just barely damp. Avoid repotting until it is utterly potbound. Use an acid fertilizer, such as Miracid, at half-strength during the growing season, usually from March to October.

In the fall, allow Gardenia temperatures to fall to about 50°F to 60°F at night and no more than 70°F during the day. You must maintain these cool temperatures through the fall and winter if you want buds to set. Once buds form it is important to maintain temperatures in the 55°F to 65°F range or they will fall off. Of course, good light and careful monitoring of the soil to keep it moderately moist is also critical during this time. There are few things more disheartening than to see fat Gardenia buds fall off because the temperature got a bit too warm or the soil a bit too dry.

It is difficult for most people to provide these conditions. Some are satisfied to keep a Gardenia as a foliage plant.

Camellia
Camellia japonica

Camellias are native to cool, misty mountainsides. Needless to say, this is not the environment most of us have in our homes and that is why this is such a troublesome houseplant. Without lots of bright light, cool temps below 60°F, high humidity, and evenly moist soil, Camellias fare poorly. In addition, most of the Camellias sold today are hybrids that are not reliable bloomers after their initial flowering at time of sale.

Because Camellias require temperatures that are not compatible with our indoor living spaces, I will go no further in providing indoor care instructions. If you receive a Camellia as a gift, try to keep it as cool as you can and keep the soil damp. Enjoy the flowers while they last and then discard the plant.

Conclusion

If you have read this far, you have learned just how challenging Azaleas, Gardenias and Camellias are when kept as indoor potted plants. All three can thrive outdoors if you are in the right geographic environment, but they are not happy with the warm environments that we prefer for our indoor spaces. That's why I recommend that you steer clear of these three otherwise lovely plants.

Bonsai

Juniper Bonsai

Bonsai (pronounced bone–sigh) plants are heart breakers. They are striking in appearance, make wonderful gifts, and they are expensive. However, most of them fail as houseplants within six months. By the time it becomes apparent that they are in trouble, it is almost always too late. That is heart breaking.

What is Bonsai?

Bonsai is not a plant species. Bonsai is a technique developed and practiced in Japan that creates miniaturized replicas of plants that are large trees or shrubs in their natural habitats. The miniaturized Bonsai is carefully pruned (both stems and roots) to create the same look that the species would have on a much larger scale in nature. Part of the Bonsai process is to use small, shallow decorative planters to maintain the scale of the miniaturized plant

A true Bonsai takes many years and a great deal of detailed, precise work to create. Consequently, true Bonsais are very expensive. Bonsais are as much pieces of art as they are living plants.

Buyer Beware

Unfortunately, there are many unscrupulous sellers of Bonsai plants. If someone tries to sell you a Bonsai at a low or discounted price, it is probably not a true Bonsai. Some dealers take a recent cutting and put it into a nice Bonsai container and then charge a lot of money while claiming or implying that it is an ancient Bonsai. Only purchase a Bonsai from a reputable plant retailer who can tell you the name of the plant species, provide good care instructions, answer all your questions and will stand behind your purchase if you have problems.

Bonsai Plant Species

Almost any plant species can be miniaturized and used for Bonsai. However, it is customary to use plant species that have tree-like characteristics. Juniper is the most commonly used species for Bonsai. Other popular choices are Japanese maple, Boxwood, Cypress, Ficus, Jasmine, Yew and Pine. All of these species have bark covered stems and trunks and interesting foliage.

Why Bonsais So Often Fail as Houseplants

All too often when people purchase a Bonsai they are not told, and do not find out, what species of plant they have. Without knowing the species of your Bonsai you will not be able to find out the care that it requires because different plant species have widely varying light, water and temperature requirements. Assuming that all Bonsais have the same care requirements is where most Bonsai problems begin.

Related to the identity problem is the temperature problem. The majority of Bonsais sold are plant species that are not tropical in origin. Juniper, for example, is native to Zones 3–7 where temperatures typically drop well below freezing for much of the winter. That means they will not survive constantly warm household temperatures.

Unless you have an unheated room in your home that also has good light, then a Juniper Bonsai and many other non-tropical Bonsai species will not be good choices for you. Without the cold temperatures that they require, they are unlikely to make it through the first winter in your heated home.

Bonsais That Will Work for You

Fortunately, there are Bonsai species that are tropical in origin and can live in our year-round warm homes. However, you must get a proper species identification of your Bonsai so you can be sure it is tropical in origin.

The most common tropical Bonsais are Ficus, Jasmine, Jade, Gardenia, Podocarpus, and Polyscias. None of these require cold winter dormant periods and all are commonly used as regular houseplants.

So when acquiring a Bonsai, don't stop with the label "Bonsai." Find out what plant species it is and make sure it is a tropical species that does not require a winter dormant period.

Caring for Your Bonsai

The care of your Bonsai will depend on the species that you have, but a few generalizations about tropical Bonsais can be made. (Note: Caring for non-tropical Bonsais is addressed in the next section.)

Light: Virtually all Bonsais need bright indirect light at a minimum. That means you will have to place it on a windowsill or table in front of a window that is uncovered throughout the day. The window exposure required would depend on the species you have.

Water: The best way to water a Bonsai is by submerging the container in plain water until bubbles stop surfacing. This technique may not work if your Bonsai soil is covered with light pebbles that wash away when submerged. If so, you will have to drip water in from the top very slowly until you see a bit running through the drainage holes in the bottom of the container. When you do water, it is important that you saturate all of the soil. Pouring water too rapidly will cause the water to spill over the rim of the pot and not properly penetrate the rootball.

How often you water is very much related to the species you have as some species such as Jade need to dry out quite thoroughly while others such as Ficus like the soil to stay moist at all times. In any case, you can expect that due to the small size and limited amount of soil around the roots, Bonsais will need to be watered more often than non-Bonsai plants.

Fertilizer: Fertilize your Bonsai as you would your other houseplants. Use a fertilizer that is diluted to half-strength with plain water

Repotting: Unless you plan to take on Bonsai as a serious hobby, I don't recommend that you ever try to repot your Bonsai. That is because you never move a Bonsai into a larger pot; you prune the roots so that the Bonsai can stay in the same container indefinitely.

Pruning: Bonsais can quickly become overgrown if they are not pruned regularly. If you are squeamish about pruning houseplants, then Bonsais are not for you! In general, your goal is to maintain the original size, shape and proportions that your Bonsai had when you purchased it. It took many years for the professional artisan to get it just right, so it is your job to maintain — not improve — that look.

Pests: Bonsais are just as prone to pests as any other plant of the same species. Be vigilant and treat any pest problems immediately. A small plant can quickly become overwhelmed by a pest infestation. (See Chapter 10 for information on treating plant pests.)

Non-Tropical Bonsais

Juniper, Cedar, Cypress, Japanese maple, Ginkgo, Boxwood and Yew are among the more popular species used for Bonsai. However, all of these are non-tropical in origin and are poor choices to keep as houseplants. If you were given a non-tropical Bonsai species as a gift, then do your best to identify its species and get appropriate care instructions for that species. Remember, if it is non-tropical in origin, then you will have to find a way to keep it as cool as possible.

If you have an unheated room or a somewhat protected outdoor location for your non-tropical Bonsai, then you have a good chance of succeeding with it. It is probably best to keep your non-tropical Bonsai outside year round, but it will need protection from strong winds, animals and severe cold. Of course you will have to make sure it is also getting appropriate light and water for the particular species.

Bonsais that are grown outdoors grow faster than indoor Bonsais. That means you will need to invest more time in regular root and to pruning.

Summary

If you have or plan to get a Bonsai, be sure to identify the plant species so you will know how to research proper care for it. If you want to keep your Bonsai indoors, limit your choices to Bonsai species that are tropical in origin

Finally, if you are truly serious about your Bonsai and want to adopt it as a hobby, then get a good book on Bonsai that diagrams the proper ways to prune the roots and the plant. You may also want to check the following websites:

http://bonsai-bci.com

http://www.absbonsai.org/

Bromeliad

Guzmania Bromeliad

How would you like to have a plant that never needs repotting, can adapt to a wide range of light, can be put on a weekly watering schedule, never needs fertilizer, does well in high or low humidity and produces a large spectacularly colored flower that lasts for 2 to 6 months? There is such a plant and it is a Bromeliad.

Bromeliad is a large family of plant species that has many diverse members. The most familiar is the Pineapple plant that often shows up in supermarkets. Another common Bromeliad species is commonly known as Spanish moss and is often used by florists. However, there are other Bromeliad species that have brilliantly colorful flowers that last for up to 6 months in good conditions.

Although Bromeliads are unusual looking and have unusual care requirements, they are one of the easiest of all flowering plants to care for. Plant owners too often overlook them. In this chapter, I will focus on the care of the more popular flowering Bromeliad species, such as Guzmania and *Aechmea fasciata*.

Monocarpic Epiphytes

Okay, those two words either got your attention or made you decide to skip this section! Those are technical terms that refer to a couple of special Bromeliad features. Bromeliads are "monocarpic." That means they produce only a single flower (or fruit) before they die. However, that single flower is very long lasting and the plant's demise is a slow one, often taking up to 3 years. During that time, 1 to 3 offsets (called babies or pups) are produced to carry on the species.

An epiphyte is a plant that grows up in the air as opposed to in the ground. Now that does not mean that epiphytic plants simply float in the air like clouds. Rather,

Bromeliads

they grow up in the crotches of tree limbs high above the ground, usually in tropical rain forests. This is important to know because it affects the way that they are potted and watered. Many Orchid and some Fern species are also epiphytes.

Potting

In nature, most Bromeliads grow in high places where their roots are surrounded by circulating air. But these regions are also bathed daily with warm rain and high humidity. That tells us that the roots must be potted in a very porous potting mix that will retain some moisture but also keep air circulating around the roots.

Some Bromeliad species are grown outside of pots entirely. The fine roots may be attached (along with some moss) to a piece of wood or tree bark. Some small Bromeliad species are sold in novel ways, such as inside a small seashell. You can do this with epiphytic plants because their roots are adapted to exposure to the air.

However, the more common flowering Bromeliads are usually sold in small 5 or 6-inch pots filled with a porous or epiphytic potting mix that contains lots of moss, coarse bark chips and perlite. Because Bromeliad root systems are small and fine, they do not need repotting. Never put a Bromeliad in a standard soil-based potting mix. If you don't like the looks of the plastic nursery pot, then simply place the entire plant and pot into a more decorative planter. Double potting is fine; repotting is not.

Light

For best results and to prolong the flower duration, keep your Bromeliad on a north or east windowsill where it will get lots of bright, mostly indirect light.

However, if you would enjoy your Bromeliad more if it were placed in the center of the living room and far from a window, then you can do that although the flower may only last for 2 months in low light.

Water

If your Bromeliad is properly potted and in good light, a weekly thorough watering will be just right for it. In low light, watering every two weeks is more appropriate. Because of its unusual epiphytic roots, the soil should be quite dry deep into the pot before watering. This plant will survive drought, but it will not survive waterlogged soil and roots.

The customary practice of keeping the cups or vases formed by the Bromeliad leaves filled with water has been discredited. Indoors, where air circulation is poor, the cups often rot. In addition, applying water only to the cups will deprive the roots of needed water. Keep the soil barely damp and it will not be necessary to water the cups.

If your tap water is on the hard side, then you should use only filtered, distilled or rainwater to water and mist your Bromeliads.

Fertilizer, Humidity & Temperature

Bromeliads are slow growers and use nutrients in minute quantities. At most, your Bromeliad should be fertilized no more than every two months with a fertilizer diluted to half strength. It will not suffer if you never fertilize.

Although Bromeliads grow naturally in warm, humid climates, they are surprisingly adaptable to dry indoor air as long as the soil and roots are watered properly. Misting and using humidity trays will do no harm, but they are really not necessary in dry climates, although you may be informed otherwise.

Bromeliads do not tolerate cold temperatures very well. However, this is not a problem in most homes where temps are kept above 60°F. If you move your plants outside in the summer, it is best to move your Bromeliad back inside in the fall when night temps start to fall below 60°F.

After the Flower Dies

No flower lives forever, but Bromeliad flowers are the longest lasting among all houseplants. Somewhere in the 2 to 5 month period, your Bromeliad flower will start to get dry and brown. This happens slowly, staring at the tip of the flower and working its way down over the course of several weeks. This is normal and irreversible, so don't feel you have done something wrong and don't try to fix it. When the flower no longer looks attractive, simply cut it off at its base and discard it.

After the flower has died, you will be left with a handsome foliage plant, at least for a while. Continue to care for it as you have while it was in flower, although providing lots of bright indirect sunlight is important now. Resist the urge to repot your Bromeliad at this time.

If you are observant, you will notice two things. First, you will see new plants emerging from the soil alongside the original plant. These baby plants are called offsets or "pups." Second, you will notice at some point that the leaves of the original plant are starting to die back. This is also part of the normal life cycle of the monocarpic Bromeliad. As the original or "mother" plants gradually dies, new plants emerge to carry on the species.

The dying of the original plant is often a very slow process taking a year or even longer, but it is inevitable. Accept this mother plant die-back and simply remove unattractive leaves as they discolor. At some point you will want to remove all of the faded leaves from the mother plant. During this time, your focus should be on the health of the pups, not on the dying of the mother. If the pups are healthy looking, then you are providing proper care.

Propagation

The pups can be left on the mother plant or they can be severed and potted up separately. If you choose the latter, then wait until the pups are about one-third to one-half the size of the mother and have at least five leaves before separating them.

Remove the soil where the pup attaches to the mother plant. Most of the time the pup can be pulled away from the mother with a firm but gentle tug. Otherwise, cut the pup low on the woody part of the stem that attaches the pup to the mother. Allow the severed pup to sit in the open air (out of the sun) for a day before potting it. Pot the severed pup in a small pot filled with a mix of peat moss and perlite. Keep this mix damp and place it in bright light away from direct sunlight. Keep temps above 65°F. You may want to place it inside a clear plastic bag to help maintain high humidity for the first month after it is potted up.

It may take several years before the offsets are mature enough to flower. Make sure they stay tightly potted in pots no more than 6" in diameter. Provide lots of very bright light and of course keep watering properly.

After they reach maturity, you may want to put the Bromeliads in a clear plastic bag along with a ripe apple for 7 to 10 days. The ethylene gas given off by the ripening apple will help stimulate new flowers.

Trying to propagate Bromeliads from seed is impractical. The seeds of some hybrids are sterile. Those that are not sterile must be pollinated. It may take up to a year for the seeds to mature enough to remove them for germination.

Different Bromeliad Species

Guzmania is my personal Bromeliad favorite. It has shiny dark green strap-like, arching leaves with tall flowers in brilliant red, yellow, orange and purple colors.

This is a great choice if you would like an eye-catching splash of color in your home. It produces multiple pups.

Vriesea species look quite similar to the Guzmania, but their flowers have an unusual flat, feather-like shape. It usually produces only one pup.

Aechmea fasciata (Primera), also known as the Silver Vase plant is another popular choice. Its leaves are wide, light green and covered with a silvery powder or dust, giving them a unique appearance. It is best not to try to wipe off this silvery film. The flower is very tall, large and pink. The large leaves and flower make it appear to need a larger pot, but it doesn't.

Neoregelia is a small, short Bromeliad with spectacularly colored foliage near its center and a small flower sitting low in the center of the plant. This is a good choice if space is limited or if you want a stable plant that will not easily tip over.

Cryptanthus is similar in shape and size to the *Neoregelia*, although a bit larger. The leaves come in a variety of subdued colored stripes. It is sometime called Zebra Plant. The flower is small and insignificant.

Tillandsia species are often called air plants. This species includes Spanish moss seen growing from and hanging from tree branches in warm climates. Although some Tillandsias produce colorful flowers, most are more notable for their wispy foliage and ability to survive in strange places. They can be mounted on pieces of wood bark or driftwood. They can be placed inside of small seashells or small glass containers. When grown outside of a pot, it is best to take them to a sink and drench them once or twice per week when the air is dry.

Epiphytic Air Plant (Tillandsia)

The *Ananas* species includes the pineapple plant. It is often sold as a potted plant. Its flower is the fruit we all know and it grows on a flower spike above the leaves. On top of the fruit is a crown of leaves that can be used to propagate another pineapple plant. This is a novelty plant and when potted, the fruit is not particularly large or tasty.

Propagating a Pineapple

Many of us kids like the experience of growing a pineapple from a store-bought pineapple. To propagate a pineapple, use a fresh pineapple that has healthy leaves on the crown. Twist or cut off the crown (leafy stem) just above the fleshy part of the fruit. Strip away the leaves from the lower inch of the crown. Place the crown in a narrow vase or glass filled with water that will allow the bare stem to stay in contact with the water, but hold the leaves above the water. Place it in a bright spot that is protected from direct sun. Keep the water level in contact with the bare stem at all times. Change the water weekly.

Roots usually appear within a week or two. When the roots are an inch or more long, put it into a 4- or 6-inch clay pot using a damp soilless, peat-based potting mix. Water thoroughly whenever the top inch of soil feels dry. Gradually increase the light until it ends up on a sunny windowsill.

Pineapple plants do best in direct sun and warm temperatures (above 60°F). If you move yours outside in the summer, introduce it to direct sun gradually over the course of two weeks. You can increase the chances of flowering by keeping it quite potbound in a peat-based potting mix. Water thoroughly whenever the top inch of soil feels dry. Fertilize regularly at half strength when it is in good light and growing vigorously.

For more information on Bromeliads, go to the Bromeliad Society International website at http://www.bsi.org.

Bromeliad (Pineapple)

Chinese Evergreen
(Aglaonema)

Red Aglaonema in 6" pot

Aglaonema 'Silver Bay'

The primary virtue of Aglaonemas is that they do not require as much light as most other plants. There are many hybrids that offer a range of variegated leaf patterns in shades of green, yellow, white and even red. Chinese evergreens come in small sizes suitable for tables and windowsills and in sizes large enough to be placed on the floor. However, even the largest Aglaonemas don't grow much taller than 2 feet.

Light

Aglaonemas do best in very bright but indirect light but can survive nicely in low light. The best location for this plant is in front of a north or east window. If the window faces south or west, then the plant should be protected from the direct rays of the sun that shine through the glass, especially in the afternoon. In direct sunlight, the leaves will bleach out. The lowest light this plant will tolerate is natural light good enough to read newsprint comfortably throughout the day. That means no more than about 6 feet from the nearest window. Artificial light from incandescent lights may be good for reading, but is not adequate for plant health.

Chinese Evergreen is a terrific office plant because it thrives under overhead fluorescent lights in interior offices or cubicles that lack natural light. You can also keep it under a fluorescent lamp at home if the lamp is left on for at least 8 hours per day.

In general, the darker varieties of Aglaonema do better in low light. That may help you select an appropriate Aglaonema from the many hybrids available.

Repotting

Aglaonemas have long, fairly thick white roots that are quite fragile. These roots grow slowly, especially if the plant is located in low light. It is rare that Chinese Evergreens need repotting. You may see some roots wandering out of drainage holes, but that does **not** mean they need a bigger pot. In fact, unnecessary repotting is likely to cause root rot. If your plant reaches the point that it requires a thorough watering every 2 to 3 days, then it may be a candidate for a pot one size larger.

If you find the plastic nursery pot unattractive, then purchase a decorative planter that is large enough for you to put the nursery pot inside. This double-potting (cachepot) is much easier and better for the plant than repotting directly into another planter. For more information on repotting see Chapter 1.

Water

If your Chinese Evergreen is properly potted and left in its nursery pot and given good light, then a thorough watering once per week will be just about right. However, it is important that you monitor the soil moisture closely and not rely on the calendar to decide when to water. Allow the top quarter of the soil to dry before watering thoroughly. With this plant it is best to err on the side of dryness, especially if it is in low light where it will not use as much water.

Temperature & Humidity

Aglaonemas prefer warm temperatures above 60°F. Normal home temperatures are fine but it must be protected from cold drafts coming through open doors and windows in winter. Low humidity is not a problem for Chinese Evergreens.

Fertilizer

In good light, Aglaonemas can be fertilized monthly at half the recommended label strength as long as the plant is putting out new growth. In low light, do not fertilize at all. Fertilizer is not medicine and should not be used to treat plant problems. Nor should it be used to force faster growth.

Pests

Mealybugs are the most common pest problem for Chinese Evergreens. Look for tiny bits of soft, white cotton-like substances on the backs of leaves and along leaf stems, especially in crevices where the leaf stems attach to the main stems. A thorough spraying with a solution of water, alcohol, and dish soap will usually solve the problem. Scale insects and spider mites are less common pest problems

Mealybugs on leaf

on Aglaonemas. Chapter 10 provides detailed information on identifying and treating these indoor plant pests.

Symptoms

Yellow leaves tell you something is wrong, but don't reveal just w hat that is. Bright yellow leaves are more likely to indicate under watering, whereas soft, pale yellow leaves are more indicative of over watering. Keep in mind that yellowing and loss of some lower leaves is a normal reaction of the plant as it adds more new leaves on top. As long as you are not losing more foliage than you are gaining, it is not a cause for concern.

Distorted or discolored new growth is usually a sign of rotting roots resulting from overwatering or using a pot that is too large.

Soft, mushy lower stems can result from either over or under watering, but too much water is more likely.

Discolored leaves will not repair themselves. They can be removed without adversely affecting the overall health of the plant.

Pruning

Aglaonema stems do tend to grow tall and become leggy. If left unpruned, gravity will prevail and start to cause outer stems to lean outward and down. Lots of folks mistakenly think this calls for a larger pot but the only solution is pruning.

Any stem that looks leggy because of lower leaf loss or that starts to lean over the edge of the pot should be pruned back. The stems are soft enough to cut back easily with scissors or a knife. Cut the leggy stem back to the place where you would like to see new foliage growth emerge. This is usually a height 3–6 inches above the soil. Regular pruning not only eliminates older leggy stems, but it helps to keep your Chinese Evergreen shorter and more compact — the way it was when you purchased it.

Pruning never hurts the plant, so don't worry about doing it incorrectly. For more information on pruning, see Chapter 11.

Propagation

Aglaonemas can be propagated quite easily by rooting healthy stem cuttings in water. When the cuttings have developed roots at least an inch long they can be moved into a very small pot with fresh potting mix of peat moss and perlite. Because Aglaonema stems do not generate new stems or branches, it is best to root and pot several stem cuttings together in the same pot.

Flowering

Although Aglaonemas do produce flowers, they are rather small and not very colorful. You can leave them on until they start to fade or you can cut them off when they first emerge. A few Aglaonema varieties also produce bright red berries.

Corn Plant
(Dracaena fragrans 'Massangeana')

The Corn Plant, as *Dracaena fragrans* 'Massangeana' is more commonly known, is one of the workhorses of the indoor landscape. It is seen in offices, building lobbies, restaurants and homes all over the world. It is a relatively inexpensive plant that will survive as well as any in low light. Because it has a tall and slender profile, it fits in many locations (low light corners) where other plants will not An even better choice for low light, narrow spaces is the Dracaena 'Lisa,' described in the next chapter.

The Corn Plant has a reputation for hardiness primarily because it does well in moderately low light. However, it is vulnerable to too much light, overwatering and unnecessary repotting. In addition, it will not survive for long in dark places where the light is inadequate even for this plant.

Canes

The Corn Plant is often sold in the cane form. This refers to the very thick, bark-covered trunks of staggered heights that are rooted in soil and have foliage only at their tops. In tropical regions, *Dracaena fragrans* grow as very tall trees with bare trunks, much like Coconut Palms. Nurseries cut these tall trees down and chop them into one, two, three and four-foot long sections. These leafless sections or canes are then rooted by positioning them upright in damp potting material. The top ends are sealed with wax to prevent fungal infections prevalent in very damp tropical environments. As the damp potting material triggers root growth, bright indirect light promotes secondary stems with leaves to sprout from the tops of the canes. Although the canes can be rooted individually, it is customary to put multiple canes of staggered heights in the same pot. This creates a single pot with leaves at staggered heights. Although the individual canes can be separated, doing so would defeat this purpose. Separating them also stresses them and I don't recommend trying it for any reason.

The thick 'canes' never grow taller or thicker. All future growth is in the secondary stems that sprout from the tops of the canes. These secondary stems can grow much taller than the canes, however. If you want to shorten or propagate this plant, you cut the secondary stems, never the thick canes. (See section on Propagation below). Although it is possible to saw through the canes and root them as nurseries do, it is very difficult to do outside of a carefully controlled nursery or greenhouse environment. That is why I recommend using only stem, not cane, cuttings to propagate more plants. **Note:** The popular *Yucca elephantipes* is also grown in a cane form and is often mistakenly identified as a Corn Plant. Although these two plants look very similar, the Yucca requires much more light than the Corn Plant. Yuccas have thicker, more rigid leaves that come to a sharp point and whose edges are sharp enough to cut your skin. See page 263 for information on Yucca cane care.

Light

The Corn Plant is a low light plant that thrives in bright, but indirect, sunlight. Direct sunlight shining directly on the leaves will cause the leaves to turn a pale green. This is because in nature Dracaena 'fragrans' grows only in deep shade and cannot adapt to direct sunlight. On the other hand, that does not mean it grows in the dark! Low light means light that is bright enough to comfortably read newsprint all day long. Generally that means that it should be located within a few feet of an uncovered north window or no more than 8-10 feet from a tall south-facing window. In an office setting, it will do fine under overhead fluorescent lights that are turned on eight hours per day.

If you place this plant is a dim corner or far from a window or keep your window covered, then this plant will gradually deteriorate. And so will any other low light plant. See Chapter 3 for a thorough discussion of light for indoor plants.

Water

Because the Corn Plant is usually in low light and has a small root system, it does not use as much water as many other potted plants. In general, wait until the top quarter of the soil feels dry to the touch before watering thoroughly. This drying out rarely occurs more than once per week and often takes up to two weeks, assuming that it is potted in the right sized pot. If you keep the soil too moist, the roots will gradually rot but you won't see any signs of this until it may be too late.

Symptoms

If the leaves of your Corn Plant look slightly wilted and the edges develop a wavy contour, then you are probably not watering enough. If the leaves wilt permanently and don't recover after watering, then root rot has probably already set in. As the root rot progresses, the secondary stems may shrivel or turn soft and dark and the bark on the canes will become loose and papery. At that point the canes are beyond recovery.

Dry brown tips usually indicate excessive drying of the soil or an abundance of minerals in the soil caused by using hard water or too much fertilizer. (Someone will advise you that low humidity is the cause, but that is not true. This plant will do very well in low humidity, as well as low light.)

Brown/yellow tips are signs of excessive water or too little light.

Corn plant leaf spotting has multiple possible causes. Among them are soil that is too dry; roots are compacted at the bottom of the pot; soil pH becomes too acidic; and mineral salts from excess fertilizer or hard water have built up in the soil. Here is what you need to do:

- Pull the plant out of the pot. If you find only one or two large roots at the bottom of the rootball, then cut them off, add a little soil to the bottom of the original pot and put the plant back in.

- If you find a mass of large roots wrapped around just the bottom of the rootball, then pull them loose and cut the big ones off. Add an inch or two of fresh soil to the bottom of the original pot and put the plant back in.

- If you find a mass of roots completely surrounding the entire outside of the rootball (sides as well as bottom), then loosen these roots and repot the plant into a pot one size larger. Never add soil to the top of the rootball.

- If your local tap water is hard, then use filtered or distilled instead.

- If you have had your corn plant for many years, then the soil may have become too acidic. You can remedy this by adding some horticultural lime to the soil.

Leaning Canes

Corn plants develop long, thick roots with few of the finer root networks that characterize most other indoor plants. This limited root structure means that the canes often become wobbly or start to lean off-center in their pots. The tendency to "fix" this by adding soil or moving it to a larger pot is the wrong thing to do. (See the section on Pot Size that follows.)

The proper solution is to push the leaning cane back to the vertical position or a little beyond. Then press the soil in tightly around the cane so that it will stay in place.

Pot Size

The Corn Plant rarely needs repotting. An unnecessarily large pot will keep the soil too moist for too long and rot the roots. That is fatal.

If you think your Corn Plant needs repotting, remove it carefully from its pot while the soil is still damp. If you see a mass of roots wrapped around the base of the rootball and below the soil, then cut off that mass of roots. Add an inch of soil to the bottom of the original pot before reinserting the trimmed rootball back into it.

If a mass of thick roots completely encircles the entire rootball, then loosen those roots and move the plant into a pot one size larger. This repotting is rarely needed, so think twice and read Chapter 1 before doing this.

If you don't find any mass of roots, then leave the rootball and its pot as is and be confident that it should not be repotted.

Fertilizer

In low light, potted plants do not need fertilizer. Such plants grow slowly and use nutrients in very minute quantities. If you fertilize unnecessarily, the build up of excess soil mineral salts (nutrients) will cause leaf tips and edges to develop brown edges and spots. If your Corn Plant has been in the same pot for several years and is very healthy, then fertilize it three of four times per year but at half the dilution rate listed on the label. (See Chapter 8 for more detail on fertilizing your potted plants).

Water Quality

Most Dracaenas, including the Corn Plant, are vulnerable to foliage damage when irrigated with hard water. If your tap water is hard, use distilled, filtered or rainwater as an alternative. The normal amount of chlorine and fluoride added to tap water will not harm Dracaenas, but hard water and water treated with softening agents will.

Pruning

Although Corn Plants grow slowly, in time they can become leggy looking or too tall for their space. You can cut these too-tall secondary stems back to a shorter length, but leave at least one to two inches of secondary stem above the cane from which they will grow. New growth will emerge on the cut stem just below where you make the cut and grow upwards from there.

Propagation

The pruned off stems (see above) can be rooted in plain water or in a small pot filled with damp, porous potting mix. Trim the lower portion of the stem cutting so that it is no more than 2 to 4 inches of bare stem below the lowest leaves.

Flowers

Yes, Corn Plants can and do flower indoors! It often surprises Corn Plant owners when they first discover these odd-looking growths emerging from the tops of the stems. The flower stems or spikes are 6 to 10 inches in length with rather indistinct looking flowers along the stem. These flowers have a strong, sweet aroma that some people love and others find overpowering. You can  decide for yourself and if you don't like the aroma, simply cut off the entire stem.

Getting your Corn Plant to flower requires patience, as it is usually older plants that have been in the same pot and location for at least several years that bloom. However, once they reach flowering maturity, Corn Plants will reliably flower once or twice per year thereafter, usually in the late fall and/or late spring, provided you don't discourage flowering by repotting or relocating the plant.

After a couple of weeks, the flowers start to dry and turn brown; it is best to cut off the entire flower stem before the dry flowers start to drop to the floor. They are not only messy, but also very sticky. Cutting the flower spike will not harm the plant.

Removing Dead Canes

It is not uncommon for one or two of the shorter canes in a single pot to gradually die back. This often occurs because the shorter canes are shaded by the taller canes and do not receive enough light. If all of the foliage dies on a cane, then it will not recover and it is best for appearances sake to remove the dead cane. Grasp the dead cane firmly and twist it in place until it spins freely. Then pull it up and out of the pot. It will come out cleanly without spilling soil or disturbing the roots of the other canes. Fill in the vacated hole by pressing in the surrounding soil.

Sometimes a new shoot will emerge right at the soil line and attached to a dying cane. This is usually the last gasp of the dying cane and the new shoot rarely survives. You may want to try cutting it off from the cane and rooting it in a very small pot with a porous potting mix.

Conclusion

The Corn Plant is a good plant because it does well in low light and because it fits in tight spaces, especially corners. However, it is also a bit fragile and resents too much water, sun and fertilizer.

Dracaena 'Janet Craig' & Dracaena 'Lisa'
Dracaena deremensis

Dracaena 'Janet Craig'

Dracaena 'Lisa' in bloom

7-foot Dracaena 'Lisa' in 9" pot. No natural light

These two closely related members of the Dracaena family are two of the very best low light plants. They are grown in heights up to 6 feet. Both have very dark-green, naturally glossy leaves that are long and strap-like, similar to those of the more common Corn Plant. The 'Janet Craig' is usually shorter and more bush-like in shape. The 'Lisa' is taller and grows on canes. It fits well in corner spaces where there is not a lot of light and not much horizontal space. (The Dracaena 'Michiko' is almost indistinguishable in appearance and care from the 'Lisa.')

The 'Lisa' is one of my personal favorites because I often have need for plants that fit in narrow spaces and don't need much light. The better quality 'Lisas' are moderately expensive and I suspect that is why they are not as available in the big box discount stores as the Corn Plant.

Light

'Janet Craigs' and 'Lisas' grow naturally in the deep shade of tropical forests. That means they do well in low light and do not tolerate direct sunlight at all. Both plants do well close to a north window or far enough away from other window exposures that the sun's rays do not fall directly on the foliage at any time during the course of the day. They also do well under fluorescent lights that are left on for at least 8 hours each day. That makes them very good plants for interior offices without windows or basements with overhead fluorescent lights.

Remember, low light does not mean no light. All plants must have at least 8 hours of daily light that is bright enough for you to read newsprint comfortably. If you do not have that much light, then no live plant will survive for long.

When exposed to direct sunlight, these Dracaenas will develop yellow and brown spots on their leaves.

Pot Size

Because 'Janet Craigs' and 'Lisas' are most often used in low light, they tend to grow slowly and that means they rarely need repotting. Generally, it is best to leave them in their original black plastic nursery pots for at least six months. If you find that after that your Dracaena needs water every few days, then it may be time to move it into a pot one size larger.

Dracaena 'Lisa' planted in volcanic cynders and double-potted

Sometimes these plants develop lots of roots at the base of the rootball. If you see roots wandering out of bottom drainage holes, then take it out of its pot and look for a mass of roots at the bottom of the rootball. If you find that mass of roots, then use sterile pruners to trim them off. Add an inch or soil to the bottom of the same pot and put the trimmed rootball back in.

Contrary to popular belief, a small pot will not retard the growth of the plant. In fact, plants grow best when they are moderately potbound. See Chapter 1 for further information on repotting.

Water

'Janet Craigs' and 'Lisas' prefer to stay in damp, but not wet soil. If they are properly potted in good soil and the right sized pot, then it is best to water them as soon as the top inch of the soil feels dry.

If the soil gets too dry, leaf tips and edges will turn dry and brown. These discolored portions of the leaves can be trimmed off with sharp scissors, but it is best to avoid letting your plant get quite so dry in the future.

If you don't allow the soil to regularly dry out a bit at the surface, then the roots will gradually rot and you won't know it until the leaves turn a dull yellow and the stems become soft and shriveled. At this point it is often too late, so it is best to avoid keeping the soil too moist.

Soil Quality

Most *Dracaena* 'Janet Craigs' and 'Lisas' are grown in peat-based, soilless potting mixes that are both porous and able to retain water easily. Garden soil intended for outdoor use is too dense or heavy to use with these plants.

Some of the better quality 'Lisas' are grown in a mix incorporating volcanic cinders. You will know this as soon as you try to press your finger down into the soil. The cinder mix is hard, sharp and nearly impenetrable. However, it is very porous and does retain water quite well. Unfortunately, it is very hard to determine the moisture content of this potting mix because you cannot get your finger into it. You will have to experiment a bit if your Lisa is in this cinder potting mix. Usually a moderate amount of water once per week is about right. Just make sure that you don't leave the pot standing in water for more than a few hours. Once you get the hang of watering this unusual mix, your plant will prove to be healthier than it would otherwise be in a standard potting mix.

Fertilizer

Fertilizer is not medicine so never use it on ailing plants. 'Janet Craigs' and 'Lisas' are slow growers so they use very limited nutrients. A liquid fertilizer that is high in nitrogen content should be diluted to half the recommended label strength and applied about 4 times per year as long as the plant is healthy. If you skip the fertilizer altogether, it is not likely to harm the plant in any way. See Chapter 8 for more information about fertilizing.

Temperature and Humidity

All Dracaenas are tropical in origin. As tropical plants they need protection from cold. Temps in the 60°F to 80°F. range are recommended. The 'Janet Craigs' and 'Lisas' are sensitive to cold temperatures and drafts so it is best to keep them away from drafty windows and doors. For this reason and because they do not do well in strong light, they are not good candidates to move outside, even in the warmer months.

Sudden exposure to cold temperatures or freezing drafts will cause leaves to turn dark and soft. Once leaf tissue is damaged by cold, it does not recover, so trim off the damaged leaves. If the roots were not damaged by cold (roots are more insulated than leaves), then the plant will survive and healthy, new growth will emerge.

Normal household humidity levels are fine for Dracaenas. They have proven to do well even in heated indoor environments where humidity levels are desert-dry. Of course, in warm dry air, moisture will evaporate more quickly from the soil and the leaves, so more frequent watering may be necessary in winter. Otherwise, humidity levels are not an important consideration for Dracaenas.

Pests

'Janet Craigs' and 'Lisas' are mostly pest-free. Occasionally, mealybugs will show up on newly emerging leaves or hiding in crevices where leaves attach to stems. Fortunately, they are fairly easy to spot because their white, cotton-like covering shows up well against the dark green background of the leaves.

Mealybugs are best treated with a spray solution of rubbing alcohol and water with a squirt of liquid soap. The best prevention is vigilance. Read Chapter 10 to learn how to identify and treat these plant pests. Inspect the leaves and stems carefully for pests before you purchase a plant. After purchase, be sure to check your plant at least monthly for pests and treat them promptly and thoroughly.

If you keep the soil too moist or if your plant was grown in poor quality soil, then a fungus gnat problem may develop. The adult gnats have wings and fly about, but the larvae feed on decaying roots in the soil. Thus, it is important to treat fungus gnats as a soil pest problem. The flying adults will die of their own accord after a week. See Chapter 10 on treating plant pests.

Pruning Leggy Plants

'Janet Craigs' and 'Lisas' are slow growing plants and do not need pruning very often. However after many years they can outgrow their space and the stems may start to lean precariously or push up against the ceiling.

Stems can be pruned off at any height and then new growth will emerge just below the pruning cut and grow upward from there. The pruned off tops can be inserted in the same pot where they usually root or they can be propagated in separate pots.

Propagation

'Janet Craig' and 'Lisa' stems root quite readily in damp soil or in plain water. Use the smallest pot that the cuttings will fit into and filled with a standard peat-based, soilless potting mix. If you root the cuttings in water, wait until you have several roots at least an inch long before moving them into small pots as described above

Flowers

Very occasionally, 'Janet Craigs' and 'Lisas' will flower. The flowers don't look like the petaled flowers we see in the florist's shop. Some people describe the flowers as "strange looking growths." After a week or two they will dry and can be pruned off. If you don't like them, you can prune them off at any time without harming the plant.

Dracaena marginata

Sometimes called Dragon Trees, *Dracaena marginatas* are one of the most popular indoor plants and have been for many years. Although they come in many sizes, it is the taller Marginatas of 4 feet or more that are most popular. They are usually grown with multiple stems at different heights in the same pot. Depending on how they are grown, some very interesting shapes are created. Sharply curved stems are not uncommon. This makes a very sculptural looking plant with a hint of the exotic that makes them appealing.

Marginatas are so-named because of the thin red edge along the margin of each leaf.

This is a relatively fast-growing plant and that means it can be sold without a large price tag. However, as with most fast-growers, their life span is typically shorter than slower growing species. It is not uncommon for Marginatas to do very well for several years and then rather abruptly take a turn for the worse and never recover. Enjoy this plant, but don't become too attached to it!

Buying a Marginata

Close inspection of the foliage on a Marginata can tell you a lot about how it was grown and what its light requirements will be.

When grown in strong direct sunlight, Marginatas produce thick, spiky leaves that stand upward rigidly from the stems. Such a Marginata will struggle to adapt to anything other that an indoor location that provides direct sunlight for most of the day. It will have to be placed directly in front of and close to an uncovered window.

Marginatas that have been adapted to reduced light or shade, have thinner, darker green leaves that arch gracefully from the stems creating a fountain-like effect. For most people, a Marginata with this softer foliage is a better option for indoor use. Although it still requires lots of bright indirect light and should be no more than 3 or 4 feet from a sunny window, it does not require the intense direct sunlight that the Marginata with spiky leaves requires.

Repotting

Unless you acquire a Marginata in a very small pot (8 inches or less) with roots bursting through the drain holes, **do not** repot this plant…*ever*. Once a Marginata is moved indoors to reduced light (relative to the nursery where it was grown), its growth rate will slow down and so will its need for nutrients and water. The roots will **not** need more room. If you add more soil you will prevent the root zone from drying out properly and that can be fatal for a plant that develops root rot easily. For more information on repotting see Chapter 1.

If you find the plastic nursery pot unattractive, then purchase a decorative planter that is large enough for you to put the nursery pot inside. This is much easier and better for the plant than repotting directly into another planter.

Water

If your Marginata is properly potted and left in its nursery pot, then it is best to water it as soon as the top quarter of the soil feels dry. Pour in water slowly so that the entire rootball is saturated and a bit of water runs through the drainage holes. It should reach that level of dryness again within 10 days or less. If it doesn't, then add less water next time.

Not allowing the soil to dry out adequately between each watering will eventually cause root rot and kill your Marginata. When roots start to rot, leaves will turn pale, wilt and fall off in bunches. The stems will turn soft and mushy. By then it is often too late to save.

On the other hand, if you consistently under water a Marginata, the leaves will wilt and turn brown and dry. The leaves will perk up after the soil has been watered, but the brown leaves will not recover.

Needless to say, it is better to err on the side of dryness with this plant.

It is important to know that as this plant ages, its need for water declines. The quantity or frequency of water that was appropriate when the plant was new to you will no longer work as it gets older. It is the inadvertent overwatering of older Marginatas that often shortens their lifespan.

Temperature & Humidity

Dracaena marginatas are moderately tolerant of cool temperatures as low as 55°F, if the temperatures drop gradually. Normal home temperatures are fine for a Marginata, although it should be protected from very cold drafts through open doors and windows. They are tolerant of low humidity.

Fertilizer

In good light, your Marginata will put out new leaves regularly. Fertilize monthly at half the recommended label strength as long as the plant is growing vigorously. Fertilizer is not medicine and should not be used to treat plant problems.

Pests

Unfortunately, Marginatas are magnets for spider mites. These very tiny dust-like specks show up on the bottom and top sides of the leaves. Before you purchase a Marginata and after you acquire one, inspect the foliage very carefully in very bright light so you can spot these critters before they infest your entire plant and start spinning their tiny webs. Chapter 10 provides detailed information on identifying and treating spider mites, but generally a thorough spraying with soapy water is effective.

Even if your Marginata does not have spider mites when purchased or has never had them, continue to inspect the foliage at least monthly. In the right conditions — warm, dry air — spider mites can reproduce at a furious rate and quickly take over your Marginata.

If the thought of having to cope with spider mites spooks you, then a Marginata is not the plant for you!

Discolored Leaves

Brown leaf tips on older leaves will occur in anything other than perfect conditions. If they bother you, trim them off at a sharp angle with scissors. Lower (older leaves) that yellow and die are also quite normal as they are replaced on top with newer leaves. Excessive leaf yellowing is usually due to improper watering. A mottled appearance to the leaves is usually a sign of a spider mite infestation. Discoloration of leaves on or near the tip ends of stems probably means that you have been keeping the soil too damp and root rot has already set in.

Pruning

Healthy Marginatas can quickly outgrow their space because of their tall, fast-growing stems. Tall stems also lose a lot of their lower leaves even when healthy. An overgrown plant does not mean it needs a larger pot. Sooner or later (sooner than you think!) your Marginata will need to have some of the stems pruned back. It is best to prune them back before it is really obvious that they are too tall for their space or starting to lean over precariously. Marginatas can be pruned at any time of the year. Any stem can be cut back and new growth will soon emerge just below the point on the stem where you make the pruning cut. So prune back to the point where you would like to see new growth emerge. Pruning will help eliminate leggy stems that have lost lower leaves and help keep your plant looking fuller and more compact.

Branching

Some Marginatas branch more freely than others. Although pruning will sometimes promote branching of stems, in general there is not much you can do to make your Marginatas develop branches.

Propagation

Marginata cuttings do not root easily because the stems usually rot before the roots develop. Air-layering is the most effective way to propagate more plants from the stems. See Chapter 12 to learn how to air layer.

Dieffenbachia

The most interesting thing about this plant is its common name — Dumb Cane. Dieffenbachia, like most members of the Aroid plant family, contains oxalic acid which can cause tissues of the mouth and throat to swell up when it is eaten. Such swelling can render a person unable to speak, hence the name "dumb" cane. The oxalic crystals can also irritate the skin so it is best to wear gloves when pruning a Dieffenbachia. Needless to say, this is not a good plant to have in a household with toddlers and plant-chewing pets.

Dieffenbachias are popular because they have attractive green and white variegated leaves in a wide variety of patterns. Some species are nearly all green and others are mostly white. Some varieties are quite small and remain that way. The popular Dieffenbachia 'Tropic Snow' has very large leaves, very thick stems and grows rapidly. All Dieffenbachia species and varieties have the same basic care requirements.

Light

Dieffenbachias can adapt to moderately low light, but they do best with lots of indirect sunlight. Try to place your Dieffenbachia very close to a north or east window or several feet back from or to the side of a west or south window. A few hours of direct sun falling on the leaves is okay, but bright indirect light all day long is best.

In low light, growth will be very slow, new leaves may be smaller and the stem space between the leaves will be elongated. Variegated varieties may revert to all green. In low light, lower leaves die and you will be left with long, leggy stems. Too much direct sun will cause leaves to turn a pale green color.

Water

If your Dieffenbachia is properly potted, then it is best to water it as soon as the top quarter of the soil feels dry. In low light, it is better to allow the soil to dry out a bit deeper before watering thoroughly. Don't allow the pot to sit in water for more than a couple of hours. If you consistently under water a Dieffenbachia, you will find leaf edges turning brown and lower leaves will yellow and fall off prematurely. Overwatering will cause the roots to rot and the plant will languish, developing dull yellow leaves that fall.

Repotting

Like most potted plants, Dieffenbachias do best when they are kept quite pot-bound. If there is enough soil in the pot to keep the roots properly moist for at least three days between thorough waterings, then it is usually best to leave the roots undisturbed in the existing pot. If your plant is so potbound that it requires water every few days, then it is appropriate to move it into a pot one size larger.

The large-leafed, thick stemmed *Dieffenbachia* 'Tropic Snow' tends to grow very tall and the large leaves soon make it top-heavy. The stems start to bend and lean and soon become unsightly. The common assumption is that this problem can be fixed with a larger pot. That is a mistake. Leaning stems can only be fixed by pruning. (See Pruning below).

Temperature & Humidity

Dieffenbachias prefer warm temperatures above 50°F. Normal home temperatures are fine, although Dieffenbachias should be protected from very cold drafts coming from open doors and windows. Dieffenbachias are unaffected by low humidity.

Fertilizer

Dieffenbachias are not particularly heavy feeders. If yours is in low light, the growth rate will be slow and growth cannot be forced with fertilizer. In low light, it is best to skip fertilizing altogether. In good light, fertilize your Dieffenbachia monthly at half the recommended label strength as long as the plant is growing vigorously. Fertilizer is not medicine and should not be used to treat plant problems.

Pruning

Healthy Dieffenbachias, especially the larger varieties such as 'Tropic Snow,' can quickly become leggy and/or outgrow their space. It is best to prune a Dieffenbachia back before it is really obvious that it needs it. It can be pruned at any time of the year.

Very tall Dieffenbachias stems usually start to lean or bend under the weight of their very heavy leaves. Sometimes the stems even snap. I regularly see these plants propped up with stakes and poles and broom handles. There is nothing wrong with this, but it certainly is not a very pretty sight. A better option is to prune back these tall stems as soon as they start to become unwieldy. Cut the stem back to a foot or less, leaving a short stem stub. New growth will soon emerge from near the top of this stub and grow up rapidly from there. The result will be a much shorter, but more compact and manageable plant. Pruning will also help eliminate leggy stems that have lost their leaves.

Pruned off stems will root quite readily in small pots of damp potting mix and in the soil at the base of the existing pot, if there is room to insert it.

When you prune, be sure to wear gloves and avoid getting sap on your skin and in your eyes or mucous membranes. Dieffenbachia does not give off toxic fumes, so do not be unnecessarily alarmed, but do be careful when cutting leaf and stem tissue.

Propagation

Dieffenbachias can be propagated by using tip stem cuttings. A tip cutting has a green, non-woody stem with no more than 4-6 leaves. Leave no more than six inches of bare stem below the lowest leaves when propagating. Insert cuttings into a small pot filled with a porous potting mix of 2 parts peat moss and 1 part Perlite. Keep this mix damp, provide bright indirect light and warm temperatures and you should have some healthy roots within 4-6 weeks. In many instances the cuttings can be inserted in the soil of the same plant from which it was cut.

Branching

Dieffenbachias do not branch. Each stem grows straight up. For this reason, most nurseries plant more than one stem in each pot. This helps fill out the plants and give it a more lush appearance. Don't worry, that does not mean their roots are overcrowded and that they should be separated. Leave the roots undisturbed.

Pests

Dieffenbachias are susceptible to spider mites, mealy bugs and occasionally scale insects. If soil quality is poor or if the soil is kept too moist, then fungus gnats may become a problem. See Chapter 10 for information on identifying and treating these plant pests. As always, keeping your plants healthy is your best protection against plant pests.

Ferns
Filicopsida

Ferns remind us of cool, damp forest floors where ferns often grow. Although the Fern family (*Filicopsida*) includes dozens of different species that grow in regions all over the world, most ferns commonly used as houseplants do come from environments where the soil is moist and the light is low. That tells us that they must have their soil moisture and their light attended to carefully. Even a single episode of forgetting to water can be fatal to a fern. Almost overnight, a fern can go from lush fronds to dry, crispy foliage — a most disheartening sight. If you expose a fern to direct sunlight for more than a few hours, the fragile fronds will bleach out and turn a sickly, pale green-yellow.

What all true ferns have in common is that they never flower and they reproduce from spores usually found on the undersides of fronds. (The misnamed Asparagus Fern is not a true fern because it does flower, produce seeds and is actually in the Lily family.)

In this chapter, I will first provide an overview on the care of ferns generally. Following that, I will discuss some of the unique qualities and care for some of the most popular fern species used as indoor plants.

Roots and Water

Most fern species grow in damp locations, such as the floor of a tropical or semi-tropical forest where the soil never dries out. Consequently, the roots of ferns are adapted to and require constantly damp soil. These roots are fine in texture, somewhat fragile and do not penetrate deep into the soil because moisture is always available near the surface.

For our potted ferns, we need to duplicate this root environment as closely as possible. That means that ferns should be watered as soon as the soil feels almost dry or just barely damp. If you allow the top inch of the soil to dry — as we do with many of our other potted plants — then your fern will react by wilting and dropping fronds. At the other extreme, if a fern's soil is kept constantly wet or soggy, then the roots will rot and the plant will die. So monitor the soil moisture of your fern carefully if you want to keep it for a long time.

Light

Ferns do best in low and medium light. They are naturally adapted to shady and semi-shady conditions. They are best placed close to a north or east window that does not provide more than a couple of hours of direct sunlight falling on the fronds each day. Too much sun causes the fronds to turn pale green in color.

But that does not mean you can stick your fern in a dark corner or place it across the room from the nearest window. Even low light ferns require sufficient natural light to comfortably read newsprint all day long. Unlike some other low light plants, ferns do not fare well in artificial light alone. If your office or basement has no windows, but good overhead fluorescent light, a fern is probably not a good plant choice. (See Chapter 4 for better low light plant options.) In poor light, ferns will develop weak, under-sized new fronds and the plant will gradually become thin and lose its naturally lush appearance.

Water Quality

Many fern species are sensitive to excessive mineral salts around their roots or in the air. If your local tap water is on the hard side, use filtered, distilled or rainwater instead. Likewise, do not use hard water to spray or mist your ferns. Pesticides that are okay to use on other plants are often damaging to many fern species. Never use any pesticide on a fern unless the label states specifically that it is okay to use on ferns. Finally, ferns are not good to use in swimming pool areas as the chlorine levels in pool water are at toxic levels for ferns

Soil, Repotting & Pot Size

Ferns require soil that retains water. That means a good fern potting mix is rich in peat moss, leaf mold or ground bark chips but minimizes porous material such as sand and Perlite. A good fern potting mix should be able to retain water so that the soil does not dry out for about a week following a thorough watering.

Many ferns are grown in pots that are shallow in proportion to their width. The reasons for this are twofold. First, ferns have shallow roots. Second and counter-intuitively, shallow pots retain moisture longer than deeper pots. If you only have a taller pot available for your Fern, it is best to use a layer of drainage material in the bottom of the pot so as to effectively shorten the rootball and help the soil stay moist longer.

Because fern roots are fine and not particularly extensive, ferns rarely need up-potting to larger pots. However, a vigorously growing Boston Fern is a exception to this rule. Generally, a fern's pot should be large enough to retain moisture for about a week before drying out. If you are struggling to water frequently enough to keep the soil damp at all times, then repot your fern into a pot one inch larger.

Humidity

Nearly all ferns are native to areas that have naturally high humidity levels. As potted plants, ferns benefit from increased humidity, although this is not a necessity for many fern species. The popular Boston Fern, for example, does quite well in low humidity environments. On the other hand, the delicate Maidenhair Fern fares poorly outside of a greenhouse or terrarium where high humidity levels can be maintained. For humidity-loving Ferns, daily misting or moving them to the bathroom will not help very much.

Temperature

Ferns grow in many parts of the world from warm tropical regions to bitterly cold temperate zones. The fern species that do best as indoor plants are native to tropical and semi-tropical regions. However, it is best to learn what the temperature limitations are for your fern before you make any assumptions

Fertilizer

Ferns have tender roots and do not use large quantities of mineral nutrients. There is a greater danger in burning fern roots by using too much fertilizer than the danger of depriving a fern of essential nutrients. Organic fertilizers are a bit gentler on tender fern roots than standard commercial fertilizers. In any case, it is best to always dilute the fertilizer to half the label strength and apply no more than monthly. Fern fertilizer should have a higher proportion of nitrogen to the other two major nutrients (phosphorous and potassium) so a fertilizer with a 3-1-1 ratio is best for ferns.

Pruning & Trimming

Most ferns do not require much pruning as they are not fast growers and rarely outgrow their space. However, many Ferns will need trimming or removal of older fronds that have discolored or died. Once a frond becomes discolored, it will never return to its original color so it is best to remove it. If a lot of fronds are dying, then you need to figure out what is causing the problem and correct it.

Propagation

Ferns do not have flowers and do not produce seeds. They do produce spores, which are tan in color and appear on the undersides of certain fern fronds. Some spores are large and look like raised moles on the skin. Others are as fine as dust particles and may appear massed together as a brown patch on the undersides of frond tips. The spores are often mistaken for scale insects. See Chapter 10 on Plant Pests. Propagating fern spores is difficult and time consuming and is best left to the professionals so I won't get into it here.

An easier way to propagate many Fern species is by division. That is done by removing that plant from its pot and using a large knife, slicing straight through the rootball from top to bottom. Although some of the roots will be cut through, there will be enough other roots in each section of the rootball for the sections to survive. The divided sections can be put into their own separate pots that should be just barely large enough to accommodate them. Do this only with healthy Ferns.

Some Fern species such as the "foot ferns" can be easily propagated by cutting off sections of the furry "feet" or rhizomes. These rhizome sections can be pinned in place on the surface of constantly damp potting mix. In time they will put down roots into the moist soil and after that, they will start to produce fronds from the top sides of the sections.

Pests

Ferns are relatively pest-free. However, they do occasionally attract scale insects, which are hard to identify because they do not look like insects as we think of them. In fact, scale insects appear as slightly raised, oval bumps on the undersides of fronds and along frond stems. They are easily mistaken for spores on ferns. Not only are scale insects hard to identify, they are also hard to eradicate. White, cotton-like mealybugs are easier to identify and are also found on fern species. Both scale insects and mealybugs secrete a sticky substance called honeydew, but spores do not. So if you find any stickiness on fern fronds, you can be sure you have a pest infestation. More detailed information on these pests can be found in Chapter 10.

Because fern fronds are sensitive to many foreign substances, you will have to test spray any pesticides or cleaners, including oils and soaps, before treating an entire plant. Do this by applying the spray onto a single healthy frond and wait a week to see if that frond reacts negatively to that particular spray. Only if it does not should you proceed to spray the entire plant.

Frankly, if your fern develops a pest infestation, it is probably best to discard the plant. Otherwise, you may never entirely eradicate the pests and must be prepared for an ongoing treatment plan.

Boston Fern (Nephrolepis exaltata 'Bostoniensis')

This is the fern most commonly used as an indoor potted plant. Its popularity is attributable to its rapid growth and tolerance of low humidity, moderate light, and even occasional watering lapses. On the flip-side, it can be a messy houseplant as older fronds inevitably die and leave a residue of crispy brown leaves below. However, if you are new to ferns, this is probably a good one to start with.

Boston Ferns have long, draping fronds and look best in hanging baskets or on raised pedestal planters. It is best to locate them immediately in front of a north or east window. In good light, Boston Ferns use lots of water and often require thorough watering more than once per week. Never let the surface of the soil get completely dry or you will end up with lots of dead leaflets.

In good light, Boston Ferns grow rapidly. As they grow, their roots soon fill up the pot, sometimes even pushing the rootball upward so that the surface of the soil is even with the rim of the pot. This condition makes watering difficult and it is best to either up-pot one size or prune the roots or divide the plant. To root prune a Boston Fern, use a sharp knife to slice off an inch of rootball (roots and soil) from the bottom and a half-inch around the sides. Then add some soil to the bottom of the original pot, place the pruned rootball back in the pot and fill in the sides with fresh potting mix.

Normal home temperatures are fine for this fern, but it is best to avoid unusually warm, dry conditions. It can be moved outside to a shady location when temperatures are safely above 50°F.

Boston Ferns often produce thin, thread-like runners called stolons. When put in contact with damp soil, these stolons will produce new plants as long as they remain attached to the mother plant. This is hard to do, but it is okay to cut these stolons off if you don't like their appearance. Eventually they die back on their own.

Rabbits Foot Fern & Bears Paw Fern
(Davallia fejeensis & Aglaomorpha meyeniana)

These ferns are unusual in that they are epiphytic, meaning they grow above the ground attached to damp tree bark, and they have rhizomes or stems that are covered with fur-like material, hence their unusual common names.

The rhizomes of these ferns do not grow under the ground and they should never be buried within a pot. Rather let them wander over the surface of the soil and out over the edge of the pot. In many instances, these rhizomes will grow around and envelop the container they are potted in. In fact, some of these ferns are grown in very porous containers made out of tree fern. These ferns are easily watered by dunking them into a sink or bucket filled with water. They can also be watered by hose or under a shower and then letting them drip dry. As with other ferns, never let the soil get too dry.

Not only do the rhizomes wander out of the soil, but they also push out new fern fronds. If you want to propagate an epiphytic fern, simply cut off a section of the rhizome with one or more fronds attached. Then pin the cut section on the surface of a pot filled with damp soil. Do not cover the rhizome cutting with soil as you would other plant cuttings. The surface contact with damp soil will trigger the rhizome to put down roots into the damp soil and you will soon have a new plant.

These ferns can tolerate a bit more light than most ferns, but still no more than a couple of hours of direct sun each day and keep it in a light shade when outdoors. They are not low light plants so they must be within a few feet of a window. They are tropical in origin and temperatures should be kept above 55°F.

Bird's Nest Fern *(Asplenium nidus)*

This is an unusual fern with large green glossy leaves that emerge from a central crown creating a nest-like appearance. Each leaf has a very dark central rib running lengthwise and is an interesting contrast to the deep green leaves. Symmetrically spaced brown spores appear on the undersides of the fronds and should not be mistaken for scale insects.

Lots of bright, mostly indirect light is best for this fern. Right in a north or east window is best. It is a warm-loving plant so keep temps above 60°F. Cool temperatures and drafts will cause newer leaves to develop dark spots and spoil their appearance.

Water the Bird's Nest Fern as you would other ferns, keeping the soil evenly moist by watering whenever the surface of the soil feels almost dry. Improper watering will cause leaf spotting.

This is a slow growing fern with new leaves that emerge from the central crown. It is extremely rare that a Bird's Nest Fern will ever need a larger pot. It is normal for some of the older fronds to gradually discolor as they age and are replaced with new fronds. This is not a cause for concern as long as it is not losing more than it is gaining. Prune off older leaves once they start to discolor.

As with other ferns, be alert for scale insects and mealybugs, although this fern species is more resistant than most and easier to treat.

Unfortunately, this fern cannot be propagated by division or cuttings.

Asparagus Ferns
(Protoasparagus densiflorus and *Protoasparagus plumosus)*

As mentioned previously, this is not a fern despite its misleading common name. I include it here simply because you might logically search for information on it in this chapter.

Plants in the *Protoasparagus* and *Asparagus* genera, including the edible *Asparagus officinalis*, are in the Lily family. They have underground rhizomes or fat tubers that cause them to quickly outgrow their pots when they are in good light. They produce clusters of tiny white flowers and red berries containing seeds.

Unlike true ferns, Asparagus Ferns love lots of direct sunlight when indoors and dappled light when outdoors. They do best when hung or placed right in your sunniest window.

A with true ferns, water your Asparagus Fern when the surface of the soil feels dry, although the Asparagus Fern can tolerate drought better than a true fern. If allowed to get too dry, the needles may yellow but the plant will recover when it is properly watered again.

In good light, this plant will soon outgrow its pot. However, it is still best to delay up-potting until the soil dries out within three days after a thorough watering. A standard shaped pot one size larger is best. If your Asparagus Fern outgrows its pot and you don't want to move it into a larger pot, then root pruning is the solution. Follow the instructions for root pruning in the section above on Boston Ferns.

The biggest problem with Asparagus Ferns is their attraction to pests, especially spider mites, but also scale and mealybugs. You must be constantly vigilant in checking weekly for any signs of pests. Unlike true ferns, the Asparagus Fern is more tolerant of various sprays used to treat these pests. More detailed information on these pests can be found in Chapter 10. For persistent pest infestations, the best solution is to cut off all of the stems right to the soil line and spray the remaining stubs and soil surface with a solution of water, soap and rubbing alcohol. With good light and proper watering, you will soon see lots of new stems emerging from the soil. This technique can also be used to rejuvenate an older plant that has lost lots of needles and thinned out.

Asparagus Ferns do best in cooler temperatures and fresh air. Both will help deter pests. You can move these plants outside once temperatures are safely above 45°F in the spring and keep them outside until temperatures fall below

40°F. in the fall. Indoors in winter, keep your Asparagus Fern away from heating elements.

Maidenhair fern *(Adiantum raddianum)*

This is one of the most delicate and fragile of the commonly used ferns. The tiny green leaves at the ends of dark stems are thinner than paper and easily bruised. But the airy manner in which they display themselves out over the plant makes them utterly appealing. It also triggers a natural desire to touch them. Unfortunately, they bruise very easily and handling them is not recommended.

Maidenhairs do best in terrariums where humidity levels are high. They develop brown frond edges when humidity levels are too low so they are impractical plants in areas where winter heating systems dry up the air. Humidifiers can remedy this, but daily misting will not help nor will keeping them in a bathroom.

Maidenhairs like bright but indirect light and must be protected from direct sun. Close to a north window is the best location. They prefer constant environments so find an appropriate location for this fern and avoid relocating it.

Because they are such fragile plants and because their root systems are small, it is best if they are not repotted.

Water as you would any other fern, but be sure to use clear or distilled water that is free of mineral salts.

Normal household temperatures are fine as long as it does not get above 80°F or below 60°F.

Maidenhairs are generally pest resistant, but if you do get a pest infestation that may doom the plant because they are so sensitive to any sprays used to treat insect pests.

Staghorn Fern *(Platycerium bifurcatum)*

This unusual looking fern is one of my personal favorites. Words cannot describe this unusual looking plant with fronds that are reminiscent of a stag's antlers. It is truly a remarkable looking plant.

Like the Rabbit's Foot Fern, it is epiphytic, but it does not have rhizomes. It grows in tropical regions where it has roots that attach themselves to the crotches of tree limbs above the forest floor. Nature designed it to produce layers of flat, round, paper-thin shields that catch and trap nutrient debris and water when it rains. These shields start out green but turn brown as they age. Out of the center of these flat shields grows the green antler-like fronds that absorb the sunlight and produce patches of fine spores on the tips of the fronds. The fronds of this plant are covered with soft white fuzz that many folks mistake for dust or pests or mold. This fuzz consists of tiny hairs that help the Staghorn retain moisture and nutrients so don't rub or wipe them off.

If you want an unusual sculptural looking conversation piece for your home, the Staghorn should be given serious consideration. But read this first so you will have a good idea of its special care needs.

Staghorn Ferns are sold in small pots of soil; attached to slabs of bark or wood; and in large open baskets. Although it is possible to maintain this plant in a small pot and soil, I recommend that you transfer a potted Staghorn to a slab or a basket.

Wire is usually used to attach the Staghorn shield to the wooden slab. The wood slab can then be hung flat against a wall for an interesting display. In most cases, you will need to take it down once or twice per week and soak it in the sink or shower to properly water it. It cannot be watered in the conventional manner using a watering can. Once it is attached to a wooden slab, it is difficult to ever move it or reattach it to something else.

Another way to keep a Staghorn is to place it inside of an open basket lined with sphagnum moss. Depending on the size of the basket, more than one Staghorn Fern can be placed inside the basket. In any case, the shield and the fronds should poke through the open portions of the basket. Press the sphagnum moss in around it to hold it in place. You will have a hanging basket with the fronds protruding outward into space at odd angles — very unusual indeed! In time, the individual plants will produce more and more shields that will cover the outer portion of the basket and produce even more fronds. Eventually the entire basket will disappear from sight as the shields completely envelop the basket.

As with the slab-mounted Staghorn, the basket Staghorn will have to be soaked at least once per week and allowed to drip dry a bit before returning it to its preferred location. This plant grows slowly, but over the course of several years it will become ever-larger and heavier. Keep this in mind if you decide to get one.

Staghorn Ferns prefer lots of bright indirect light such as you get close to a north or east facing window. Protect it from direct sunlight, but do not put it far from the window. In poor light, new fronds will be thin and weak. In light that is too strong, the deep green fronds will become a paler shade of green.

Staghorns tolerate cool temperatures quite well and can even withstand mild freezes for short periods if the low temperatures are introduced gradually. For best results it can be placed outside when spring temperatures are above 50°F and left out in the fall until temperatures drop to 40°F. It will also tolerate temperatures into the mid-80s.

As with other ferns, watch carefully for signs of scale insects and treat them promptly when detected.

Brake or Hand Ferns *(Pteris species)*

These are mostly small, slow-growing ferns that are sometimes used in terrariums and in dish gardens. Follow the general instructions outlined at the beginning of this chapter — indirect light, moist soil, small pots, and moderate temperatures.

Holly Fern *(Cyrtomium falcatum)*

This is an unusual fern in that its leaves are shaped like Holly leaves and they are glossy and leather-like in texture. It prefers cool temperatures and will tolerate temperatures down to freezing for short periods.

Brake Fern

It is less temperamental than many other ferns, but it does need protection from direct sunlight and dry soil. In good light, it will grow quite rapidly and become larger than many fern species.

Button Fern *(Pellaea rotundifolia)*

This fern has small, round leaflets along each frond. They are shiny and leathery in texture. It has a low, spreading profile and works well as a ground-cover to fill spaces between other plants.

This fern is not quite as fragile as some other ferns as long as it gets good bright indirect light and the soil is kept moist. It tolerates low humidity as well as temperatures to freezing for short periods.

Button Fern

Mother Fern *(Asplenium bulbiferum)*

This is an unusual fern that, when mature, produces tiny plantlets along its fronds. These plantlets drop off and root easily if left in contact with damp soil. This fern is a lighter shade of green and grows quite quickly and large in good conditions. Provide lots of bright indirect light and temperatures in the 45–75°F. range. It is a bit less temperamental than many ferns, but avoid letting the soil dry out too much.

Ficus Tree
Ficus benjamina

No indoor plant is more popular than the tree-like *Ficus benjamina*. And no indoor plant is a greater source of agony than the *Ficus benjamina*. It is commonly called "weeping fig" because it is in the fig family and the branches hang down in a weeping manner. I think there is more to this nickname than that. Weeping fig sheds leaves (tears) so easily that it causes many owners to cry out in despair! More Ficus trees are discarded prematurely than any other indoor plant. Why is that these trees that look so gorgeous in the plant shop seem to fall apart so quickly at home?

And why do I claim that *Ficus benjamina* is the hardiest and most long-lived indoor plant that you can own? Read on.

The Problem Is Light

Ficus trees *must* have lots of sunlight. If you don't have a nice, largely unobstructed sunny window to locate a Ficus tree, then you had best select another plant. There are dozens of houseplants that thrive in areas beyond the reach of the sun's rays, but the Ficus is not one of them.

The leaves on *Ficus benjamina* are unusually light sensitive. New leaves are suited for the light level they received at the time they emerged. If that light level changes subsequently, then many of those leaves will drop off. Replacement leaves are adapted to the new light level. For this reason, Ficus trees are notorious for dropping leaves every time they are relocated. They go through a process called acclimatization, which means they must adapt to any change in light intensity.

These trees are usually grown outside in warm climates in full sunlight. The better nursery growers move them into shaded areas for 6 weeks before they sell them so that the trees will have an easier time adapting to the lower light levels inside the home. Unfortunately, many discount growers skip this important step and the result is that the trees have a much more traumatic adjustment to go through after they are sold.

What To Do With Your New Ficus Tree

It is common and even expected that Ficus trees will shed lots of leaves when they are moved to a new environment. Although you can't stop the leaf loss completely, there are some things you can do to ensure that lots of new replacement leaves appear in due time.

- Don't add to the trauma by repotting. Wait until the acclimatization is complete before repotting. Even then, it may not be necessary.

- Give your new Ficus as much direct sunlight as possible. A south-facing window is best. After it has acclimated, you can move it to a less bright location, such as a north window, if you prefer.

- Water the rootball thoroughly. Make sure the soil is packed in tight around the circumference of the pot so the water doesn't just run right through without soaking the rootball. Water again thoroughly when the surface soil feels dry.

- Don't fertilize it until it has finished adjusting and is putting out healthy new growth.

- Prune off interior branches that have lost most of their leaves.

You will notice that new leaves form from tiny green points at the ends of the branches. This new growth will be acclimated to its new environment.

Eventually, many of the original leaves will drop off and be replaced by lots of new leaves. This process can take up to six months, so be patient.

Practical tip: Once a week give your Ficus a vigorous shake to loosen all the leaves that are destined to fall off soon anyway. Then clean them all up at once. It's easier than picking up a few leaves every day.

There is nothing mysterious about Ficus trees. They don't like to be moved. They don't like dry soil. They prefer more light rather than less. They thrive outside in direct sun, but they will survive indoors with a minimum of bright indirect sun all day long. That is a wide range of light to which they can adapt. In general, give them as much light as possible, but avoid moving them unless you are willing to deal with a lot of leaf shedding.

Ficus trees are finicky, but very tough to kill

When given adequate light and proper water, weeping figs will live longer than any other indoor plant. They can survive bouts of occasional over or under watering. They don't need misting or high humidity and they can survive all indoor temperature extremes, including cold drafts. Although sudden environmental changes will cause Ficus trees to shed leaves for a while, be patient because this is temporary and the Ficus tree will recover nicely.

Pruning

Pruning Ficus trees is as much art as it is science — like cutting hair. Try to visualize how your tree will look with certain branches cut back and also how it will look as the new growth comes in. I have successfully pruned back Ficus trees enough that there was not a single leaf remaining. In time, I had a beautiful tree with all new growth. Plunge in and have fun!

How to Prune A Ficus Tree

Healthy Ficus trees are wonderful to prune, once you overcome your initial hesitancy, because you really can't go wrong. They put out new growth soon enough that they quickly cover over any mistaken cuts. Just trust that the new growth will come in after you do your pruning. With experience you can learn to shape them as you see fit.

Generally, Ficus trees respond well to regular and even heavy pruning. You should routinely prune out all of the dead twigs and weak growth in the center of the tree and also prune some outer growth as well. Keep in mind that new growth always emerges at the ends of healthy stems and branches.

Here are three pruning approaches to use.

1. Remove up to one third of the outer growth on all the stems and branches. This will shrink the overall canopy of the tree by one third. This approach

will yield a smaller and fuller Ficus tree. It is great for Ficus trees that have outgrown their space.

2. Selectively prune back up to one third of the longest individual stems and branches into the center of the tree. This will open up the center portion to more light. The cut back stems will now produce new growth and fill in the sparse center area. When done regularly, this technique will maintain the existing size of the tree without making the pruning obvious.

3. Combine the first two.

White Sap

Ficus trees "bleed" a white, slightly sticky sap. This is normal. This sap is a mild skin irritant for some people. So be advised and use gloves when pruning. This sap also will permanently stain cotton fabric.

Propagating

Ficus trees can be propagated by stem cuttings. Tip cuttings with green stems and fewer than a half-dozen leaves can be rooted in damp potting mix in a small pot that is placed inside of a clear plastic bag. This plastic "tent" will preserve the moisture in the soil and maintain moisture in the surrounding air while roots are forming. Leave the plastic sealed for 4-6 weeks before gradually opening it to household air.

To propagate larger stem cuttings, you will have to use the air-layering technique, which is described in detail in Chapter 12.

Moving Your Ficus Outside

If your Ficus is doing reasonably well indoors, then you should leave it there. Here's why. Ficus leaves are very sensitive to even subtle changes in light. Moving your Ficus from indoors to outdoors is a dramatic change in light that puts it under considerable stress. Old leaves fall off and are replaced with healthy new growth. Ficus trees are tough plants that thrive in direct sunlight. By the end of the summer, an outdoor Ficus will probably look good again (provided you water it heavily). However, you will have to move it back inside in the late fall and it will have to readjust to the dramatically lower light all over again. You will spend most of the winter picking up fallen Ficus leaves. I recommend against this because most people do not want to look at a declining tree for 6-plus months every year. If you are prepared to accept that, then go ahead and move it outside for the summer.

If you have lots of direct light inside, then the winter adjustment process will not be as severe. Yet, in that circumstance, there is no benefit to moving it outside in the first place because it gets enough light inside.

It is preferable to find a permanent indoor location for your Ficus with lots of direct or bright indirect light and leave it there. It will reward you by stabilizing and not constantly dropping leaves.

Repotting

Ficus trees can manage quite well even when potbound, provided they get enough water. Really saturate the soil when you water, allowing the Ficus to sit in the excess water for an hour or so to wick it up. If the soil stays damp for several days or more, then I would advise against repotting. If it dries out again in a day or two, then repotting is probably warranted. If so, use a pot one size larger, usually 1 or 2 inches wider at the top.

You may observe roots growing out of the drainage holes of your Ficus pot. In most cases you can simply cut off these roots where they emerge from the pot. These are tough plants and it will not harm them.

Repotting a large Ficus tree is a big project requiring at least one extra pair of hands to help with the lifting. I recommend root pruning and returning the plant to its original pot. After you have removed your Ficus from its pot, use a long sharp knife (a machete is ideal) to slice off approximately an inch of rootball all around the sides and bottom. Put an inch or so of fresh soil in the bottom of the pot, place the root-pruned Ficus back into the pot, and fill in the sides of the pot with fresh soil.

Unexpected Leaf Drop

Sometimes a well-established Ficus tree that has not been moved in a year or more will experience a sudden spurt of inexplicable leaf loss. The leaf drop seems to occur after a prolonged period of sustained growth. This is because, at some point, a Ficus has as many leaves as it can support in the available light, i.e. it is maxxed out. It continues to grow and put out new foliage at the end of its branches, but it now has to sacrifice some of the older leaves to survive. This phenomenon usually occurs in the winter months when the day length is shorter. The best thing you can do in this circumstance is to prune your Ficus back as much as you can stand. This will curtail the leaf drop and help keep your tree full and bushy in its center.

Pests

Scale insects and mealybugs are the most common Ficus pests. Often they go undetected until the owner notices stickiness on the leaves and on furnishings under the tree. The best treatment is a silicon plant cleaner called Brand X. Horticultural and neem oil sprays are also effective. Insecticidal soap sprays and many pesticides often cause increased leaf drop. Never spray Ficus trees when they are exposed to direct sunlight or high temperatures. See Chapter 10 on Plant Pests.

Enlarged stem growths: Gall

Rarely, Ficus trees may develops one or more bark-covered, roundish growths attached to stems. This growth is called gall and is usually caused by a bacterial or fungal infection. Sometimes the infection will have other negative effects on the tree. Most of the time, it has no effect. There is no "cure" for gall.

If it is only one branch or stem that has the gall and it appears to be dying, you can prune off that branch, including the gall. Disinfect your pruners after cutting the infected branch. The rest of the tree is probably OK, but you can never be sure. If the rest of the tree starts to die back, then you will have to discard the tree.

White Balls of Sap

You may find small globules of hard white sap on the underside of Ficus leaves just above where the leaf attaches to the leaf stem. Don't worry, these are not insects or eggs or any other worrisome problem. It is a normal production of many Ficus trees and requires no treatment.

Fiddle-Leafed Fig
Ficus lyrata

Fiddle-leafed Figs are so named because the shape of their leaves is reminiscent of a fiddle. They have been around for many years, but have gained popularity recently because of their unusual sculptural look. They are often used as specimen plants that stand alone creating a dramatic statement in a large open space.

This plant comes in two overall forms or shapes. One is the standard shape that has a single tall trunk topped with multiple branches with many large leaves. The other is a bush form that has multiple smaller trunks growing from the soil with leaves all along the stems. The latter form has a more slender profile. Both require the same care.

The Fiddle-leafed Fig is a close relative of the popular Ficus Tree (*Ficus benjamina*) and Rubber Plant (*Ficus elstica*). The individual leaves on each of these family members are very different, but they are close relatives in the Fig family.

Like all members of the Ficus family, *Ficus lyrata* has a white sap that flows readily when a stem or leaf is cut. It is a mild skin irritant and may stain fabric.

Light

Ficus lyrata do best when they receive at least several hours of direct sunlight every day. It is best located right in front of an east or west window, or back a bit from a south window. It can adapt to a location right in front of a north window, but it will not be able to hold as many leaves.

Inadequate light is the most common problem with maintaining this plant. If it does not receive enough light, the leaves will discolor and fall off, especially lower leaves and those in the center portion of the plant that does not receive as much light.

When purchasing a *Ficus Lyrata*, look for one that has very deep dark green leaves as that is a good sign that the nursery has acclimated the plant to reduced light. Plants grown in high light have lighter green leaves and have a harder time adapting to the reduced light they receive indoors.

Water

If your Lyrata is properly potted and left in its nursery pot, then it is best to water it as soon as the top surface of the soil feels dry. Pour in water slowly so that the entire rootball is saturated and a bit of water runs through the drainage holes. If you consistently under water a Lyrata, you will find leaves developing large brown spots along the edges of the leaves and many leaves falling off. You want to avoid this because a brown spot on a large leaf is very noticeable and it never recovers its green color.

Overwatering is rarely a problem unless the plant does not receive enough light or if it has been moved into a larger pot that retains water for too long. This will cause the roots to rot and the plant will languish, developing dull yellow leaves that fall off.

Repotting

Like most indoor plants, the Lyrata does best when kept moderately potbound. If you find the plastic nursery pot unattractive, then purchase a decorative planter that is large enough for you to put the nursery pot inside. This double-potting is much easier and better for the plant than repotting directly into another planter.

Over time, Fiddle-leafed Figs develop very thick roots that start to show through the surface soil and smaller roots that may creep out of drainage holes. Surprisingly, this does not necessarily mean the plant needs a bigger pot. If there is enough soil in the pot to keep the roots properly moist for at least three days between thorough waterings, then it is usually best to leave the roots undisturbed in the existing pot. Wandering roots can be cut off where they emerge from the drainage holes. Surface roots can be covered with a top dressing such as Spanish moss.

If your Lyrata is so potbound that it requires water every few days, then it is appropriate to move it into a pot one size larger. See Chapter 1 on when and how to repot properly.

Temperature & Humidity

Ficus lyratas are quite tolerant of cool temperatures as low as 50°F, if the temperatures drop gradually. Normal home temperatures are fine for a Lyrata, although it should be protected from very cold drafts from open doors and windows. They are tolerant of low humidity.

Fertilizer

In good light your Lyrata will put out new leaves regularly often in spurts. Fertilize monthly at half the recommended label strength as long as the plant is growing vigorously. Fertilizer is not medicine and should not be used to treat plant problems.

Discolored leaves

Fiddle-leafed Figs that don't receive enough light or water develop leaves with brown leaf spots and edges. Because the leaves are so large, these spots are very noticeable and disheartening to discover. Unfortunately, there is no way to remove these brown spots once they emerge. If the spot is not too large, you can leave it alone. Otherwise, you will have to remove the entire leaf. The spots are not a disease and are not contagious. The reason to remove discolored leaves is to make the plant look better.

Of course, it is best to avoid them in the first place. If you notice leaf spots developing, that is a sign that you need to improve the light and/or the watering to prevent further damage.

Pruning

Healthy Lyratas can quickly outgrow their space because of their rigid stems and large leaves. It is best to prune them back before it is really obvious that they are too large for their space. Pruning will also keep the plant from becoming unbalanced looking. Lyratas can be pruned at any time of the year. Any stem or branch can be cut back and new growth will soon emerge just below the point on the stem where you make the pruning cut. So prune back to the point where you would like to see new growth emerge. Pruning will help eliminate leggy stems that have lost lower leaves and help keep your plant looking fuller and more compact.

When you prune, be prepared to staunch the free flow of white sap. The sight of this might make you think you have permanently damaged the plant, but you haven't. The sap flow will stop on its own, but it will stop sooner if you put a damp piece of paper towel or cloth over the wound. The sap is a skin irritant so you may want to use gloves when pruning a Ficus and be very careful not to get the sap near your eyes.

Another way to control growth and prevent lower leaf loss is to pinch out new leaf shoots as they emerge. This is most effective at maintaining your Fig as it is.

Propagation

Lyratas can be propagated by using tip stem cuttings. A tip cutting has no more than 4-6 leaves. Older, larger cuttings with woody stems do not root as readily as tip cuttings. Insert the cuttings into a small pot filled with a porous potting mix of 2 parts peat moss and 1 part Perlite. Keep this mix damp, provide bright indirect light and warm temperatures and you should have some healthy roots within 4-6 weeks. You can also try inserting the cuttings in the base of the existing plant.

Larger stem cuttings can be propagated by air layering. See Chapter 12 to learn how to air layer.

Branching

Some Lyratas branch more freely than others. Although pruning and pinching will sometimes promote branching on stems, in general there is not much you can do to make your Lyratas develop branches.

Pests

Another reason for the popularity of Fiddle-leafed Figs is their general resistance to plant pests. Occasionally scale insects and mealybugs may infest them, but that is not common. If soil quality is poor or if the soil is kept too moist, then fungus gnats may become a problem. See Chapter 10 for information on identifying and treating plant pests.

Ivy
(Hedera helix)

The term Ivy is often used to describe any hanging or climbing plant. However, it is most commonly used as shorthand for the English Ivies or Hedera helix varieties. This is one of the few plant species that is frost hardy that also does well as an indoor plant. So you may see Ivies attached to the outside of brick buildings in New England (the Ivy League colleges!) or growing inside on a window-sill almost anywhere. This is a highly adapt-able plant, but it can be quite difficult until it is well established in its environment. This chapter is limited to Ivies that are grown in-doors as potted plants. Other hanging plants,  such as Philodendron and Pothos are discussed in a separate chapter.

Light

Hedera Ivies do best in bright indirect light. A north or east windowsill is ideal. However, they can adapt well to direct sun on south and west-facing window-sills, provided they are kept properly moist. I don't recommend Ivies for low light areas that are more than a few feet away from an uncovered window. But I do concede that Ivies can adapt even to low light, although the growth rate will be very slow and the risk of overwatering and root rot is higher in low light.

Potting

Pot size is critical for Ivies. They must be kept potbound in small pots and they do best when their roots are undisturbed. It is a rare Hedera Ivy that needs re-potting, so resist the temptation to make it grow bigger by moving it to a larger pot. More light and proper watering will increase its growth rate; a larger pot will not.

If you don't like the appearance of the plastic pot that it comes in, then obtain a slightly larger decorative planter that is large enough for you to accommodate the plastic grow-pot. This double-potting will disguise the unattractive pot without repotting and disturbing your Ivy's roots.

If your Ivy is so potbound that it requires a thorough watering every couple of days, then you can move it into a pot that is no more than one inch wider and deeper. See Chapter 1 on repotting for further information on this poorly understood topic.

Water

Ivies, especially new ones, are not very tolerant of even minor watering lapses. Inconsistent or improper watering will kill your Ivy very quickly.

Assuming your Ivy is in the right-sized pot (see above) and in good light, then you should water it as soon as the surface of the soil becomes dry. This will usually occur every 3 to 10 days, depending on light, humidity, temperature, etc. Water it thoroughly until a bit of water trickles through the drainage holes, but don't leave it sitting in any water that will not evaporate within an hour. Do not water your Ivy from the bottom.

If your Ivy is located in reduced light away from a window, then you will have to allow the top half-inch of soil to dry out before watering. This is because plants in lower light need less frequent waterings and are more prone to overwatering.

If you keep the soil too moist, you will deprive the roots of oxygen and they will rot quickly. Root rot is fatal and there is no cure for it. On the other hand, if you allow the soil to dry out too much — even once — the tender roots will dry up and die. The symptoms of roots that are over or under watered are quite similar — dry leaves and brittle stems.

Small Ivies and those that are still adjusting to their new homes require almost daily monitoring so make sure you water them as soon as the surface soil gets dry. That does NOT mean they need daily watering. It is simply a warning that watering a day or two too late or too soon can cause Ivies to deteriorate quickly.

After an Ivy is well established — moderately rootbound and adjusted to the light and growing vigorously — it is a bit more tolerant of occasional watering lapses. Watering also gets easier because you learn from experience just how often your particular Ivy in the location you have selected needs to be watered. Of course, if you decide to relocate your Ivy, then the plant's adjustment and your learning curve will start all over again!

Temperature & Humidity

Hedera Ivies can withstand sub-freezing temperatures and summer heat, so temperature is not much of an issue for Ivies. However, it is best to avoid sudden big changes in temperatures, such as prematurely moving your Ivy outside from your warm home to the cold outdoors.

Likewise, Ivies do well in both high and low humidity environments.

That said, Ivies prefer cooler temperatures and higher humidity levels. This is primarily because spider mites thrive in warm, dry air and spider mites just love to feast on Hedera Ivies. See more below on treating spider mite infestations.

Hedera Ivies are good choices for a cold windowsill or an unheated room or a chilly entranceway, locations that are not good for most other houseplants.

Pests

Hedera Ivies are magnets for plant pests. Spider mites are the most common pest found feeding on Ivies, although mealybugs and scale insects also find Ivies appealing. That means thorough weekly inspections for these critters are an essential part of your care routine for Ivies.

Spider mites are very tiny and difficult to spot. Look for them on the undersides of leaves in good light. They appear as tiny specks of dust, but dust does not collect on the bottoms of leaves. As the spider mite infestation advances, they make very tiny webs. Misting will cause water droplets to adhere to the webs and make the webs easier to spot. By the time the webs become noticeable, the spider mite infestation is fairly well advanced. Spider mites will leave the foliage with a permanently mottled appearance as they remove little pinpricks of chlorophyll from the leaves. Spider mites are best treated by thoroughly drenching all leaf and stem surfaces with a soap and water spraying.

Scale insects appear as oval, slightly raised bumps about an eighth of an inch long and are usually found along leaf stems or on the undersides of leaves. In the juvenile stage, scales are translucent and take on the color of the leaf or stem surface. As they mature, scales develop a hard, dark brown shell that is more visible. These scales are easily scraped off the plant tissue with a fingernail. As the infestation increases, these sucking insects will secrete a sticky substance called honeydew that falls onto leaves, furniture and floors. This stickiness is the most obvious sign of scale and the one that most people notice first. Treat scale insects by spraying your Ivy thoroughly with a solution of 5 parts water, 1 part rubbing alcohol and a squirt of liquid dish soap

Mealybugs are actually a distinct type of scale insect. They develop a soft, white outer coating as they mature. This gives the appearance of tiny bits of cotton found in nooks and crannies where leaves join stems. For this reason, they are more noticeable than other scale insects. Treat mealybugs as you would scale insects described above.

Another pest problem common to Ivies is **fungus gnats**. Fungus gnats usually go unnoticed until they reach the adult stage. As adults, they have wings and they fly about and look like tiny black gnats. Before they mature, their larvae live unseen in the upper surface of a plant's potting soil. In good light, the larvae can be seen as minute worm-like things with dark heads swimming about the surface of the soil following the application of water. Fungus gnats are almost always a sign that you have kept the soil too moist and that the roots are rotting. If you find these flying critters on a newly acquired Ivy, return the Ivy rather than trying to treat it because the chances are good that someone else has been overwatering it and the roots are already rotted. See Chapter 10 for all plant pest treatment options.

Fertilizer

Ivies do not need much fertilizer. If you have a healthy Ivy that is growing vigorously and has not been repotted in a year or more, then you might consider applying any complete fertilizer at half the label recommended strength every other month. Too much fertilizer will burn tender roots.

Pruning

You will observe that new growth on Ivies is always at the ends of each stem or vine. The vines do not branch out and they don't generate new growth from below the soil. That means that over time the vines will grow ever longer and that can be a problem.

When these vining plants do not get enough light or if they are improperly watered, they will lose some of their older leaves — the leaves closest to the soil. As older leaves die and new growth is added at the ends of the vines, you may end up with very long, bare stems with a limited number of leaves at the ends of these bare stems. New leaves will never grow in along these bare stems to replace the older ones that have died.

Selective pruning is the only way to cure and prevent your Ivies from developing these long bare stems. If this has already happened, then you should cut back every bare stem to within two inches of the soil. This may leave you with a bunch of leafless stubs and an ugly plant. However, before long you will see new leaves start to emerge at the ends of these stubs. In time, you will have lots of new growth filling in the pot and no more bare stems.

To keep your Ivy full and compact, it is best to prune back long stems before they start to lose older leaves. Every month or so, select the longest vine and cut it back to within a few inches of the soil. The long stem won't be missed, but new growth will soon emerge in the center of the plant and grow out from there. The pruned off vine can be rooted in water (See section on Propagation below).

When pruning, always cut the stems just above where the leaf stem attaches to the vine. The purpose is to avoid leaving a long unattractive stub above the leaf.

Propagating Ivies

Ivy cuttings root quite readily in water. Shorter cuttings with fewer than six leaves do best although much longer stems will also root pretty easily. Remove the lowest leaf from the cutting. The bump (called a node) where the leaf stem was attached to the main stem is the point where roots will develop. Thus, it is important that this node is covered with water at all times. Never let the water level of the cutting container fall below these nodes on the cuttings.

When new roots are an inch or more in length, the cuttings can then be moved to a small pot filled with damp potting mix.

If you want to start a new plant, it is best to use at least ten cuttings and even more is preferred. The reason for this is that if you start with say four cuttings, then your plant will never have more than four vines no matter how old the plant or how large the pot. So if you want a luxurious plant with a dozen or more vines, then you will have to start with at least a dozen or more cuttings potted up together in a small pot. Take as many water-rooted cuttings as you can hold between your fingers and hold them tightly together while you insert the rooted ends into a 4-inch pot and fill in the pot with potting mix with your free hand. Keep the soil evenly moist and the rooted cuttings in a warm, well-lit location.

Fixing an ailing Ivy

If your Ivy develops one or two stems that have mostly dry leaves, that is an early warning that you have a watering problem — allowing the soil to get too dry or keeping it too moist. Correct the watering and you may be able to limit the damage to those few stems.

If your Ivy has many stems with leaves that have died, then it is probably too late to correct the problem. Sometimes a few stems will survive, but the dead vines are never replaced and the plant will always look sparse. It may be best to take some healthy tip cuttings and start a new plant.

Ivy Topiaries

Hedera Ivies are often used as topiaries because they have long, flexible stems and small dense leaves. They can be used to wind around wire frames of various shapes. These topiaries have unusual shapes and are often used as gift plants.

Ivy topiaries are not easy to care for. They have the same light and water requirements that I described above and they are equally pest-prone. But they have some unique problems as well.

Some topiaries have more than one pot embedded within the wire forms. You have to poke around through the foliage to find all of the pots. Pots that are embedded above the lower pot are hard to find and even harder to determine the soil moisture level. Just do your best.

Another problem is that when watering an upper pot, the water may drain through and into the lower pot, making it harder to control the watering of the lower pot.

To maintain the unique shape of an Ivy topiary, you have to either trim off stems as they grow outside the original contours or you have to try to weave the new long stems around the frame so that the original shape is maintained. I recommend the former, unless there are bare spots that need filling.

Conclusion

Hedera Ivies are popular and commonly available plants that are adaptable in their light and temperature requirements, but very particular about their watering needs. They are also pest prone. So this is not a plant for folks who like to be able to neglect their plants from time-to-time, but it is a wonderful plant for those who like a challenge and monitor their plants carefully.

Jade Plant
Crassula ovata

The Jade Plant is a succulent houseplant. That means it has thick, fleshy leaves and stems and it comes from a dry region, although it is not a desert plant. It is a popular houseplant because of its unusual shape, deep green leaves and because it is relatively easy to care for as long as you don't over water or repot it. Older Jades have an unusual ancient look to them that many people appreciate. In fact, many Jade Plants live for a long time and are passed from one generation to the next within families. Those that have survived for a long time have usually been well appreciated, but never fussed over. Here is some information that will help you keep your Jade Plant for a long time.

Light

Jades are often mistakenly described as low light plants. They are not. They will survive in very bright indirect light, such as on a north windowsill, but they will thrive if they get several hours of direct sun every day. In any case, they must be very close to and in front of an uncovered window. As with many succulents, they will survive for quite a while in low light. But at some point, they will rather suddenly drop leaves and fall apart if they don't get adequate light.

The edges of Jade leaves develop a reddish color when given lots of direct sun. Without direct sun, they will grow more slowly, develop thinner stems and smaller leaves, and use less water. In general, try to provide as much indoor light as possible.

Outdoors, the light is much more intense than inside. Direct outdoor sunlight is too much for Jades. If you move your Jade outside when temps are above 50°F, keep them in light to moderate shade. Keep in mind that with the increased light and air circulation outside your Jade will use more water.

WARNING: If your Jade has been growing in reduced light and you move it suddenly to very bright direct sun, the change may be too great and the direct sun may cause the older leaves to turn a reddish purple in color. If you want to increase the light, do it gradually. If your Jade is doing well where it is, then don't move it.

Water

Jades are semi-succulent and need to dry out more than other non-succulent plants. Allow the soil of your Jade to dry about halfway down into the rootball before watering thoroughly. Some people wait for the leaves to shrivel just a bit before watering, just to be on the safe side. This plant is adapted to survive periods of brief drought so it is best to delay watering if you are unsure. Keeping the soil around the roots constantly moist will result in root rot. When that occurs, the leaves will shrivel and die and the stems will turn soft and mushy and break off easily. At that point it is usually beyond recovery.

Repotting

Jades have small, fine root systems that do best when contained in small pots. Jades rarely need repotting during their long lives. That is why it is best to avoid repotting unless absolutely necessary. Wait until it reaches the point that the soil will retain only a couple of days supply of water, i.e., it needs to be watered thoroughly every two days.

Mature Jade Plants can stay in the same pot — typically no larger than 8 or 10 inches in diameter — for decades.

If and when you repot be sure to use a sandy, well-drained potting soil and a terra cotta pot to keep your jade from tipping over as it grows larger and becomes top heavy.

Fertilizer

Fertilize sparingly at half strength only during the warmer months and only when your plant is putting out healthy new growth. Use a fertilizer that has a higher proportional nitrogen content. If your Jade has a problem it is highly unlikely that fertilizer will fix it. I have seen decades old Jades that have never been fertilized and they do just fine. Do *not* use fertilizer as medicine to cure any Jade problems.

Pests

Mealybugs are normally the only pests that bother jades; watch for tiny bits of cotton-like mealybugs hiding in the spaces where leaves attach to stems. To treat them, mix a spray consisting of 1 part rubbing alcohol with 5 parts of water and add a squirt of liquid soap. Be sure to spray all leaf and stem surfaces thoroughly. The common practice of applying alcohol with a Q-tip is not effective because it misses the ones you can't see. It is also best if you repeat this treatment again in 5 to 7 days to catch any crawlers that you missed the first time. After that, you should check your plant weekly to see if they return.

If fungus gnats are a problem, that is a sure sign of overwatering and root rot. See Chapter 10 for more specific information on identifying and treating plant pests.

Leaf Drop and Other Jade Problems

Sometimes older jades that have not been regularly pruned reach a point where they cannot support new leaves without shedding old ones. So they shed lots of older leaves. New growth then emerges at the ends of the stems. The way to counter this is to prune back your jade by as much as one-third every year or two. (See section on Pruning that follows.)

If a Jade Plant has been improperly watered (usually too frequently) by a small amount, it will not affect the plant for a long time. This is also the case if you have not provided enough light or have repotted into a larger pot. However, in all of these instances the roots gradually rot and die and can no longer supply the plant with water. The plant responds by dropping leaves. If the stems appear soft, mushy or shriveled, then it is probably too late. Otherwise, prune the plant back, allow the soil to dry out almost completely, withhold fertilizer, and look for signs of healthy new growth.

When stems appear soft, mushy or shriveled, then it is often too late. However, if you still have some healthy stems, it may be salvageable. Prune it back and re-move all stems that are soft. Move the plant to your sunniest windowsill. Water it very sparingly and do not fertilize it. As insurance, it would be a good idea to take cuttings from the healthy stems. See the Cuttings and Propagation section below on how to do this.

With very old Jades, sometimes the soil becomes severely compacted and de-prives the roots of oxygen. If the soil stays moist for a week or more following a thorough watering, then this may be the problem. Use a thin pointed object, such as a knitting needle to probe and aerate the soil.

Pruning

It is not uncommon for Jade stems to break off unexpectedly. This is because most folks are afraid to prune their Jades and gravity eventually wins out. Jades respond very well to regular pruning. Cut stems back as much as you can stand. New growth will emerge just below the point of the pruning cut. Regular pruning will help keep your Jade more compact. The pruned off sections can be easily propagated to make new plants. (See section that follows.)

A Jade is not hard to prune. Use a sharp, clean knife, pruners or scissors. Cut off any stems/branches that are too long or leggy. Cut them as far back as you like, but make the cut just above a leaf node so that you don't leave a large leftover stub. Remember that you will get new growth at the point to which you cut back. How much you cut back is more of an aesthetic than a horticultural issue. Prune it to maintain the shape and size that you want. Most inexperienced pruners tend to be too tentative and don't prune as much as experienced pruners. So prune away and don't worry!

Cuttings and Propagation

Taking cuttings is the easiest way to propagate more Jades. Smaller, green-stemmed Jade cuttings root more readily than older, thicker cuttings. Allow the cut stems to callus over night by exposing them to the dry air. Then insert the cuttings in a small pot filled with a porous mix of peat moss (2 parts) and perlite (1 part) that is kept barely damp. Moisten it lightly whenever the surface feels dry to the touch. Provide good light.

The rooted cuttings will stay in this small pot for a very long time even after roots are established. After six months you can start using a very dilute fertilizer once per month.

Jade stem cuttings can also be rooted in plain water, but there is some risk that the stems may rot before the roots develop. Once the roots are an inch or more in length, the rooted cuttings can be moved to a small pot, as described above.

For very thick stems or trunks an inch or more in diameter, you may want to try air layering. This technique is described in detail in Chapter 12.

Moving Your Jade Outside

Many folks like to move their houseplants outside in the warmer months. Outside the light is much more intense than inside, so outside direct sun is too intense for Jades. Although Jades prefer direct sun when indoors, keep them shaded when outdoors.

Also, with the increase in light, temperature and air circulation outside, your Jade will use more water, so adjust your watering schedule appropriately.

In the spring, wait until nighttime temperatures are consistently above 55°F before moving your Jade outside. In the fall, nighttime temperatures can fall as low as 40°F before you need to move your Jade back inside.

Jasmine
Jasminum polyanthum

Who doesn't love the sweet smell of Jasmine? This member of the Olive family produces a profusion of small, star-shaped flowers that is as wonderful to the eye as to the nose. No wonder this is among the most popular of all flowering plants. However, it is not an easy plant and is best reserved for plant owners with some experience and success with other plants. It makes a tempting gift, but it may be a source of frustration and anxiety for someone with limited plant experience.

Although there are many Jasmine species, *Jasmine polyanthum* is the best choice for indoor winter flowering.

Timing

Jasmine polyanthum is a winter blooming plant that requires varying conditions throughout the year. During its growing season from spring through summer, it requires lots of direct sunlight and water. In the fall, it needs a gradual drop in temperatures to below 50°F. These cool fall temps are necessary for the Jasmine to set buds. When temperatures drop to freezing, it is best to move your Jasmine inside to a cool location (below 65°F) with bright indirect sunlight.

If you get all of this right, then you can expect flowers in late January or early February — just when you most need them! After its winter flowering season, Jasmine should be moved to a sunnier location and cool temperatures are no longer required.

This is a difficult regimen for most homeowners, so consider this carefully before deciding to purchase one.

Light

For most of the year when your Jasmine is not in bloom, it requires about 6 hours of direct sunlight each day. Indoors on a south-facing window is best. Once spring nighttime temperatures are safely above 45°F, you can move your Jasmine outdoors to a lightly shaded area and then gradually increase the amount of direct sunlight as the temperatures warm and the days grow longer. Do try to protect it from the hot midday sun in summer.

In the fall, keep your Jasmine outdoors where it can experience both cooler temperatures and shorter hours of daylight. These two conditions in the fall are the key to successful setting of flower buds. The light in the fall should still be direct sunlight, but must be limited to 12 hours or less. Keep your Jasmine away from any artificial lights after sundown.

Just before night time temps fall below freezing, move your Jasmine indoors to a cool location where it will get only indirect sunlight. A north windowsill is best.

Temperature

As with light, proper temperatures for a Jasmine must be seasonally adjusted. During the spring and summer growing season, warm temperatures as high as 85°F are fine. But in the fall and winter when flower buds are set and then open, cool temperatures are a must.

The gradual drop in outdoor temperature in the fall down to freezing is best to help your Jasmine set buds. It will need 4–6 weeks of temps below 50°F to do this. If you move your Jasmine indoors prematurely, it will not experience the cool temps required for full flowering.

Once outdoor temperatures drop below freezing, your Jasmine should be indoors in a cool spot where temps are in the 55°F to 65°F range. This is colder than most of us keep our homes and that is a problem because temperatures above 65°F will cause buds that formed when outdoors to fall off.

After your Jasmine has finished its winter flowering, it should be moved to a sunny windowsill and warm temperatures are no longer a problem.

In the spring when the threat of frost has gone, move your Jasmine outdoors and let it experience normal spring and summer temperatures.

Pot Size & Repotting

As with most flowering plants, Jasmine will not flower unless it is quite pot-bound. In fact, Jasmine plants rarely require repotting and usually reach their maximum in an 8 or 10 inch pot.

Repot only if your thoroughly watered Jasmine is dry enough to water again within a couple of days. Then move it up one pot size larger. Never repot or disturb the roots when the plant is in bud or flower. Late spring or early summer is the best time to repot, but only if absolutely necessary.

Watering

Jasmine does not tolerate soil that gets too dry, yet the soil must not be kept constantly wet either. When a Jasmine is properly potted, then it is best to water it thoroughly when the top half-inch of soil feels dry to the touch if the pot is 8 inches in diameter or less. If it is in a larger pot, then allow the top inch of soil to dry before watering. That means you must monitor the soil moisture content regularly, especially during the critical period when it is in bud and flower.

Humidity

High humidity definitely benefits a Jasmine. I recommend a room humidifier or a pebble tray directly under your Jasmine. It is possible for a Jasmine to flower in reduced humidity, but only if temps are kept cool and soil moisture is carefully monitored. In any case, keep your Jasmine at a fair distance from any heating sources.

Air Circulation

Jasmines benefit from the better air circulation they get when outdoors in the warmer months. When indoors for the winter, a small fan nearby will similarly benefit your Jasmine.

Fertilizer

If your Jasmine is healthy and growing vigorously and it has not been repotted in at least a year, then it may need a nutrient boost from spring through the summer. Use a balanced, complete fertilizer with a 1-2-1 ratio at half the label recommended strength and apply it monthly during the warmer months. Do not fertilize at all from early fall through the winter. And never fertilize an ailing plant. See my Chapter 8 for more specific information on fertilizing.

Pruning

In good conditions, Jasmine is a fast grower during the warmer months. It can quickly get out of hand with many very long vines. Its appearance will be enhanced if you keep it well pruned so as to maintain a full, compact appearance. In addition, flowers appear only on new growth. That means if you don't prune every year, then after a few years, the flowers will appear only at the ends of the very long stems that have developed.

I recommend pruning back your Jasmine by about half at the end of its winter flowering cycle. That means if the stems are a foot long, then prune them back to about 6 inches. After that, let it fill out to the shape and fullness that you desire and then start pinching out new growth as it emerges. Very long stems can be pruned back to a length of 6 inches or less. New growth will then grow out from just below that pruning cut. Remember, pruning does not harm the plant in any way.

IMPORTANT: Stop any pruning and pinching after July as flower buds will start to form in late summer and you don't want to remove any of them.

Propagation

Jasmine can be propagated at any time, although early spring is the preferred time and that is also the best time to prune your Jasmine anyway.

Use tip cuttings with two to three sets of leaves. Strip the lowest leaves from the cuttings and insert the cuttings in a small pot filled with a damp, peat-based potting mix. Enclose the pot and in a clear plastic tent to retain the moisture in the soil and around the leaves. Place the pot in bright but indirect light where it will not get overheated by direct sunlight. Keep it in a warm location (above 65°F). Allow 6 to 8 weeks for roots to develop, after which you can gradually remove the plastic over the course of a week. Increase the light after that.

Pests

Jasmine is a magnet for spider mites. Few Jasmine plants escape periodic mite infestations. Check the undersides of leaves regularly for signs of mites and treat them promptly and thoroughly with a soap and water spray. Keeping the humidity high will discourage and help control spider mite infestations. More detailed information on spider mites can be found in Chapter 10.

Flowering Calendar

To get your Jasmine to flower, follow this routine:

- In late winter, prune sharply and provide lots of direct sun.
- In late spring, move it outside to light shade. Repot only if utterly pot-bound. Pinch back new growth. Resume fertilizing.

- In summer, provide lots of outdoor direct sun, water and fertilizer. Pinch back new growth until August.

- In late summer, stop pinching and pruning and ease off fertilizing.

- In the fall, provide 4 to 6 weeks of cool temperatures below 50°F. There should be no artificial light after sundown. Do not fertilize and reduce watering slightly.

- In late fall, move it inside to a cool location as soon as frost threatens. Temperatures must be kept below 65°F. Do not fertilize until late spring.

- Look for flowers to open starting in late January.

This is a difficult regimen to follow. If you can provide cool temperatures for only a few weeks in the fall, it is better than not at all. If you cannot do it at all, your plant will remain healthy but it may not bloom very much. Jasmine is not an easy indoor plant, so don't get discouraged if you don't have immediate success.

Lucky Bamboo
(Dracaena sanderiana)

Lucky Bamboo plants are among the most popular plants on the market today. They are small, interesting to look at, fairly easy to care for and relatively inexpensive. They are sold in plant stores, in gift shops, in open air markets and on the street. Good fortune and good Feng Shui karma are attributed to them.

Despite their popularity, there are some basic qualities of Lucky Bamboo that are not commonly understood and those misunderstandings can lead to problems down the road.

First of all, Lucky Bamboos are not actually Bamboo nor are they even remotely related. The bare stems and small leaves do look somewhat similar to Bamboo plants, but they are different plants in all other ways. If you care for your Lucky Bamboo as if it is a real Bamboo, then you will have problems. Lucky Bamboo is in the Dracaena family and is a close relative of the Corn Plant (*Dracaena fragrans*) and the Dragon tree (*Dracaena marginata*). The botanical name for Lucky Bamboo is *Dracaena sanderiana*.

Secondly, Lucky Bamboos are rooted cuttings and are most commonly sold growing in water. Like any other rooted cuttings, they can do okay for about a year in plain water before they start to deteriorate, mostly due to lack of nutrients. Adding fertilizer helps a bit, but, as with other cuttings, if you want to keep your Lucky Bamboo for a long time, then at some point after the roots are at least an inch long, you will need to move them into a small pot filled with a peat-based potting mix. They will then grow like any other plant if they are given lots of bright light.

Light

Retailers will often promote the purchase of these and other plants by telling customers that they don't need much light. Although a Lucky Bamboo will survive for quite some time in low light, providing a lot of very bright, mostly indirect, light will keep your Lucky Bamboo from getting tall and leggy. On the other hand, more than a couple of hours of sun shining directly on the leaves each day is too much light for this plant.

The best light is what you get on a north-facing windowsill or close to an east-facing window, assuming the windows are completely uncovered during the daylight hours. In an office without a window, your Lucky Bamboo will also do well directly under overhead fluorescent lights if those lights are kept on for at least 8 hours every workday.

Water

If your local water is on the hard or alkaline side, then switch to distilled or filtered water. Normal levels of chlorine and fluoride from tap water should not be a problem for your Lucky Bamboo.

If your Lucky Bamboo is growing in water or water with decorative stones or pebbles, then it is important to keep the roots covered with water at all times. When grown in water, you do not have to worry about over watering, but you cannot afford to neglect maintaining the water level above root level at all times. In warm, dry air the water will evaporate rapidly, so be alert.

If possible, try to replace the water with fresh water every couple of weeks. Because of the unique decorative manner in which the Lucky Bamboo is often grown, it may not be possible to drain and replace the water without losing the decorative stones. If so, don't worry about replacing the water.

If you cannot determine what your Lucky Bamboo is growing in because the roots are covered with a layer of glued-together pebbles that you cannot penetrate, then it is best to remove this pebbly cover so you can determine what is going on below. That cover is there for decorative purposes only and removing it will not harm your plant. Leaving it in place probably will!

Temperature & Humidity

Lucky Bamboo is a tropical plant, unlike true Bamboos, so it requires warm temperatures above 55°F year round. This makes Lucky Bamboo an ideal indoor plant. Like many common houseplants, Lucky Bamboos do not require high humidity even though they come from areas that do. Increasing the humidity never hurts, but it is not something that is essential for healthy Lucky Bamboo growth.

Fertilizer

Lucky Bamboos grown in plain water have no long-term source of mineral nutrients. Commercial fertilizer is formulated for use in soil, not water. A few drops of a very dilute plant food or fertilizer can help sustain the plant in water for a longer period of time. Hydroponic plant food is your best choice as it is designed specifically for plants grown in a water-based medium.

Growing your Lucky Bamboo in Soil

If you want your Lucky Bamboo to live a long time, it is best to move the rooted cuttings to a small pot of soil before it starts to deteriorate. Once the lower stems start to turn yellow, you know that they have been in water for too long. Cut off and discard all unhealthy yellow stem tissue. You can then insert the healthy remaining portion in water or damp potting mix so that new roots will form.

You can transfer your entire Lucky Bamboo plant to soil at any time. Remove the stems from the decorative planter and remove the pebbles unless they are firmly entwined within the root mass. Use a small pot just barely large enough to accommodate the root mass and a little soil. Make sure the new pot has drainage holes. Use a standard peat-based potting mix to cover the bottom of the pot and to fill in around the sides of the root mass. Water it thoroughly and then do not water again until the surface of the soil is dry. Provide the same light that you did before and use a standard fertilizer monthly, diluted to half-strength.

Pruning

Lucky Bamboo stems tend to grow tall and leggy, especially in reduced light. To control height it is best to prune them back periodically anywhere along the thinner side shoots that grow out of the thicker Bamboo-like canes. New growth will emerge and grow up from a point just below where you make the pruning cuts. The pruned off portions can then be rooted in water to make new plants.

Generally, the main canes should not be pruned. Pruning will not promote branching.

Symptoms

Brown leaf tips are common on Lucky Bamboo. Hard water with an abundance of minerals is a common cause of leaf tip burn. Excess fertilizer does the same thing. Allowing the water level to drop below the uppermost roots will cause those roots to dry and result in brown leaf tips. Even a single instance of a low water level will cause this tipping on the leaves, so pay close attention to the water level.

Leaf yellowing has many causes. Both too much and too little light produce yellow leaves, although excess light causes more of a paling of the green leaves than actual yellowing. Lack of nutrients over time will also cause the leaves and stems to yellow and die. Moving your Lucky Bamboo into potting soil is the best way to prevent this.

If a thick stem turns yellow, it is dying and won't recover. However, if you cut the stem above the yellowing portion, you may be able to root that healthy, green upper portion in water just as the original was.

A mottled appearance on the leaves is usually caused by spider mites. If you suspect spider mites, drench the leaves with a solution of liquid dish soap and water.

Little bits of cotton-like substance where the leaves join the stems means you have a mealybug infestation. Treat them with a soap and water solution with some rubbing alcohol added to the mixture. See Chapter 10 for more information on identifying and treating plant pests.

Propagation

The thick main cane-like stems are not good candidates to take cuttings from to produce more plants. You will have better luck with the shoots that grow off of the main stems because this is younger growth. You can cut these shoots at any point along their stems and root them in water. New growth will usually emerge on the original shoot just below where you made the cut.

Cuttings from your Lucky Bamboo root easily and allow you to share them with others or to design your own Lucky Bamboo planting using a small shallow dish and stones of your choice.

Cutting the Ties

Many Lucky Bamboo are sold in little bundles of stems held together with a pretty bow or tie. Although these ties are decorative, they also keep the stems in place. There is no reason to remove these ties except to separate the stems. It is okay to do this, but it may spoil the symmetry of your Lucky Bamboo. If you do cut the tie, be sure to replace it when you are finished removing a stem or stems so that those remaining don't fall apart like so many Pickup Stix.

Curves, Curls & Bends

Lucky Bamboo growers are very inventive in creating new looks with these plants. The plants come in all sizes ranging from a few inches to 6 feet or more in height. If you purchase a short one, don't expect it to ever develop into a thick-stemmed, very tall plant.

Some of the most exotic looking Lucky Bamboos are grown so that they have curved and even spiraled stems. I am often asked how to do that. It is not easy for you to do in your home, but I will explain the principles involved anyway.

Lucky Bamboo stems will grow and lean toward the light if it is not coming from directly overhead. Using that principle of nature, growers attached the stems to a rigid surface and then position the growing tip in the direction of the light, which is the direction they want the stem to curve. The plant must be repositioned relative to the light constantly in order to get

Lucky Bamboo (for Valentine's Day)

the stem to curve in a full spiral. This is a slow and tedious process and one that I have never taken on! But that's how it's done.

Conclusion

Now you know and understand just what this unusual plant is and how it got that way. You are equipped to keep it happy and healthy for a long time.

What else can I write except, "Good Luck!"

Ming Aralia
Polyscias

Polyscias balfouriana

Ming Aralia varieties

This challenging plant species is one of my all-time favorites because of the interesting way that it grows and the interesting leaf shapes that it has. It is an expensive plant, but one that has good value because it will last a long time and give great pleasure when properly cared for. I will say that my professional services are called on more regularly for this particular plant species than for any otherexcept for the very popular Fiddle-leafed Fig.

Folks spend lots of money on specimen Ming Aralias and then worry when they shed leaves or get pests and quickly call on my assistance. In most cases, the problems are relatively minor and the Aralias recover.

Names and leaf shapes

There are several popular species of Polyscias available. To the untrained eye, the foliage can be so different looking that you might not recognize them as being related. *Polyscias balfouriana* (photo on left), sometimes called "dinner plate" Aralia, has small, oval leaves that are dark green. There is a less-common variegated Balfour variety that has green and white leaves. *Polyscias fruticosa* or Ming Aralia has lacey, feathery foliage. Some of these species are further distinguished from one another by their foliage. Hence there is the carrot-top Aralia, the celery-top Aralia, fern-leafed Aralia and lace Aralia.

You may want to go online and search for images of Polyscias to see the many foliage shapes available. I am sure you will find at least one that appeals to you.

Growth Habit

All of these Aralias develop thin, bark-covered stems as they age. These stems give the appearance of small trees. For that reason they are sometimes used as Bonsais. The foliage may be dense in very good light or rather sparse, but not unattractive, in reduced light. In fact, as the stems grow taller and lower leaves fall, the plant takes on a very unusual sculptural appearance. All of the Polyscias have a tall and slender profile so they are often the perfect plant when space is limited, but good light is available.

Polyscias respond very well to pruning. This allows you to shape them as you prefer. See more below on just how pruning is done.

Light

Polyscias are not low light plants so you cannot stick them in a corner away from the nearest window nor will they fare well with just artificial light. They thrive in locations that have lots of bright indirect sun all day long with a few hours of direct sun. Right in front of a north or east window and a bit to the side of a west or south window are all fine. Make sure the window is uncovered. Keep your Ming out of a corner and no more than a few feet from the nearest window.

If your Aralia gets too much direct sun — more than a few hours — then the leaves may become a lighter shade of green and even yellow. If the light is too limited, then some foliage will drop off and the plant will have a sparser appearance. Improper watering will also cause leaf drop, so don't automatically assume the light is inadequate or the watering is inappropriate. You will have to consider both before making either a light or water adjustment.

Pot Size

Aralias can be quite fussy about their roots. Disturbing them by unnecessary repotting or by improper watering will cause Aralias to drop many leaves very quickly. It is a rare Aralia that needs to be moved to a larger pot. In fact, they are more often sold in nursery pots that are too large. A plant that is in a pot that is too large is a plant that is at risk for root rot. Your best bet is to hope that the nursery has grown the Aralia in the proper sized pot and for you to avoid repotting altogether. If you don't like the look of the nursery pot, then purchase a more attractive planter that is just large enough to accommodate the nursery pot. This double-potting will cover up the nursery pot without disturbing the roots of the plant.

Contrary to popular belief, a small pot will not retard the growth of the plant. In fact, plants grow best when they are moderately potbound. See Chapter 1 for further information on repotting.

Water

Aralias are not very forgiving about watering lapses and they will let you know in a hurry if you mess up. While a few leaves turning yellow is common, a lot of yellow leaves all at once is an Aralia's way of signaling that something is awry. If your Aralia has not been recently moved or repotted, then a spurt of yellow foliage is a sure sign that something is wrong with your watering routine.

If an Aralia is in the proper-sized pot and it is getting good natural light in normal home temperatures, then it is best to water it thoroughly when the top inch of soil feels dry. If your Aralia is in a pot less than 10-inches in diameter, then water when the top half-inch of soil is dry. The soil should reach this level of dryness approximately every 7 to 10 days. If it takes longer than that, then provide less water when you water. If it takes less than a week for the soil to dry, just water it when it gets that dry rather than waiting for the calendar to roll around to the right day.

Having said all of that, I also suggest you monitor and observe your Aralia carefully. If you are following this watering routine, but you are getting a lot of yellow leaves, then adjust your watering routine a bit to see if that helps. This is a process that requires trial and error and an understanding that every plant and its environment is unique and you must be adaptable rather than slavishly following any rules of thumb — including mine!

Once Aralias become well-established in their existing pots and in their existing locations, they are much easier to care for and even a bit more forgiving about watering lapses. So be patient and flexible early on and things will become easier as you go along.

Pruning Leggy Plants

Left unpruned, most Aralias become quite leggy after a while. They lose lower leaves when they are moved, when the light changes and when they get too little or too much water. New growth comes in at the tip ends of stems so the lower stems end up looking sparse. Some folks like this look and if you are one of them, then pruning is not necessary.

However, if you feel like you would like to see more dense foliage and less bare stem on your Aralia, then pruning is the only way to accomplish that. Pruning is the plant care technique that is most commonly avoided for a variety of reasons. But if you want to keep your Aralia looking full and compact, learning to prune is essential. See Chapter 11 for more information on pruning.

Once you overcome your inhibitions, pruning an Aralia is quite simple. Any stem that is tall and leggy can be cut back at any point along that stem. New growth will then emerge starting just below that point on the stem and grow upward from there. If a stem has 18 inches of bare stem and a few inches of foliage at the very top, then cut that stem down to a height of a few inches. You will end up with a shorter plant, but in a few weeks it will be more lush with new foliage and in a few months most of that height will be regained.

After a few successful stabs at pruning, you will discover that it is not hard; that it does not harm the plant; and that you can be creative with your pruning to achieve the size and look that you prefer.

Pests

The pests most likely to show up on an Aralia are mealybugs that look like little bits of white cotton. Other less common Aralia pests are scale insects that are identified by their tell-tale stickiness on the foliage and spider mites that spin very fine webs across the foliage.

The best prevention is vigilance. Read Chapter 10 to learn how to identify these plant pests. Inspect the leaves and stems carefully for pests before you purchase a plant. After purchase, be sure to check your plant at least monthly for pests and treat them promptly and thoroughly. My chapter on treating plant pests explains safe and effective ways to deal with any pests that may show up on your indoor plants.

Temperature and Humidity

Aralias are tropical in origin. As tropical plants they need protection from cold. Temps in the 60°F to 80°F. range are ideal, although Aralias will survive temperatures a bit cooler if they are introduced gradually. For a variety of reasons, Aralias are not good candidates to move outside, even in the warmer months. If you don't have a suitable year-round indoor location for an Aralia, then it is best not to get one.

Sudden exposure to cold temperatures or freezing drafts will cause leaves to drop off in large handfuls and stems will turn soft and dark. If the roots are not damaged by cold, the plant will usually recover.

Normal household humidity levels are fine for Aralias. They have proven to do well even in heated indoor environments where humidity levels are desert-dry. Of course, in warm dry air, moisture will evaporate more quickly from the soil and the leaves, so more frequent watering may be necessary in winter. Increased humidity will help deter spider mites somewhat, but otherwise, humidity levels are not an important consideration for owning an Aralia.

Fertilizer

Fertilizer is not medicine so never use it on ailing plants. If your Aralia is healthy and growing vigorously and has not had soil added in at least a year, then any complete fertilizer applied at half-strength once per month is appropriate, but not essential. Read Chapter 8 to learn more on why fertilizing is often over-rated.

Propagation

Aralias are not the easiest plants to propagate, but they are hardly impossible. Aralias require regular pruning anyway, so you may as well take a shot at propagating the pruned off portions.

Take a handful of small, 5 to 6 inch green tip cuttings and insert them in a small pot filled with a peat-based potting mix. Place the pot inside a clear plastic bag and blow it up with your personal supply of carbon dioxide. Seal it and provide lots of bright, but no direct sunlight. After 4 to 6 weeks, gradually unseal and open the plastic bag over the course of a week. By then, the cuttings will either have rooted or rotted. Chapter 12 explains this technique in greater detail.

Ming Aralia from cutting and kept potbound

Even if you do everything right, the propagation success rate is not much more than 50%, so don't get discouraged if you fail the first few times.

Flowers

Occasionally, potted Aralias will flower. The flowers don't look like the petaled flowers we see in the florist's shop. Some people describe Aralia flowers as "strange looking growths." The flowers mostly remain green in color with a hint of white. They may even go unnoticed. After a few weeks they will dry and can be pruned off. If you don't like them, you can prune them off at any time without harming the plant.

Money Tree
Pachira aquatica

The Money Tree or Fortune Tree is currently very popular and is sold not only in plant shops, but also in green markets, supermarkets, street fairs, health stores and discount stores. Many folks are taken by its petite size and interesting braided trunks. Others like its feng shui and believe it will bring good luck and fortune.

Because this plant is so popular and sold in so many places, it is often grown in many different sizes, shapes and containers. This variety makes it difficult to provide general care instructions, so read this chapter with that warning.

Light

Pachira does best in lots of very bright, but mostly indirect sunlight. Many retailers will tell you that this is a good low light plant. Although it will survive in low light for quite a while, eventually it will drop many lower leaves and develop long, spindly stems that bend over under the weight of the leaves. It does best on a north or east windowsill or for larger specimens, on the floor in front of a north or east window. More than a few hours of direct sunlight each day may cause older leaves to become a pale green or yellow.

Pot Size

Most Pachiras are sold in small pots, even shallow bonsai dishes. The natural inclination is to move the plant to a larger pot so the roots have more room to grow. In nearly all instances this is not a good idea, especially while the plant is still adapting to its new environment. So no matter how uncomfortable your Pachira may look to you, leave it in its existing pot. If that pot is unattractive, then use a more attractive pot that is just large enough to put the existing pot inside. See Chapter 1 for more information about repotting.

Water

How much and how often you water your Pachira will depend on the size of the pot. I have seen Pachiras sold in tiny 3-inch pots and in very large 14-inch pots and everything in between. In general, plants in small pots that are quite root bound will need more frequent watering than those same plant species in larger pots.

If your Pachira is potted in a shallow bonsai dish or in a very small pot, then it will need a thorough watering at least once per week and more frequently if the leaf stems start to droop in between. It is hard to overwater a Pachira in a small or shallow pot.

Pachiras in larger pots are best watered only when the top one to two inches of the soil are dry to the touch. If the leaf stems start to droop, then you are waiting too long before watering. When you do water, always add enough water until a small amount runs through the bottom drainage holes. If the pot is small and does not have drainage holes, then fill it with water once per week.

Pachira can be sensitive to excess mineral salts, so if your local tap water is on the hard side, use filtered, distilled or rainwater instead.

Braided Trunks

Money trees are most commonly sold with braided trunks. Typically three to five separate stems are grown together in the nursery and braided while they are still green and flexible. They do not grow that way naturally. As these braided trunks age, they develop a hard, brown bark covering. These braided trunks are often cut off just above the braids. Multiple green stems then emerge from these pruned trunks and grow upward from there and produce the leaves. I do not recommend attempting to braid these newer stems nor should you try to unbraid the lower stems.

Pruning

Pachiras tend to grow tall and leggy after a while. This is particularly true if they are getting less than ideal light. Thus, it is a good idea to to either pinch out new shoots as they emerge or prune back some or all of the Pachira stems periodically. You can cut the stems all the way back to the main braided trunks. If your plant is healthy, new shoots will emerge from just below where you make the pruning cuts and grow upward from there. Pinching will maintain the plant at its existing height.

Propagation

To propagate this plant, you will need a healthy green stem cutting with several leaf stems attached and an exposed node at the bottom of the cutting. A single leaf stem will not propagate because it does not have a node. Nodes are those little bumps on stems out of which leaf stems grow. The node remains even after the leaf stem drops off. New roots will grow from a node that is exposed to water or moist soil.

Cuttings can be placed in plain water and, if you are lucky, roots will gradually emerge after a month or more. However, it is not uncommon for the leaves to die before new roots form sufficiently to supply water to the leaves. As an alternative, place the cutting in a small pot filled with a porous, peat-based potting mix and then place the whole thing inside of a clear plastic "tent." That will keep the moisture inside. See Chapter 12 for more detailed information on propagation techniques.

Temperature

This is a tropical plant that does best indoors year-round with temperatures above 60°F, although it will tolerate lower temperatures for brief periods. When grown as a potted plant, it is quite fragile and does not hold up well outdoors in the warmer months unless it is protected from wind and rain, as well as cool temperatures.

Fertilizer

As a potted plant, the Pachira is not a heavy feeder. A standard fertilizer applied at half-strength monthly when it is growing vigorously is more than enough to meet its nutritional needs.

Humidity

Although Pachira is native to boggy regions that are normally high in humidity, it has proven to hold up quite well in very dry, artificially heated indoor environments. Increased humidity never hurts, but it is not necessary for your Pachira.

Pests

Mealybugs, scale insects and spider mites may feast on Pachira so be alert for them. See Chapter 10 to learn more on identifying and treating these plant pests.

Sticky sap

It is not uncommon for tiny beads of clear sap to appear on leaf stems. This is not usually a problem and can be ignored. However, these natural plant secretions are easily confused with similar secretions from scale insects. If you are getting a lot of stickiness on the top sides of the leaves and you find slightly raised brown bumps on the undersides of leaves immediately above, then you have a scale infestation that must be treated. See Chapter 10 for more information on scale insects.

Norfolk Island Pine
Araucaria heterophylla

The Norfolk Island Pine is one of the very few needled plants or trees that will survive indoors as a houseplant. Although it is a conifer, it is not in the Pine family of plants as its common name suggests. It is native to Norfolk Island, a small island in the ocean between Australia, New Zealand and New Caledonia. This is a semi-tropical location where temperatures rarely fall below freezing.

Most conifers are native to colder climates and are adapted to cold winters. That is why Pines and Cedars and Spruces do not fare well indoors where temperatures are warm all year round. So the Norfolk Island Pine nicely fills our need for a needled indoor plant. Many folks decorate this plant at Christmas time knowing that this is one Christmas tree that will survive the holidays and still be available for years to come, as long as it is properly cared for and that includes not putting it outside in the cold.

Growth Habit

The Norfolk Island Pine grows in spurts. Typically once or twice per year it will send a shoot up from the top and from that will grow a tier of new horizontal branches. Then nothing more will happen for another 6 months to a year. This plant has a single growing tip at the top of its main stem. That means that it grows only taller and does not branch. A common problem with these trees is that after many years, they outgrow their indoor spaces. In good indoor conditions, they can grow up to a foot per year and eventually reach the ceiling. At that point, the top will have to be pruned and that means removing the growing tip. Once that is done, the tree will gradually — usually over the course of several years — begin to die.

There is no solution to this problem, but you should keep this space requirement in mind before you acquire this plant. Moving it outside, except in semi-tropical climates, is not an option. Providing a bit less than ideal light and keeping it potbound and un-fertilized will help slow its growth. So this is a rare indoor plant where deliberately providing less than ideal conditions may pay off in the long run by keeping its growth rate in check.

Light

This plant does require good light from a nearby window. Although it does not require hours of direct sunlight, it must have abundant indirect sunlight all day long. Directly in front of a north or east window or just off to the side of a south or west window would be fine. In any case, the tree should not be more than 3 or 4 feet away from the uncovered window.

Younger Norfolk Pines are often more adaptable to reduced light levels, but even so, they should be close to a nearby window. In inadequate light, lower branches will gradually drop off and new growth — always at the top — will be smaller and less vigorous. Exposure to too much direct sunlight will cause the needles to develop a lighter shade of green.

Temperature

Although this plant will survive temperatures close to freezing, it is best not to expose it to temperatures below 45°F. This is not a plant that can survive outdoors year-round unless you live in Zone 10 or higher.

On the other hand, temperatures above 80°F, especially without good air circulation can be detrimental to this plant. So if you live in a hot, dry climate, then it is best not to move it outdoors during the hot summer months.

Pot Size & Repotting

Until a Norfolk Pine is well acclimated to its indoor environment, it can be very finicky about proper watering. Having the wrong pot size will make proper watering very difficult, if not impossible. This is not a fast growing plant so it rarely needs a larger pot. It is best to keep it in its existing pot until the soil is a solid mass of roots. Then move it into a pot one size larger, using a standard soilless, peat-based potting mix. Once it gets to a 12- or 14-inch pot indoors, it is unlikely to ever need a larger pot.

Multiple Plants in One Pot

Many nurseries place several small Norfolk Pines in the same pot. This creates a fuller looking plant and allows the nursery to sell it in a smaller (shorter) size. These individual plants do not need to be separated and, in fact, it is usually not a good idea to attempt it. Untangling the roots is too traumatic. Not to worry, as these multiple plants will not crowd each other out. However, if the pot looks too crowded visually, then the solution is to prune back a few of the individual plant stems. Remember, once a stem is cut, that stem will die. So be very sure before you prune any stems.

Watering

Careful watering of younger, less-established Norfolk Pines is very important. Improper watering will quickly lead to the loss of lower branches and those lower branches are never replaced as new growth is always at the top of each stem. If you are not careful, you will end up with a very tall, bare main stem with a few branches at the top. There is no remedy for that situation.

If your Norfolk Pine is properly potted, then it is best to water it as soon as the top half-inch of soil feels dry. For plants in larger pots (10 inches or more) that are better established, it is best to allow the top 2 inches of soil to dry between waterings. If your plant is quite potbound, then it may need water as soon as the soil surface is dry to the touch.

If the roots of this plant are allowed to become too dry, most if not all of the needles will quickly dry up and become brittle. This is most likely to happen with smaller plants, which can go from damp to very dry in just a couple of days. If it does happen, it rarely recovers.

Humidity

High humidity definitely benefits a Norfolk Pine, but it is not essential. I have successfully maintained these trees in office environments where the air is desert-dry in the winter months. Nonetheless, I recommend a room humidifier or a pebble tray directly under your tree. It is also best to keep it as far as possible from a heat source as warm, dry air creates a condition conducive to spider mites.

Air Circulation

This tree grows naturally close to the ocean where breezes are abundant. So good air circulation is beneficial, especially if the air is very warm. A small fan or an open window in warm weather will do the trick.

Fertilizer

If your Norfolk Island Pine is healthy and growing vigorously and it has not been repotted in at least a year, then it may need a nutrient boost from spring through the summer. Use a balanced, complete fertilizer with a 2-1-1 ratio at half the label recommended strength. Apply it monthly during the warmer months. Do not fertilize at all from early fall through the winter. And never fertilize an ailing plant. See my Chapter 8 for more specific information on fertilizing.

Pruning

This is a rare indoor plant that does not benefit from pruning. That is because it has a single growing tip that will cause the plant to slowly die if it is cut off or damaged. However, if you have multiple plants in a single pot, you can prune some of them out if the plant looks too crowded. Don't try to separate the roots.

NOTE: Be careful if you move this plant. If the top growing tip is accidentally damaged, it will prevent future growth.

Trimming

If your tree becomes too wide, the tips of the horizontal branches can be trimmed off, but that often upsets the symmetry of the tree, so I don't generally recommend it. Trimming these tips will not kill the tree the way that pruning off the top growing tip does.

As the tree grows taller, it usually loses some of its lower branches with old age. The first sign is that the needles on these lower branches discolor a bit and become dry and brittle. In fact, if you run your hand along a branch, some of the needles will come loose in your hand. Once this starts to happen with a branch, it is only a matter of time before it loses all of its needles on that branch, so you might just as well prune off the entire branch sooner rather than later.

Propagation

There is no practical way to propagate your Norfolk Island Pine. If you have multiple plants in a pot, it is theoretically possible to separate the individual plants and put them in separate pots. However, this is a tricky task and it is easy to end up losing all of the plants as a result of the trauma done to the roots. If a friend is envious of your Norfolk Pine, resist the urge to share it with them by dividing or cutting it. Have them get one of their own.

Pests

This plant is generally pest-resistant, but occasionally may become infested with spider mites, mealybugs or scale. Look for tiny webs between needles, white cotton-like bits on the needles or stickiness on or under the branches. More detailed information on these pests can be found in Chapter 10.

Conclusion

The Norfolk Island Pine makes an interesting addition to your indoor plant collection because of its unusual needled appearance. It can live a long time indoors, but you must have a good location for it so it can get adequate light. In addition, understand that if you are successful, this tree will eventually outgrow its space and you will have to find another home for it. Finally, it cannot be propagated so you cannot share it nor can you take a cutting to carry on after it is too big for your home.

Peace Lily
Spathiphyllum

The Peace Lily is a popular indoor plant with its broad, dark green leaves and dramatic white flowers that rise above the canopy of leaves. It is called a Peace Lily because the flowers are reminiscent of the white flag of peace. There are dozens of varieties of this popular plant due to successful hybridization. Peace Lilies come in sizes from under 6 inches to heights and widths of 5 feet and more. There are even variegated (green and silver) varieties now on the market.

The first thing that Peace Lily owners usually notice about their care is that they wilt pathetically if allowed to get the least bit too dry. This wilting can occur quickly (within a few hours and literally overnight) and will result in the leaves sagging over the rim of the pot. Surprisingly, a badly wilted Peace Lily will recover just as quickly and dramatically once it is watered.

Light

In their native habitat, Peace Lilies grow on the floor of the rainforest in deep shade. Thus, Peace Lilies do not tolerate direct sunlight well at all. When exposed to direct sunrays, the leaves will turn a pale sickly green and sometimes brown. The best light is bright indirect light. That would be right in front of an unobstructed, uncovered north window. It might also be in front of a south window that is covered with the sheerest of curtains. Or it could be right under overhead office fluorescent lights. Any window with the shades drawn will not provide adequate light. And any direct sunlight is too strong for Peace Lilies. If the light is inadequate, leaf tips will turn brown, although that can also happen as a result of improper watering. **NOTE:** In low light, Peace Lilies will flower less frequently and will need less frequent watering.

Water

You probably have already discovered that Peace Lilies do not tolerate dry soil. Although Peace Lilies do recover from wilting, each time they are allowed to wilt the recovery is less complete and a few leaves will turn yellow and some leaves may develop dry, brown tips.

On the other hand, constantly soggy soil will cause Peace Lily roots to gradually rot unnoticed. It may take several months or more for symptoms of too-wet soil to show up. Those symptoms include a slight wilting of leaves that don't recover from watering and also leaves that turn a dark brown or black color. Once the symptoms of overwatering start to show, it is usually too late as the roots have already stopped functioning.

Ideally, you water your Peace Lily just before it starts to wilt. With a healthy new Peace Lily, that occurs when the surface of the soil feels slightly damp. With older or newly repotted Peace Lilies the top half-inch or so of soil may need to dry before it reaches the wilt point and needs water. It is the failure to recognize this change that an aging Peace Lily makes that most often leads to their demise.

Once the soil has become very dry, it is sometimes hard to re-wet the soil. If this happens, allow the pot to sit in several inches of water for an hour so that it can wick up the water and become completely saturated. Then wait until the plant has just begun to wilt a bit before watering thoroughly once again.

SPECIAL CAUTION: Because new Peace Lilies wilt so quickly, there is a natural tendency to avoid this pathetic sight by watering too frequently. In addition, most Peace Lily owners fail to realize that their plant needs less frequent water as it ages. More Peace Lilies succumb to root rot than any other cause.

HINT: Every couple of months let your Peace Lily start to wilt. This will tell you how long it can go or how dry it can get before it really needs water.

Water Quality and Fertilizer

Peace Lilies are sensitive to the buildup of certain minerals in the soil. If your local tap water is on the hard side, then use filtered, distilled or rainwater for your Peace Lilies. It is also important not to overdo the fertilizer (another source of minerals) as too much can damage leaf tips.

Fertilize only when your Peace Lily is growing vigorously. Mix it at half strength and apply it monthly. Any balanced fertilizer is fine, but one with a higher middle number (5-10-5, for example) will help promote flowers a bit more than other formulations. However, don't overdo it because the buildup of excess nutrients will cause the leaves to spot.

Repotting

Peace Lilies are more inclined to produce flowers when they are potbound. Moving your Peace Lily into a larger pot may discourage flower production and, worse, may lead to root rot. It is best *not* to repot, if at all possible. If your Peace Lily dries to the wilt point every 2 or 3 days, then it might be ready for a pot one size larger. Otherwise leave it in its existing pot. (For more detailed information, see Chapter 1).

Soil

If you do repot, you can use a standard potting mix, but one that that contains little or no perlite and superphosphate because they are potent sources of fluoride that can cause browning of leaf tips and edges.

Temperature

Peace Lilies don't like temperatures below 60°F. When exposed to chilly temperatures, growth rate slows and leaves become limp and turn a dark color. Trim off damaged leaves, as they will not recover. Keep the plant warm and reduce water frequency and fertilizer until the plant recovers. If the temperatures are so cold that the roots freeze, then damage will be extensive and the plant will not recover. Always protect your Peace Lily from cold drafts.

Trimming

Leaf tips and edges will turn yellow and brown for many different reasons including improper water, too much or too little light, poor water quality and too much fertilizer. Try to determine the cause and eliminate it to prevent further damage to the leaves.

Discolored leaf edges and tips will not recover. Use sharp scissors to trim the discolored leaf margins and tips. Cut so that the original contour or shape of the leaf is maintained, i.e., so that it does not look obviously cut. This will make your Peace Lily look pretty once again. In some instances it may be better to remove the entire leaf rather than trying to trim it ever smaller. Press down inside the base of the stem with your finger until it snaps off.

Propagation by Dividing

Typically there are multiple Peace Lily stems growing out of the soil. These multiple stems help support one another and create a more compact, fuller looking plant. In general, it is best to leave these multiple stems together in the same pot. However, if you are determined to share your prized Peace Lily with someone, you can divide or separate the multiple stems by slicing down through the rootball and in between the stems. The severed portion should be potted into the smallest pot that it can be squeezed into. Do this at your own risk, as Peace Lilies often rebel when their roots are disturbed. You may end up with two dead plants rather than one healthy one! Division is the only practical way to propagate a Peace Lily.

Flowering

Why don't my Peace Lilies bloom any more? This is a common question with many explanations. Most Peace Lilies sold today are hybrids that have often been genetically selected to produce certain characteristics such as very large leaves or a darker green color or variegated leaves. This is often done at the expense of continued flower production.

Many hybrids are timed to produce a large burst of flowers at point-of-sale, but then only flower sporadically thereafter. Unfortunately, there is nothing you can do to alter the genetic structure of your plant. Peace Lily blooms last one to three weeks, depending on the environment. Don't expect them to bloom all year long; they do need to rest sometimes. Cut off the flower and its stem as soon as the flower starts to turn brown.

That said, there are several things that you can do to promote flowers within these genetic limitations:

- Provide bright indirect light rather than low light
- Keep your Peace Lily potbound
- Fertilize monthly at half strength

If that doesn't work, then enjoy your Peace Lily as the lovely foliage plant that it is.

Green Flowers

Sometimes new flowers emerge and are green rather than white. It's all in the genes and there is nothing you can do about it. Nearly all Peace Lilies sold today are hybrids that are "designed" to produce a flourish of white flowers at point-of-sale. After that, the flowering tends to be more sporadic and the flowers often revert to green.

Discoloration Of Leaves

Brown and yellow spots on the edges of leaves are very common with Peace Lilies and sometimes hard to eliminate. Unfortunately, there are numerous causes of these symptoms, including natural aging. If these symptoms appear on only a few of the older (lower) leaves, then it is just natural aging as healthy new leaves replace the older leaves. If it is more extensive than that, then continue below.

Possible causes of leaf discoloration include:

- Change in light or temperature (particularly cold)

- Using hard water

- Irregular watering

- Roots wandering out of the drainage holes

- Buildup of fertilizer in the soil

- Accumulation of minerals in the soil

Make sure you are providing proper light and temperature as described above. Monitor your watering as indicated previously. If you see roots wandering out of the drainage holes (rare), then simply snip them off unless a larger pot is warranted (rarely). The buildup of fertilizer and the accumulation of mineral salts in the soil usually happens in older plants. If your tap water is hard, use filtered, distilled or rainwater for your plants. Never use fertilizer at more than half the recommended rate.

If you seem to be doing everything right and are still getting new brown tips or leaf spots, then add some horticultural lime or gypsum to the soil. Sometimes it is just easier to trim off the discolored leaf edges when they appear and not worry about it.

However, if newly formed leaves are discolored, then that is more serious and usually is a symptom of root rot. Often, it is too late by the time this particular symptom appears.

Torn leaves usually result from people brushing against the very thin and easily torn leaves. This damage is not due to insects.

Humidity

Low humidity is not the cause of leaf spotting on Peace Lilies. Many times people don't realize that plants need more water when the humidity is low because of increased evaporation. If the roots get too dry, especially if the soil is over fertilized, brown spots will appear on the leaves as a result of the underwatering, not the low humidity. Many people are confused on this point.

Moving Peace Lilies Outside

Many indoor plant owners like to move their plants outside during the warmer months. The Peace Lily is not usually good plant to move outside, for several reasons.

- Cold temperatures below 60°F can cause damage

- Outdoor light, except in deep shade, is too intense for this low light plant

- The thin, fragile leaves are easily torn by strong breezes and precipitation

Longevity

Finally, I will note that Peace Lilies do have a tendency to decline as they age. They are not a particularly long-lived indoor plant although this can vary with particular varieties and overall care. When it comes to frequent flowers and a long life, keep your expectations low with your Peace Lily.

Orchid
Phalaenopsis

The orchid family of plants is the largest plant family with over 30,000 different species. The Cattleya orchid is the orchid most commonly used as a cut flower and is often seen in corsages and boutonnieres. However, the orchid most popular, available, and commonly used as a potted plant is the *Phalaenopsis* or moth orchid. This is the orchid that is the easiest to care for in the home and office environment. It has also been hybridized so that the flowers come in a multitude of colors and patterns. Except where otherwise noted, the information in this article refers to the care of the *Phalaenopsis* orchid. For information about the dozens of other Orchid species, check with the American Orchid Society at www. aos.org or 561-404-2000.

Orchid Potting Mix

Orchids are epiphytes, as opposed to terrestrials. That means that their roots are adapted to grow attached to the bark of trees in tropical rain forests where their roots are exposed to the humid air. They don't grow in soil. Their roots are never covered, but are constantly bathed in moist air and frequent rain showers. That is what you are trying to duplicate, as much as possible, when you grow an orchid. These Orchids produce aerial roots that are thick and covered by a special material called velamen that is silvery in color and changes to light green when it is wet. These plump roots absorb and store water for the plant.

All of this explains why orchids are potted in a mix of bark chips and other very porous material such as Sphagnum moss.

Orchid roots like to adhere to damp bark chips on one side of their roots, but they prefer to have the other side of their roots exposed to the air and rinsed with water periodically. If the bark chips are too small, then they will cover the roots on all sides and not allow sufficient air circulation. Large chips work better.

Watering

The hardest thing about orchids is when and how to water. Err on the side of under watering — once per week is sufficient in most cases. When the potting mix appears dry as far into the pot as you can see, take it to a sink and let the water wash over and through all of the roots and potting mix for about 15 seconds. You will notice that most of the water runs right out so you don't have to worry about adding too much water. Let the excess water drain out and return it to its usual spot. If the plant looks healthy, you are probably on the right track.

Repotting

Every 6 months or so check the condition of the roots and the potting mix. Soak the pot and the roots before you try to remove it from the pot. That will make it easier to remove. When you get it out of the pot, remove all loose bark chips and other material. Healthy roots have a plump, silvery appearance. Dead or dying roots are soft or shriveled, brown or black in color.

If you find an abundance of rotting bark chips and soft, rotting roots, then you have been watering too frequently — not too much, but too often. If you find many dry, shriveled roots and shriveled plant tissue, then the roots are getting too dry. This is an indication that you need to water more frequently.

Cut off any unhealthy roots with sterilized scissors. Remember, it is normal for some older roots to die back as they are replaced with healthy new roots. So don't be surprised to see some dead roots at any time. This is not unlike foliage plants that drop some lower leaves as they add new growth on top. No reason to be alarmed.

Within one to two years, even large bark chips begin to decompose and need to be replaced. Repot your orchid in fresh orchid mix. Use a clay pot, preferably one with side drainage holes to provide extra air circulation to the roots.

Light

Moth orchids do need lots of bright light, but it must be filtered or indirect. Direct sunlight can scorch the leaves or turn them a pale shade of green. Inadequate light will cause new leaves to be very dark green and soft. An unfiltered, unobstructed north-facing windowsill is ideal. Any other windowsill would need a very sheer curtain or slatted blinds to protect the orchid from the sun's direct rays at certain times of the day.

Moth orchids also grow very well under fluorescent lights that are no more than 12 inches away.

Fertilizer

Orchid fertilizing can be a very esoteric art and unnecessarily complicated. Here is a simplified version of orchid food basics.

Most orchids are potted in media that do not readily provide nutrients — bark chips, peat moss, coir, lava rock, etc. In general, orchids need a balanced liquid fertilizer during their foliage growth or non-blooming period. Balanced means the three analysis numbers are similar (20-20-20, for example). Orchids potted in bark chips need more nitrogen, so the first number should be higher than the other two (30-10-10 for example). As the blooming time approaches or when buds begin to form, it is best to switch to a higher phosphorous content. So you want the middle number to be higher in proportion to the others (15-30-15, for example) to promote flowers. Do this in the month or so preceding expected bloom or when the flower spike starts to emerge.

It is best to use a dilute liquid fertilizer with every watering. Most fertilizer dilution rates are based on a once per month application, so if you are watering weekly (4 times per month), then dilute it with 4 times as much water or 1/4 the amount of fertilizer recommended on the label. In addition, recommended fertilizer rates are based on ideal growing conditions, which few of us can provide. Damage from excess fertilizer is a more common problem than under fertilizing, especially with Orchids.

Temperature and Humidity

Moth orchids must have warm temperatures all year long. Always keep temperatures above 65°F. In the fall, nighttime temperatures down to 55°F for several weeks will help promote flower spikes. Protect your orchid from cold windowsills and drafts in the winter.

Although orchids grow naturally in humid areas, they can adapt to the low humidity of our indoor spaces. Humidifiers and pebble trays will help your orchid. Misting will help keep the leaves clean, but it does not significantly increase the humidity.

Flower Spikes

Orchid flowers grow on stems called spikes that emerge from the base of the plant. They open gradually, stay open for one to three months, and then die off gradually. Remove each flower as it withers. When the last flower has faded, cut off the flower spike just above the third node (bump) on the stem, counting up from the bottom. If you are lucky, you may get a secondary flower spike with a few more blossoms. Otherwise, you will have to wait until the following year for a new spike and flowers.

Roots Outside the Pot

Moth orchids typically grow new roots that climb over the top of the potting mix and over the rim of the pot. This is fine and there is no need to cover them up. Just make sure they get a good soaking when you water your orchid. These roots will absorb and store water for the plant and benefit from occasional misting. The next time you repot, these roots can be covered with the fresh potting mix or they can be left outside the pot.

Orchid Pests

Orchids are fairly resistant to plant pests and relatively easy to treat. You should be alert for scale, mealybug and spider mites. Scale will appear on the undersides of leaves as soft translucent bumps or as hard brown bumps. They scrape off easily with a fingernail.

Mealybug looks like little bits of cotton. Spider mites appear as tiny specks of dust and give a mottled appearance to the leaves.

Remove scale insects and mealybugs by wiping all leaf surfaces with a soft cloth soaked in rubbing alcohol. Use a soapy cloth to remove spider mites.

Orchid Planters

Many florists and high-end plant dealers are now selling Orchids in beautiful glass and ceramic planters that are cylindrical or cubic in shape. The problem with these stylish planters is that they are sealed and without drainage holes in the bottom. This makes them nearly impossible to water properly beyond the life of the flowers or about one month. The florist may tell you that it is okay to do this because there is drainage material in the bottom. Don't believe it.

In addition, you pay a premium for these special planters and the cost of planting the Orchids into these planters. If you can afford it and don't mind discarding the Orchid after it finishes flowering, then enjoy the design of these Orchid planters. If your Orchid is already in a sealed planter, leave it until it has finished flowering; then repot it into a planter with drain holes.

However, it is preferable to buy one in a container that has multiple drainage holes. That container can then be inserted inside of a slightly larger, more decorative planter of your choice. This allows you to remove the inserted container, take it to the sink and water it as described above before putting it back in its display planter.

Conclusion

Orchid growing is different, but not difficult. It takes a while to figure them out, but they are quite forgiving and hardy over the long run. Be patient, be willing to experiment, and be sure to enjoy the whole process.

Palms

Palm species are very popular indoor plants because they inspire thoughts of vacations, tropical beaches and a leisurely lifestyle. They are the classic potted plant that was used even back in Victorian days of the 19th century.

Despite their popularity, Palm species are often a source of heartache for their owners as they can be difficult to care for. Palms are also a source of confusion.

Identity Crisis

There are many Palm species readily available in the retail market. Unfortunately, they are often not labeled as anything more than Palm. The problem with that is that different Palm species have widely varying care requirements. Some need direct sunlight while others must always be in the shade. Some Palms like constantly moist soil while others need to dry out quickly between waterings. Finally, there are some plant species that are mistaken for Palms or called Palms because they look like Palms but are not actually in the Palm family. Examples are Sago Palm, Ponytail Palm, Dracaena *marginata*, and Dracaena *massangeana*. If you have one of these, then don't read this Bulletin for care advice because those are *not* Palms!

So your first task is determining just what Palm species you have. You may need to go on the Internet and search for Palm photos or look in some plant picture books that will help you identify your particular Palm.

What Palms Have in Common

Palms are native to tropical or semi-tropical regions so most Palm species are not frost hardy. That makes them good indoor plants.

Unlike most trees and other plant species, Palms have a single growing tip. That means all new growth is at the top of each stem and if that top, growing tip is damaged or pruned off, that stem will slowly die. So your Palm cannot be cut back if it gets too tall, but fortunately Palms are slow growers indoors so this is not often a problem.

Palms cannot be propagated via cuttings. They must be grown from seed (this takes a very long time) or by dividing multiple Palms that are grown in the same pot. However, I don't recommend this because division spoils the appearance (fullness) of the original Palm and is a risky procedure that often compromises the roots. If you want to share your Palm, it is best to purchase another one.

There are two general types of Palms — those that have feather-like fronds and those that have fan-like fronds. A frond is the arching stem with its multiple leaves along each side. Examples of feather-like fronds are found on Areca Palms, Kentia Palms, Majesty Palms, Date Palms and Bamboo Palms. Examples of fan-type Palms are Rhapis Palms, and Chinese Fan Palms.

Beyond these qualities, Palm species have little in common. In the next chapters I write about the most popular Palm species individually and describe their unique care requirements.

Majesty Palm
(Ravena rivularis)

This is one of the most popular Palms because the Big Box stores can sell these large plants for not very much money so they promote them heavily. They appear to be a great bargain, but they are invariably a big disappointment! So much so that it is just about the only plant that I strongly recommend that you ***do not buy!***

This is one of the few Palm species that grows rapidly in warm outdoor climates. That is a big reason they are cheap to buy. Unfortunately, they do not adapt well to indoor environments where light is reduced and air circulation is minimal. In addition, discount growers do not take the time-consuming step of gradually acclimating these Palms to reduced light.

If you already have a Majesty Palm, lower your expectations and do your best as these plants rarely look good after a year as an indoor potted plant.

Light, Potting & Temperature

Indoors, the Majesty Palm should be placed in front of your sunniest window. Do not repot it, although you can place the plastic grow-pot inside of a larger decorative planter to enhance its appearance.

If you can move your Majesty Palm outdoors in the warmer months when temps above 55°F), it will fare better. However, you will need to place it in light shade or dappled light where it is protected from direct outdoor sunlight, which is much more intense than indoor light.

Watering

Indoors or out, keep the soil moderately moist at all times, but not wet. This can be nearly impossible if the soil mix is not a good one with lots of aeration. If you have any watering lapses with Majesty Palms, you pay the price with fronds that turn yellow or tips that turn brown. Water it thoroughly when the surface of the soil feels dry. If it is outside in warm weather, then that may mean watering every couple of days.

Fertilizer

When they are growing vigorously, Majesty Palms require lots of fertilizer, particularly the minor element magnesium. Use a fertilizer with a 4-1-6 ratio and be sure the fertilizer includes magnesium. Avoid Miracid or any other fertilizer that lowers the pH and prevents the nutrients from being absorbed. Fertilize monthly at full strength when outdoors and at half strength when indoors. Use a standard complete fertilizer that you dilute in water. Avoid fertilizer sticks that create "hot spots" and can burn roots.

Humidity and Pests

Majesty Palms are spider mite magnets — another reason why this plant is not a particularly good choice. There doesn't seem to be any way to prevent spider mites on this plant, so you must be vigilant in watching for early signs of these critters. (See Chapter 10 for more information on spider mites). Good air circulation and high humidity will help deter the spider mites.

Trimming, Pruning & Symptoms

Brown leaf tips and yellowed fronds are inevitable. Discolored tips can be trimmed off with scissors and yellowed fronds should be pruned off completely. This will keep your Majesty Palm looking good as long as you have it, but eventually you will probably want to toss the entire plant. Just remind yourself that you didn't spend a lot of money on it!

Areca Palm
(Formerly Chrysalidocarpus lutescens, now Dypsis lutescens)

This is another fast grower and is difficult to keep looking good because it is a demanding and unforgiving plant, although not as problematic as the Majesty Palm. Areca can be identified by its distinctive yellow lower stems.

Light

Areca Palms must have very bright natural light all day long. Right in front of an east or west window is best. Without bright light, you are fighting a losing battle. Outside in the warmer months (above 60°F), keep your Areca in light shade where it is protected from direct outdoor sun.

Watering

Water thoroughly and then water again when the top inch of soil is dry. Never let the Areca sit in water for more than an hour or so. Arecas are very sensitive to hard or alkaline water. If your local tap water is hard or alkaline, then switch to distilled or filtered water for the Areca. Also, avoid fertilizing it.

Potting

Generally, it is best to avoid repotting your Areca unless it is drying out every couple of days. Read Chapter 1 before you repot.

Humidity and Pests

Arecas don't fare well in low humidity. Like many Palms species, they are very prone to spider mites. Check the undersides of the fronds regularly for signs of spider mites (dust-like particles under the leaves). Misting helps deter mites, but doesn't make much difference as far as raising humidity. Raising the humidity with a pebble tray or humidifier will help keep the spider mites at bay. Chapter 10 has more information on treating pests and mites.

Trimming, Pruning & Symptoms

If the light and water conditions are not right, the Areca reacts by getting brown tips and yellow fronds. Trim off the discolored tips and remove the yellowed fronds completely to keep your Areca looking good.

As a final note

Arecas grow quickly and don't last very long. That is why they are relatively inexpensive. Other Palm species described here, grow more slowly but last much longer. That is why they are more expensive initially but may be a better value in the long run.

Kentia Palm
(Howeia forsteriana)

Kentia Palms, Crotons, Anthuriums

The Kentia Palm is the classic elegant Palm species that has tall, graceful arching dark green fronds that are often seen in old photos of Victorian era interiors. It is a slow grower, can only be grown from seed and takes 5-6 years before it is large enough to sell. For that reason, Kentias are expensive. (Do not confuse the cheaper Majesty Palm with the Kentia.) However, Kentias do not require much light and are largely pest resistant. With proper care, a Kentia will last for a very long time and is unlikely to outgrow its space. It is best to select a Kentia that is the right size from the outset rather than counting on its growing larger to fill a space.

Light

A Kentia Palm does best in a location with lots of bright indirect light (close to a north or east window), although it will survive in low light if you are very careful not to overwater. Note: Low light must be bright enough all day long to allow easy reading of small print. In low light, your Kentia will maintain no more than 5 or 6 fronds at one time, so provide brighter light if you want a fuller plant with more fronds. On the other hand, you must protect your Kentia from direct sunlight falling directly on the fronds for more than an hour or two each day. This is not a good plant to move outdoors in the summer.

Potting

Kentias are best kept potbound in pots that appear to be too small for the long arching fronds. In fact, yours will never need repotting because their root systems are quite small and unless they are kept potbound, they tend to fall over in their pots. If you do not rotate your Kentia regularly to provide equal exposure to light, it will start to lean severely in the direction of the light.

Newer, better quality Kentias are now grown in a potting mix that is mostly volcanic cinders. This may seem strange to you and hard to determine the moisture content. However, this very porous material makes it much less likely that you will inadvertently rot the roots by keeping the soil too moist.

Watering

If your Kentia is potted in the volcanic cinder-type mix, is in its original growpot and is getting adequate light, then a thorough weekly watering is probably just about right. If your Kentia is potted in a standard potting mix, then allow the top quarter of the soil to dry in between thorough waterings.

Overwatering is the most common problem with these Palms. Never let the pot stand in excess water. Overwatered Kentias will get brown tips and then yellow spots on the fronds. Underwatering will cause brown tips and the fronds will droop somewhat.

Fertilizer

Kentias are very light feeders. Fertilize once or twice per year with a complete fertilizer diluted to half strength. Use a standard complete fertilizer that you dilute in water. Avoid fertilizer sticks that create "hot spots" and can burn roots.

Temperature

Kentias will tolerate temperatures to the low 40s F for short periods. However, it I best to keep them above 52°F at all times. Thus, they can be kept in a cool indoor location that some other plants may not tolerate. However, moving your Kentia outdoors is not recommended because outdoor light is too strong so temps below 50°F are not likely to occur.

NOTE: Do keep your Kentia out of cold drafts, especially in entranceways where doors open in the colder months.

Humidity and Pests

Pests are rarely a problem for Kentia Palms. Spider mites are more likely to occur if the Kentia's soil is kept too dry than if the air is dry. Thus, you need not be concerned with low humidity levels for this Palm.

Trimming, Pruning & Symptoms

In reduced indoor light, Kentia Palms can support only a limited number of fronds at one time. That means that as new fronds emerge at the top in the center, older fronds may yellow and die. As long as the overall number of fronds is maintained, this is not a cause for concern. If you lose more fronds than you gain, it may be simply because you Kentia is adapting to reduced light. Otherwise, the light may be inadequate or your watering may be improper.

Once fronds start to yellow, they don't recover their green color, so it is best to cut off the entire frond from where it attaches to the main stalk.

If a new frond emerges and is discolored after opening, then you have a serious problem, as that new frond is the growing tip and the future of your Kentia. In most cases, a discolored new frond is due to improper watering and root damage. Correct your watering and hope for the best, but it may be too late.

Brown tips can be trimmed off with scissors and are not a serious problem unless the browning spreads deeper into the leaves. That indicates a watering problem or inadequate light.

With their long, arching fronds, older Kentias may need a little support to keep them from arching too far down and over the side of the pot. A larger pot is *not* the answer. Here is a simple trick: Tie a soft string moderately tightly around the base of all of the fronds. Then, slowly slide the string up the stems so that all of the stems are pulled together into a more upright position. The higher you slide the string, the more vertical the fronds become.

This is a plant that does best when you do less rather than more. It is a slow grower, but a plant that can last for decades if it is not fussed over too much. It is worth the price if you can afford it. Beware of Kentias that are on sale. Good quality Kentias are not discounted and poor quality Kentias can fall apart quickly even with good care.

Fishtail Palm
(Caryota mitis)

This is an unusual looking palm because its somewhat ragged looking individual leaves have the shape of fish tails. It is a look that some people love and others hate. If you are among the former, here is what you need to know.

Light

The Fishtail Palm works well indoors because it does not require a lot of direct sunlight. In fact, it does best in a north or east-facing window where exposure to direct sun is limited. However, it still must be kept close to and in front of an uncovered window. Too much light will bleach the leaves and too little light will cause weak, spindly growth.

Water

Allow the top inch or two of soil to dry and then water thoroughly so that a little runs through the bottom drainage holes. Do not use hard or alkaline water. If your tap water is on the hard side, then switch to filtered or distilled or rainwater for your plants.

Potting

The Fishtail Palm is a slow growing plant that rarely needs repotting. In fact, it will grow better when kept quite potbound. Repot only when it becomes necessary to water every couple of days to keep the soil properly moist and then only into a pot one size larger.

Fertilizer

Because Fishtails grow slowly they use up nutrients very slowly. Thus, they need only monthly fertilizer at half strength when they are healthy and growing vigorously. Otherwise, skip the plant food entirely. Use a standard complete fertilizer that you dilute in water. Avoid fertilizer sticks that create "hot spots" and can burn roots.

Temperature

Keep temps above 55°F at all times. If you move your Fishtail outside in warm weather, make sure it stays in deep shade and away from any exposure to direct outdoor sunlight.

Humidity and Pests

The Fishtail Palm is not as prone to spider mite infestations as many other Palm species. However, you still must be vigilant and check the undersides of leaves regularly for early signs of spider mites. See Chapter 10 for more information on detecting and treating spider mites. While raising humidity helps somewhat in deterring spider mites, the Fishtail Palm otherwise will do just fine in a low humidity environment as long as the soil and roots are not allowed to dry out. Misting does not raise the humidity, but it does help keep the leaves a bit cleaner.

Trimming, Pruning & Symptoms

Brown leaf tips are the most common symptom on Fishtail Palms. Letting the soil get too dry and using hard water are the most common causes of brown leaf tips. Dark brown leaf tips are caused by excess water or inadequate light.

Lower (older) fronds tend to yellow as they age. This is normal.

Discolored leaf tips can be trimmed off with sharp scissors and yellowed fronds can be pruned off at their base.

Fishtail Palms rarely become too tall for their space so pruning back for height is not an issue. However, they do tend to spread out as they age. Fronds that extend uncomfortably into your living area can be pruned off at their base without harm to the plant.

Chinese Fan Palm
(Livistona chinensis)

This is a semi-tropical Palm that will grow outdoors where temperatures do not fall below 25°F. As an indoor plant, it tolerates cooler locations and rarely grows taller than 3 to 4 feet. However, Chinese Fan Palms have arching fronds that become almost horizontal as they age. This is normal, but it means you must allow for this wide spread when you locate it in your home or office. If you have a low wide space that needs filling, this is an ideal choice as long as the light is appropriate.

Light
Provide lots of bright indirect light with a few hours of direct sun, such as an eastern window provides. A north window is also a good location as long as the

Fan Palm is close to and immediately in front of that window. Too much direct sun will scorch the fronds. Too little light will cause weak growth with undersized new fronds.

Water
Water thoroughly as soon as the top inch of soil feels dry. Excessive drying of the soil will cause the fronds to droop even more than usual. Keeping the soil constantly wet will rot the roots and you will eventually lose the entire plant

Potting
Keep your Fan Palm potbound for best results. Repot only when it becomes necessary to water every couple of days to keep the soil properly moist and then only into a pot one size larger.

Fertilizer
Fertilize monthly and at half-strength when it is growing vigorously. Use a standard complete fertilizer that you dilute in water. Avoid fertilizer sticks that create "hot spots" and can burn roots.

Temperature
The Chinese Fan Palm does best in cooler temperatures in the 60-to-70°F range, although it is adaptable to temps below freezing and as high as 80°F.

Humidity and Pests
The Fan Palm is not as prone to spider mite infestations as many other Palm species. However, you still must be vigilant and check the undersides of leaves regularly for early signs of spider mites. See Chapter 10 for more information on detecting and treating spider mites. Raising humidity helps somewhat in deterring spider mites. If you cannot raise the humidity, this Palm will do fine in a low humidity environment as long as the soil and roots are not allowed to dry out.

Trimming, Pruning & Symptoms
As with most Palms, brown tips caused by improper watering, inadequate light or hard water are common. Brown leaf tips can be pruned off to enhance the appearance of your Palm. Brown spots in the center of the fan fronds are usually caused by irregular watering. So providing a consistent watering routine is important. Speckled or mottled fronds are a sign of spider mites that are usually found hiding on the undersides of the fronds.

Coconut Palm
(Cocos nucifera)

The Coconut Palm is a novelty plant that is not easy to maintain as a houseplant. It is often sold as a seedling growing out of the cracked coconut shell that falls from tall Coconut trees. You are led to believe that this will grow into a large Coconut producing tree right in your home. It will not. In most cases, it grows to a height of 2–3 feet before succumbing to spider mites and dry, brown leaves.

If you receive one of these as a gift — I don't recommend buying one — you must keep it in a sunny window. There is no reason to remove it from its hard outer shell (coconut) or to repot it. Water it thoroughly as soon as the surface of the soil feels dry. If possible, increase the humidity and the air circulation — a fan helps.

Spider mites are a constant problem, as are dry brown leaf edges and tips. Treat the mites promptly (See Chapter 10), and trim off the brown leaf edges.

Do your best with your Coconut Palm, but keep your expectations low.

Lady Palm
(Rhapis excelsa)

Rhapis Palms and Guzmanias   Healthy Rhapis Palm

This is a fan type Palm with stems that are more upright than arching. Like the Kentia Palm, the Lady Palm has deep green fronds, tolerates low light, is pest resistant and is expensive. Unlike the Kentia, it prefers soil that is evenly moist at all times. This is an excellent choice if you want more height than width or if you tend to be a bit heavy-handed with your watering.

Light
Lady Palms are excellent medium to low light plants. They do best right in a north or east-facing window. A few hours of early or late day direct sun is fine. It will survive in low light if you are very careful not to overwater. In low light, your Lady Palm will grow more slowly and will not maintain a many fronds as it would in better light.

As with the Kentia Palm, you must protect the Lady Palm from direct sunlight falling directly on the fronds for more than an hour or two each day. It is *not* a good plant to move outdoors in the summer unless you can keep it in deep shade.

Watering

Water your Lady Palm thoroughly with clear water as soon as the surface of the soil feels dry. Do not let it sit in any excess water for more than a few hours. If you let your Lady Palm get too dry, the frond stems will droop downward. They will recover a while after you water, but it is best to avoid allowing it to reach this wilt point. In general, the Lady Palm is more tolerant of watering lapses than other Palm species because it will tolerate overwatering (up to a point) and will recover from underwatering. For that reason this is a good choice for someone who wants a Palm but is not too experienced with plants.

Potting

In good light, Lady Palms will grow faster than most other Palm species. They also have a robust root system that causes them to require repotting more often than many other indoor plants. It is not uncommon for tightly potted Lady Palms to push new stems out of drainage holes or even through thin-walled plastic pots.

If your Lady Palm is seriously potbound, then move it to a new pot that is one size larger. Use a standard potting mix that retains water but also has porous material mixed in. If you move your Lady Palm to a larger pot prematurely or to a pot that is too large, you will slow growth and risk root rot.

Temperature

Lady Palms do best in normal indoor temperatures in the 50°F to 80°F range. Avoid cold drafts and hot, dry heating vents.

Humidity and Pests

Lady Palms are virtually pest-free, although spider mites and scale insects do occasionally host on this species. Increased humidity is fine for the Lady Palm, but it will do just fine in low humidity as long as the roots are given adequate moisture.

Fertilizer

Lady Palms are very light feeders when in low light and moderate feeders when in bright indirect light. In low light, fertilize once or twice per year with a complete fertilizer diluted to half strength. In good light, fertilize monthly at half-strength.

Trimming, Pruning & Symptoms

Excess fertilizer, hard water, insufficient light, and over and underwatering will all cause tips of Lady Palm fronds to brown. Underwatering usually causes light brown tips, whereas dark tips are more likely caused by keeping the soil too moist or by inadequate light. Discolored tips can be trimmed off with pinking shears or torn off by hand to preserve the naturally uneven tip ends.

Yellow fronds are not as common with Lady Palms as it is with other Palm species. Excessive drying of the soil will cause a burst of yellow fronds several days after the drying. Occasional yellow fronds are normal and not a cause for concern. Yellow fronds can be cut off completely without harm to the plant.

As with most other Palm species, you cannot prune off the top of any Lady Palm stem with causing that stem to die. Likewise, you cannot take stem cuttings to propagate more plants.

Propagation

To propagate a Lady Palm, you have to divide the roots system by cutting the rootball in half. This is very difficult because the roots are very tough and difficult to separate or cut. I don't recommend it.

Rhapis Palm

Dwarf Date Palm
(Phoenix roebellini)

This is a symmetrical Palm that typically has a single fat stem out of which grow short, feathery fronds. Although a close relative of the Palm species that produces edible dates, this Palm will not produce edible fruit. A notable characteristic of this Palm is its long, sharp thorns that can make it difficult to handle!

Light

At a minimum, Date Palms must have lots of bright indirect light and do better if they get a few hours of direct sunlight every day. Right in front of an uncovered east or west window is best and in front of a north window is adequate. If you cannot provide enough light for this Palm, then spare yourself the heartache of watching it gradually decline despite your best efforts.

Potting

Date Palms thrive when they are potbound. They have more substantial root systems than many other Palm species, grow more quickly and may need repotting more than most other Palms. However, it is best to keep yours in its existing pot as long as a thorough watering is sufficient to keep the soil moist for at least 3 or 4 days. If not, then move it into a pot one size larger.

Watering

Date Palms are usually tightly potted and don't tolerate soil drying out. Therefore, they need to be watered thoroughly as soon as the surface to upper half-inch of soil feels dry to the touch. A subirrigation system that supplies water from below on an as-needed basis is a good option for this plant.

Temperature

Date Palms do well in normal indoor temperatures in the 50°F to 80°F range. Avoid cold drafts and hot, dry heating vents. Because they are sturdy plants and enjoy good light, Date Palms can be moved outside to light shade during the warmer months.

Humidity and Pests

Date Palms are very spider mite prone. If this Palm is under stress due to inadequate light or improper watering, mites will flourish. Warm, dry air also provides an environment conducive for spider mite reproduction.

Use a humidifier or a pebble tray to increase the humidity around your Date Palm. Misting may help deter mites somewhat but does not really increase the humidity effectively. A fine mist will help reveal the almost invisible spider mite webs as the droplets get caught in the webs. See Chapter 10 to learn more about finding and treating spider mites.

Fertilizer

Date Palms are moderate feeders when in proper light. Fertilize monthly at half-strength when the Palm is putting out new growth. Use a standard complete fertilizer that you dilute in water. Avoid fertilizer sticks that create "hot spots" and can burn roots.

Trimming, Pruning & Symptoms

As with other Palm species, the growing tip cannot be removed or damaged without causing the Palm to die. However, as the date Palm grows taller it is normal for it to lose some of its older, lower fronds. These fronds will gradually turn yellow and then brown. It is best to cut these fronds off complexly as soon as they start to discolor.

Brown tips are a very common problem with Date Palms. Hard water, excessive drying of the soil, dry air and too much fertilizer will cause brown tips. Poor light and over watering will cause the leaf tips to turn dark brown or black. Discolored tips can be trimmed off to make the Palm look nicer, but unless you correct the underlying cause, the tips will continue to discolor more and more.

Conclusion

The Date Palm is a lovely, stately Palm species, but it is high maintenance because its fragile fronds require proper watering and light; it attracts spider mites; and it has those nasty thorns! If you are up to the challenge, then this is a good Palm for you.

Chamaedorea Palms
(Parlor, Bamboo & Cat Palms)

The Chamaedorea Palms are more affordable Palms that will survive in moderate to low light, and that makes them more practical. However, the Chamaedoreas are very prone to spider mites. The Parlor Palm comes in small sizes and is rarely more than 3-feet tall. The Bamboo Palm is generally sold in sizes 4-feet or taller and has an upright, slender profile.

Parlor Palm

Light

The Parlor Palm (*Chamaedorea elegans*) is a good low light option. It does best in bright indirect light, but can survive in low light up to 6-feet away from an uncovered window. The Bamboo Palms (*Chamaedorea erumpens*) and Cat Palms (*Chamaedorea cataractum*) require medium light close to a north or east-facing window. Too much direct sun will bleach the fronds to a pale green or yellow color.

Water

The Parlor Palms and Bamboo Palms need to dry out a bit more than the Cat Palm. Allow the top inch or two of the former to dry between thorough waterings. Water the Cat Palm as soon as the surface of the soil is dry.

Potting

None of the Chamaedorea Palms are rapid growers so repotting is rarely necessary. If you do repot, be sure to move up only one size larger and be sure to use a porous potting mix.

Fertilizer

Chamaedoreas are light feeders and need only monthly fertilizer at half strength when they are healthy and growing vigorously. Otherwise, skip the plant food. **Note:** Fertilizer may promote tender new growth that is particularly favored by spider mites!

Temperature

Normal home temperatures are fine for the Chamaedorea species. Because their leaves are thin and easily damaged by wind, I don't recommend moving them outside in the warmer months.

Humidity and Pests

Although these Palms do not require high humidity to thrive, dry air does create a more favorable environment for spider mites to reproduce rapidly. Do what you can to raise the humidity when the air is warm and dry. Misting doesn't raise the humidity, but it does discourage mites somewhat.

Because these Palms are so mite prone, you must be vigilant in watching for spider mites so you can treat them early. Before they make visible webs, spider mites appear on the undersides of Palm leaves as tiny white specks of dust. Check Palm leaves weekly for mites and treat them promptly with a soap and water solution. Although less common than spider mites, mealybugs and scale insects may also enjoy tasting your Chamaedorea Palm. See Chapter 10 to learn more about identifying and treating these Palm pests.

Trimming, Pruning & Symptoms

Some yellowing of lower fronds is normal as these Palms grow taller. Excessive discoloration of fronds means there is usually a light or watering problem.

Underwatering, excess fertilizer and using hard water usually cause light brown tips. Dark tips are more likely caused by keeping the soil too moist or by inadequate light.

Discolored tips can be trimmed off to make the Palm look nicer, but unless you correct the underlying cause, the tips will continue to discolor more and more.

Bamboo Palms tend to grow quite tall and lose their lower fronds. These lanky stems can be cut back to the soil level. Once cut, a stem will cease growing, but it may trigger new stem growth from below the soil surface in addition to eliminating an overgrown stem.

Berries

The Chamaedorea Palms bear clusters of small, pea-sized fruit that may be yellow or dark red in color. They are not edible and they rarely produce new plants. In time, they dry up and fall off or you can safely remove them at any time.

Philodendron & Pothos

6" Pothos in rectangular planter

Philodendron and Pothos are two of the more commonly used and popular houseplants. They are vining or hanging plants that adapt as well as any plants to low light. These plants are also available at nearly all plant retail shops and are reasonably priced. I have included these two distinct plant species together because they look similar and are often mistaken for one another. In addition, their cultural requirements are the same.

How are they different?

Although there are many different Philodendron species available, the most common is the heart-leafed Philodendron. The leaf shape and size and the vining growth of this Philodendron are very similar to the Pothos.

The leaves of a Pothos are thicker and usually a bit larger than those of a Philodendron. Philodendron leaves are a darker shade of green than the Pothos. Although there are all-green varieties of Pothos (called

Pothos
Epipremnum pinnatum

Jade Pothos), most Pothos are variegated with splashes of white (called Marble Queen Pothos) or yellow (called Golden Pothos).

More importantly, the Pothos has proven to be hardier, faster growing and a bit easier to care for than the Philodendron.

Both plants are in the Aroid plant family that includes the ZZ Plant, Peace Lily, and Chinese Evergreen among others. Like all members of the Aroid plant family, the Philodendron and Pothos are toxic to people and pets if ingested or chewed.

Light

Pothos and Philodendron grow along the floor of the tropical rainforest under a canopy of deep shade. That is why they adapt well to lower light as houseplants. Ideally, they should be in bright indirect light, such as you find close to a north window or off to the side of a window facing any other direction. Pothos and Philodendron do need protection from the direct rays of the sun falling directly on the leaves. Too much sunlight will cause the leaves to become a pale green/ yellow in color.

As you move these plants further from the window and reduce the light, their growth rate will slow, the new leaves will become smaller in size and the space between the leaves will be elongated. Although they can survive as far as 10 to 12 feet away from an uncovered window, their appearance will gradually decline over time.

Pothos and Philodendron thrive under fluorescent lights alone, provided the lights are overhead and on for about 8 hours per day. This makes them ideal office plants in areas where there are no windows. Because these are not large plants, try putting one on your desk under a desk lamp fitted with a compact fluorescent bulb. You will need to leave the light on for about 8 hours each day, but compact fluorescents are cost-effective because they use so little energy.

Pot Size

The heart-leafed Philodendron and the Pothos are usually sold in 6-inch and 8-inch hanging basket plastic pots. Occasionally, very large plants are sold in 10-inch pots.

Whatever pot size your plant is in is probably the size it will stay in forever. That is because these plants have small root systems that do best when they are tightly potted. Unnecessarily repotting them often causes root rot. (See Chapter 1). This is particularly true of the Philodendron, which has finer roots than Pothos.

You may not like the look of that plastic pot yours is growing in. If so, then simply purchase a better-looking pot that is large enough for you to insert the plastic pot. This double potting will satisfy your aesthetic desires while avoiding repotting and disturbing the roots.

Water

When kept moderately potbound in the proper sized pot (see above) and given adequate light, Pothos and Philodendron are pretty easy to water. Wait until the surface of the soil is dry and light brown in color. Then apply enough water so that a small amount trickles through the bottom drainage holes. In most cases this is about once every 7–10 days.

If you let these plants get too dry, you will see some bright yellow leaves that will eventually turn brown and dry. Remove these leaves, water a bit more frequently and the plant will recover. In cases of severe drought, the leaves and stems will wilt and you will lose many leaves. In that case, you will have to soak the plant in warm water for 30 minutes to re-wet the soil and prune back the damaged stems sharply.

A Pothos or Philodendron that is not allowed to dry out properly between waterings will exhibit dull yellow leaves and soft wilted stems. Usually by the time these symptoms appear, root rot is already well established and it may be difficult to get your plant to recover. So, if in doubt about whether it is time to water, it is better to err on the side of dryness because the consequences of underwatering are less drastic than overwatering.

Humidity and Fertilizer

These are not important issues in caring for your Philodendron or Pothos. Both have proven to do very well even in the driest indoor heated air despite their being native to humid environments.

Both of these species have low nutrient needs so regular fertilizing is not necessary. If you fertilize with a standard fertilizer at half strength a few times each year, your plants will be fine.

Temperature

Philodendron and Pothos are tropical plants and do best in temps that don't fall below 60°F. They can survive somewhat lower temps, but growth will slow and there is a greater chance for root rot. So try to keep these plants warm, up to 85°F. Be very careful about moving these plants outdoors as they are sensitive to cold and to the intensity of outdoor light where they must be kept in deep shade at all times.

Pruning

You will observe that new growth on these plants is always at the ends of each stem or vine. The vines do not branch out and they don't generate new growth from below the soil. That means that over time the vines will grow ever longer and that can be a problem.

When these vining plants do not get enough light or if they are improperly watered, they will lose some of their older leaves — the leaves closest to the soil. Over time, as older leaves die and new growth is added at the ends of the vines, you may end up with very long bare 'strings' with a limited number of leaves at the ends of these bare stems. New leaves will never grow in along these bare stems to replace the older ones that have died.

Selective pruning is the only way to cure and prevent your plants from developing these long bare stems. If this has already happened to your Pothos or Philodendron, then you should cut back every bare stem to within 2-4 inches of the soil. This may leave you with a bunch of leafless stubs and an ugly plant. However, before long you will see new growth leaves start to emerge at the ends of these stubs. In time, you will have lots of new growth filling in the pot and no more bare stems.

To keep your Pothos or Philodendron full and compact, it is best to prune back long stems before they start to lose older leaves. Every month or so, select the longest vine and cut it back to within a few inches of the soil. The long stem won't be missed, but new growth will soon emerge in the center of the plant and grow out from there. The pruned off vine can be rooted in water (See section on Propagation below).

When pruning, always cut the stems just above where the leaf stem attaches to the vine. The purpose is to avoid leaving a long unattractive stub above the leaf.

Many folks like to have very long stems that trail up and over windows, picture frames or across desks and floors. This is reminiscent of the way these vines grow in nature. In nature, however, the vines put out roots along their stems and permanently attach themselves to moist soil and damp tree bark. That doesn't happen indoors, so trying to duplicate it with your potted vining plants eventually fails. At a certain length, the plant can no longer support any new leaves. So the older leaves start to yellow and die. That is when those gorgeous long vines start to look like scrawny strings with a few end leaves. It is best to reserve that viney jungle look for the jungle, not your home or office!

Propagating

Pothos and Philodendron cuttings root quite readily in water. Shorter cuttings with fewer than six leaves do best although much longer stems will also root pretty easily. Remove the lowest leaf from the cutting. The bump (called a node) where the leaf stem was attached to the main stem is the point where roots will develop. Thus, it is important that this node is covered with water at all times. Never let the water level of the cutting container fall below these nodes on the cuttings.

Pothos nodes

When the roots are an inch or more in length, the cuttings can then be moved to a small pot filled with damp potting mix.

If you want to start a new plant, it is best to use at least eight cuttings and even more is preferred. The reason for this is that if you start with say four cuttings, then your plant will never have more than four vines no matter how old the plant or how large the pot. So if you want a luxurious plant with a dozen or more vines, then you will have to start with at least a dozen or more cuttings potted up together in a small pot. Take as many water-rooted cuttings as you can fit into the circle of your thumb and forefinger and hold them tightly together while you insert the rooted ends into a 4-inch pot and fill in the pot with potting mix with your free hand. Keep the soil evenly moist and the rooted cuttings in a warm, well-lit location.

Hanging, Spreading & Climbing

These vining plants can be hung so that the vines trail down over the edges of the pot. Keep the vines out of reach of toddlers and pets that may find them fascinating. Philodendron and Pothos are mildly toxic to pets and people when ingested.

Pothos and Philodendron can also be placed on tables or shelves or windowsills with vines spilling over across these surfaces.

Many folks like to get their long Pothos and Philodendron vines to climb onto trellises and poles. In fact, Pothos are sometimes sold in pots that have a pole in the center with vines attached to these poles. This is called a "totem" form. In nature, when stem nodes (see section on Propagation above) are in contact with constantly moist soil or tree bark, the nodes develop into aerial roots that attach themselves to the tree bark. These aerial roots allow the vines to climb ever higher in the rainforest environment. Unfortunately, duplicating this in the home environment is nearly impossible because we don't ordinarily have constantly damp surfaces on which the vines can attach and climb. Long vines can be wrapped around a pole or trellis, but they will never develop aerial roots and affix themselves permanently.

Other Philodendron Species

There are many other Philodendron species that are commonly available and don't look at all like the heart-leafed Philodendron that I have described in this chapter. Most of the other popular Philodendron species have large leaves that come in a variety of shapes

Philodendron Selloum grows from a single main stem that may be several inches thick and that sprouts very long aerial roots that will wander out of the pot and across the room if not redirected. These long aerial roots serve no useful purpose for a potted Selloum, so you can cut them off without damaging the plant.

Philodendron Xanadu

There are many varieties of so-called "elephant ears" Philodendrons. The name refers to the shape of the leaves. Some of these varieties have purple or red undersides and green tops while others have a completely maroon or bronze color.

Other Philodendron varieties have long, pointy leaves, while others have fiddle-shaped leaves and still others have leaves with a rippled or quilted texture. Most of these are hybrids and new shapes, sizes and colors come on the market regularly.

All of the many Philodendron species have the same general cultural requirements — bright indirect light, evenly moist soil, and relatively small pots — as described above.

Monstera deliciosa is often called "split-leafed Philodendron," although it is not technically a Philodendron. It is a vining plant that does not do well when contained in a pot, becoming quite unruly unless pruned regularly. It's care requirements are similar to most other Philodendron species.

Ponytail Palm
(Beaucarnea recurvata)

This popular and unusual looking plant looks something like a palm tree, but the Ponytail Palm is not a Palm at all. In fact, it is related to the Yucca and both are in the Lily family. Yes, like all Lilies, a Ponytail Palm will flower, but that is rare when it is kept as an indoor plant.

Young Ponytails have small, swollen bases that will swell into large, bark-covered, aboveground bulbs as they age. It is this swollen bulb that gives the Ponytail its unique appearance. The swollen base allows the Ponytail to store water during periods of drought in its native habitat of Mexico.

This is a low maintenance plant that thrives more on neglect. Too much water, unnecessary repotting and poor light must be avoided for the Ponytail to do well.

Light

Ponytail Palms do best in a sunny window with lots of direct sun. In direct sun, they will grow rapidly and the leaves will be thick and sturdy.

However, Ponytails will survive quite nicely in bright indirect light, such as on a north windowsill or even under bright fluorescent lights. In this reduced light, the growth will be almost imperceptible and the leaves will be thinner, more graceful, and a deeper green in color.

Although the Ponytail is adaptable to a wide range of light, it is best to pick one location for yours and leave it there. Changing its light location is stressful and will weaken your Ponytail.

Pot Size

Maintaining your Ponytail in a small pot is of critical importance. In general, there should be no more than a half-inch of space between the widest part of the base bulb and the edge of the pot.

Many folks think this is too small for the fat bulb, but it is not. In addition, Ponytails are typically grown in shallow pots or planters because they have shallow roots that do not require deep pots.

A small pot is important because small pots do not retain water for long and it is most important that Ponytail soil dry out quickly after each watering. Remember, this plant comes from arid regions where rain is infrequent. It is adapted to withstand drought, but it cannot withstand constantly moist soil.

Water

Watering a Ponytail Palm can be tricky and the stakes are high if you get it wrong. The soil must be very porous and should dry out about half way down into the pot every week or two. If you don't allow this deep drying out to occur, the roots will gradually rot and die. You won't see any evidence of this root rot until it is too late. This is because the Ponytail will be able to live on the water stored in its bulb long after the roots have rotted and stopped delivering water to the plant.

Okay, have I scared you into avoiding watering this plant too frequently? I hope so!

Because there is little space between the bulb and the edge of the pot, it is difficult to get your finger down in deep enough to tell if the soil is dry. You may want to get a soil probe such as Soil Sleuth (available at http://www.soilsleuth.com/) or a plain wood dowel that you can stick into the soil to make a determination as to how dry the soil is about halfway down into the pot.

This is a bit complicated in the beginning, but after a while you will get a pretty good sense as to how often it takes for the soil to dry out properly after a thorough watering. Lifting the pot and feeling the weight just before and just after is another method of determining when the soil is appropriately dry.

Some people wait until the bulb feels a bit soft before watering. I think this may cause you to wait longer than is ideal for a healthy plant. In addition, a Ponytail that is dying from root rot may also start to shrivel similarly.

When you do water, water slowly all around the bulb until a bit of water starts to run through the drainage holes. Drainage holes are a must for this plant.

Temperature & Humidity

Temperature and humidity are not problems for Ponytail Palms as they tolerate a wide range for both.

If you like to move your Ponytail outside it will survive temperatures as low as 20°F, although growth will slow dramatically in colder temperatures. This is a good plant to use in a room that is on the cool or drafty side as long as there is adequate light.

Because the Ponytail is native to arid regions, it does very well in the low humidity of our winter-heated homes.

Fertilizer

Ponytails come from regions where the soil is not rich. Therefore, they do not require a lot of minerals or fertilizer. Fertilize sparingly at half the label recommended rate, but only when it is growing vigorously. Any complete fertilizer will suffice.

Pests

Ponytail Palms are relatively pest-resistant, but you do need to watch for mealybugs hiding in the crevices where the leaves attach to the central stem. Pull the leaves downward a bit so you can peer in these crevices and spot these critters early.

If you do find mealybugs, spray them with a solution of 1 part rubbing alcohol, 5 parts plain water and a squirt of liquid soap. If your spray is thorough, a single treatment is often sufficient.

See Chapter 10 for more information on identifying and treating plant pests.

Pruning and Trimming

Ponytails usually grow with a single stem and do not branch. They start small and grow slowly so their height rarely becomes a problem making pruning unnecessary.

If your Ponytail does grow too tall or if you want to experiment with getting multiple stems or "heads," then you can cut off the top. You may then get one or more stems growing from a point just below where you make the cut. This may also trigger the emergence of offsets or baby plants from the bulb.

Ponytails need to be trimmed more than they need to be pruned. It is quite normal for older leaves to develop brown tips as they age. To keep your Ponytail looking nice, use scissors to trim off these brown ends as they develop. This trimming will have no effect on the health of the plant. It will only make it look nicer.

Likewise, older leaves will, eventually yellow and die as newer leaves on top replace them. Once a leaf is more then half discolored or has been trimmed back by more than half, then it is best to remove the entire leaf.

Repotting

As with overwatering, unnecessary repotting can be fatal and must be avoided. Ponytails rarely need repotting and certainly should never be repotted right after they are acquired.

Ponytails are very susceptible to root rot and too much soil in a too-large pot will promote root rot. The soil needs to dry out at least halfway down to the bottom of the pot in between thorough waterings. If this drying out process takes more than three days, then your Ponytail Palm does not need a larger pot — even if it looks like it does.

If you determine that your Ponytail really does need a larger pot because it is drying out thoroughly every few days, then the new pot should be no more than one inch wider than the width of the ponytail bulb at its widest part. Ponytails are usually potted in shallow pots. If yours is now in a shallow pot relative to its width, then you should maintain those pot proportions when you repot.

Use a porous, soilless, peat-based potting mix. Mix about two-thirds of the potting mix with one-third perlite or sand. This porous potting mix will help discourage root rot. Avoid using any potting mixes that have moisture-retaining additives and do not tamp the soil down too hard into the new pot. Add no more than a half-inch of soil to the bottom of the new pot and do not add any soil to the top of the existing rootball, even if you see some exposed roots.

Remedy for Root Rot

If you suspect root rot, take the following steps:

1. Carefully remove the plant from its pot.

2. Look for healthy (whitish, firm) roots within the rootball. If they are plentiful, then there is no root rot and no further remedy is required.

3. If you find few or no healthy roots, then gently remove the soil and discard it.

4. Feel the lower portion of the Ponytail bulb. If it is soft and squishy or if the bark peels away easily, then your Ponytail cannot be saved. Sorry.

5. If there are a few healthy roots remaining and the bulb is still moderately firm, then it may be possible to re-root it.

6. Use a shallow pot just slightly wider then the bulb and fill it two-thirds with a damp, porous mix of half peat moss and half perlite.

7. Set the base of the bulb on top of the damp potting mix.

If you follow all of the above steps, new roots may very slowly regenerate over the course of many months. Patience is a necessary requirement here, and there is no guarantee of success.

Propagation

In general, this is a plant that you cannot propagate by cuttings or by division. Sometimes older plants will spontaneously produce offsets or baby plants attached to the large bulb. After these offsets are about two inches in height, they can be severed and rooted in a small pot filled with damp potting mix. This is a risky and a slow process, so you may be better off just leaving the offsets attached to the main plant and let them grow from there.

Bonsai

Ponytails Palms are often sold as Bonsais. In most cases they are not terribly old and should not be too expensive. However, unlike many other non-tropical Bonsais, the Ponytail is tropical and will do well as an indoor Bonsai.

Do not attempt to repot your Ponytail Bonsai. It was deliberately miniaturized so that it will stay in its Bonsai planter forever. If it truly outgrows its planter, then you will have to learn how to root prune so it can be kept in the same pot. See page 125 to learn how to care for Bonsai plants.

Rubber Plant
Ficus elastica

Rubber plants have been a popular indoor plant for a very long time. They are relatively undemanding and have unusually large, thick, leather-like leaves. Some of the Rubber Plant hybrids available today have deep burgundy leaves that look almost black and other hybrids are variegated with a mix of green and white leaves.

The Rubber Plant is a close relative of the popular Ficus Tree (*Ficus benjamina*) and Fiddle-leafed Fig (*Ficus lyrata*). The Rubber Plant is a little less demanding than its relatives.

Like all members of the Ficus family, *Ficus elastica* has a white sap that flows readily when a stem or leaf is cut. Although this white sap has been used to make latex, the primary source of latex is the Pará rubber tree (*Hevea brasiliensis*), which is in the Euphorbia family and also emits a white sap.

Light

Rubber Plants can adapt to moderately low light, but they do best with lots of natural sunlight. Try to place your Rubber Plant as close to your sunniest window as possible to encourage more vigorous growth. At a minimum, you should locate it within 5 feet of a south or west window and even closer to an east or north window. You can supplement natural light with a compact fluorescent flood light above your Rubber Plant.

In low light, growth will be very slow, new leaves may be smaller and the stem space between the leaves will be elongated. Variegated varieties may revert to all green in low light.

Water

If your Rubber Plant is properly potted (see Repotting below), then it is best to water it as soon as the top half-inch of soil feels dry. In low light, it is better to allow the top quarter of the soil to dry out before watering thoroughly. Don't allow the pot to sit in water for more than a couple of hours. Rubber Plants are more forgiving of watering lapses than most indoor plants.

However, if you consistently under water a Rubber Plant, you will find leaf edges turning brown and lower leaves will yellow and fall off prematurely. Overwatering will cause the roots to rot and the plant will languish, developing dull yellow leaves that fall.

Repotting

Over time, Rubber Plants develop very thick roots that start to show through the surface soil and smaller roots that may creep out of drainage holes. Surprisingly, this does not necessarily mean the plant needs a bigger pot. If there is enough soil in the pot to keep the roots properly moist for at least three days between thorough waterings, then it is usually best to leave the roots undisturbed in the existing pot. Wandering roots can be cut off where they emerge from drainage holes. Surface roots can be covered with a light soil, peat moss or a top dressing such as Spanish moss.

If your Rubber Plant is so potbound that it requires water every few days, then it is appropriate to move it into a pot one size larger. See Chapter 1 on how to repot properly.

Temperature & Humidity

Rubber Plants are quite tolerant of cool temperatures as low as 40°F, if the temperatures drop gradually. Normal home temperatures are fine for a Rubber Plant, although it should be protected from very cold drafts from open doors and windows.

Rubber Plants are unaffected by low humidity.

Fertilizer

Rubber Plants are not particularly heavy feeders. If yours is in low light, the growth rate will be slow and growth cannot be forced with fertilizer. In low light, it is best to skip fertilizing altogether. In good light, fertilize your Rubber Plant monthly at half the recommended label strength as long as the plant is growing vigorously. Fertilizer is not medicine and should not be used to treat plant problems.

Pruning

Healthy Rubber Plants can quickly outgrow their spaces because of their rigid stems and large leaves. It is best to prune a Rubber Plant back before it is really obvious that it is too large for its space. It can be pruned at any time of the year. Any stem or branch can be cut back and new growth will soon emerge just below the point on the stem where you make the pruning cut. So prune back to the point where you would like to see new growth emerge. Pruning will help eliminate leggy stems that have lost lower leaves and help keep your plant looking fuller and more compact.

When you prune, be prepared to staunch the free flow of white sap. The sight of this might make you think you have permanently damaged the plant, but you haven't. The sap flow will stop on its own, but it will stop sooner if you put a damp piece of paper towel or cloth over the wound.

The sap is a skin irritant so you may want to use gloves when pruning a Ficus and be very careful not to get the sap near your eyes.

Propagation

Rubber Plants can be propagated by using tip stem cuttings. A tip cutting has a green, non-woody stem with no more then 4–6 leaves. Older, larger cuttings with woody stems do not root as readily as tip cuttings. Let the cuttings heal over night in the air, then insert them into a small pot filled with a porous potting mix of 2 parts peat moss and 1 part Perlite. Keep this mix damp, provide bright indirect light and warm temperatures and you should have some healthy roots within 4–6 weeks.

Larger stem cuttings can be propagated by air layering. See Chapter 12 to learn how to air layer.

Branching

Some Rubber Plants branch more freely than others. Although pruning will sometimes promote branching of stems, in general there is not much you can do to make your Rubber Plant develop branches.

Pests

Another reason for the popularity of Rubber Plants is their general resistance to plant pests.

Occasionally scale insects and mealybugs may infest a Rubber Plant, but that is not common. If soil quality is poor or if the soil is kept too moist, then fungus gnats may become a problem. See Chapter 10 for information on identifying and treating plant pests.

Schefflera
Schefflera arboricola and *Schefflera actinophylla*

Schefflera arboricola in bloom

Schefflera arboricola in bud

This popular indoor plant is commonly called Umbrella Tree because of the way that the individual leaflets fan out from the top of the leaf stem much like the spokes on an umbrella.

Although there are many species of Schefflera, the two used most frequently as indoor plants are the *Schefflera actinophylla* and the *Schefflera arboricola*. The former has large leaves about six inches in length and thick, tree-like trunks. The latter is more shrub-like and has much smaller leaves less than three inches in length. Although their care is similar, there are differences that I will note below, referring to each by its proper botanical name.

Light

Scheffleras are often promoted and sold as low light plants, but they are not true low-light plants.

They do best with lots of bright indirect light all day long. Right in front of and close to a north or east facing window is best. A few hours of direct sun falling directly on the leaves is okay, but too much direct sun will cause the deep green leaves to fade to a paler shade of green. If the light is inadequate, lower leaves will drop off and new growth will be small and spindly.

In office environments, Scheffleras will do well without natural light if they are under fluorescent lights directly overhead and those lights are kept on for at least eight hours every day.

S. *Arboricola* will react much more swiftly to inadequate light than S. *Actinophylla*. Sudden loss of many lower leaves when an Arboricola is relocated is a common problem.

If you decide to purchase a large Schefflera, try to find a *Schefflera actinophylla* 'Amate.' The Amate variety has been bred to hold up better in reduced light, is resistant to spider mites and has thick, deep green leaves that are much more attractive than the S. Actinophylla species. The Amate variety may be a bit more expensive, but it is worth the money because it is far less fragile and a far better-looking plant.

Arboricolas come with all green leaves or with variegated green and yellow leaves. As with most plants, the variegated type requires a bit more light than the all-green variety. So if you are not sure if you have enough light, avoid the variegated variety.

Pot Size

Scheffleras do not like to have their roots disturbed and the Arboricola is particularly sensitive to unnecessary repotting. The plastic nursery pot that your Schefflera is grown in may not be very attractive, but it is almost always the right-sized pot. So resist the urge to repot your new Schefflera for at least six months while it settles into its new home. If you don't want to look at the plastic nursery pot, then get a better looking planter that is large enough to accommodate the nursery

Exposed surface roots of Schefflera

pot. This double-potting allows you to hide the ugly plastic pot without disturbing the plant and without having to get your hands dirty.

It is a rare Arboricola that ever needs repotting. Older Actinophyllas will outgrow their pots and may need to be moved up one pot size when the soil no longer stays moist for more than a couple of days after a thorough watering. By then, the rootball will be a nearly solid mass of roots. A few roots wandering out of the drainage holes are not necessarily an indication that a larger pot is required. See Chapter 1 for further information on repotting.

Water

Watering Scheffleras, especially Arboricolas can be tricky. If it is not done correctly, your Schefflera can deteriorate quickly. If your Schefflera is healthy and well-rooted (not over potted as described above), then it is best to water thoroughly from the top as soon as the top half-inch of soil feels dry to the touch. If your plant has just barely enough light, then it is best to let the soil dry a bit deeper into the pot before watering.

If the pot size and light are in order, then the soil should reach the appropriate level of dryness about once per week. If it takes much longer than a week for the soil to dry out, then check to be sure the pot is not sitting in excess water. This may also be an indication that it is not getting enough light.

If the soil dries out appropriately within 4 to 7 days, then that is fine as long as you remember to water it as soon as it is appropriately dry. If it needs water every day or two after a thorough watering, then it is probably time to move it into a pot one size larger.

Arboricolas are particularly fussy and unforgiving about improper watering. If you let them get a bit too dry or keep them a bit too moist, they will quickly drop lots of lower leaves and you will soon end up with a very leggy plant When the soil is kept too moist, the roots will start to rot and you may lose the entire plant. With under watering, you will get lots of yellow leaves, but the plant will survive. So if you are unsure, it is best to err on the side of dryness.

Large well-established Scheffleras are much more tolerant of watering lapses.

Pruning Leggy Plants

Schefflera arboricolas almost invariably get leggy as time passes. They are by nature more shrub-like than tree-like. As the individual stems grow taller, they drop lower leaves as they add new ones on top. Even healthy, well-cared for Arboricolas get leggy after a while. There is only one solution to this problem and that is pruning.

Pruning is the plant care technique that is most commonly avoided for a variety of reasons. But if you want to keep your Arboricola looking full and compact, learning to prune is essential.

Once you overcome your inhibitions, pruning an Arboricola is quite simple. Any stem that is tall and leggy can be cut back at any point along that stem. New growth will then emerge starting just below that point on the stem and grow upward from there. So if a stem has 18 inches of bare stem and a few inches of leaves at the very top, then cut that stem down to a height of 3 to 6 inches. The top few inches of the pruned-off stem can be rooted in moist soil or water to make new plants. You can prune back one or two stems selectively over time or you can prune all of them off at one time.

Pruning larger tree-like Scheffleras is more a matter of keeping them from outgrowing their spaces. Large stems can be pruned back to any height. New growth will appear just below the pruning point and grow upward from there. So be sure to prune back far enough so there is plenty of new growing room.

Pests

Schefflera actinophylla is particularly susceptible to spider mites. Scale and mealybugs also find Schefflera species to their liking. As mentioned above, the 'Amate' variety is most pest resistant and that makes it a good choice for those who don't want to deal with insect pest problems.

Otherwise, the best prevention is vigilance. Read Chapter 10 to learn how to identify the tell-tale signs of these plant pests. Inspect the leaves and stems carefully for these pests before you purchase a plant. After purchase, be sure to check your plant at least monthly for pests and treat them promptly and thoroughly. My pest chapter explains safe and effective ways to deal with any pests that may show up on your indoor plants.

Temperature and Humidity

Scheffleras are all tropical in origin. As tropical plants they need protection from cold. Temperatures in the 60°F to 80°F range are ideal, although Scheffleras will survive temperatures in the 40s if those temperatures are introduced gradually. Sudden exposure to cold temperatures or freezing drafts will cause leaves to turn soft and black. If the roots are not damaged by cold, the plant will usually recover. Very high temperatures can be tolerated by Scheffleras for short periods as long as the soil and roots get lots of water to compensate for the evaporative loss of water from the soil and through the leaves.

Normal household humidity levels are fine for Scheffleras. They have proven to do well even in heated indoor environments where humidity levels are desert-dry. Increased humidity will help deter spider mites somewhat, but otherwise, humidity levels are not an import consideration for Scheffleras.

Fertilizer

Fertilizer is not medicine so never use it on ailing plants. If your Schefflera is healthy and growing vigorously and has not had soil added in at least year, then any complete fertilizer applied at half-strength once per month is appropriate, but not essential. Read Chapter 8 to learn more on why fertilizing is over-rated.

Propagation

Scheffleras are not the easiest plants to propagate, but they are hardly impossible. Arboricolas require regular pruning anyway, so you may as well take a shot at propagating the pruned off portions unless your spouse is already complaining that you have too many plants!

Arboricolas have thinner stems so they are easier to propagate than thick stemmed Actinophylla. Use Arboricola cuttings that are about 5 to 6 inches in length with 2–3 inches of bare stem to be inserted in damp potting mix or plain water. Larger cuttings with older stems do not root as readily as young, green tip-cuttings. Inserting the cuttings inside of a plastic "tent" increases the chances of success. Chapter 12 explains this technique in greater detail.

To propagate large, thick stemmed cuttings from *S. Actinophylla*, it is best to use a technique called air layering. This technique is also described in detail in Chapter 12.

Even if you do everything right, the propagation success rate is not much more than 50 percent, so don't get discouraged if you fail the first few times.

Snake Plant
Sansevieria

Sansevieria in rectangular planter

The Sansevieria is commonly known as a Snake Plant or somewhat disparagingly as the Mother-in-Law's Tongue. This slender upright plant has a reputation as being virtually indestructible and an easy plant for anyone to keep alive in any conditions.

Unfortunately, the conventional wisdom about this common houseplant is mostly wrong. Indeed, it is a plant that thrives on neglect, but other than that the conventional wisdom is mostly inaccurate. If you have failed with this plant it is not because you have a black thumb, but because you were not given good information about how to care for it.

258 Don't Repot That Plant!

Light

The Sansevieria is *not* a good low light plant, although plant books and plant retailers often describe it as such. If you keep this plant in low light it will do just fine for about a year or maybe two. Then it will gradually fall apart and leave you with a mess of stinking leaves. I mean stinking because when the roots and stems of this plant start to rot or die, the odor is very unpleasant! So if you want a low light plant that will live for many years, the Snake Plant is *not* a good choice. (See Chapter 4 for better low light plant selections.)

The more light a Sansevieria receives, the better it does. At a minimum it must have bright indirect light all day long, such as you get on a north windowsill. Better yet, place it in a sunny window where direct sun is abundant.

Water

As with most succulents, the Sansevieria does best when the soil is allowed to dry out very deep into its pot. It can easily withstand drought, but cannot tolerate soil that is evenly moist. Keeping the soil constantly moist is the surest way to kill this plant, so resist the urge to water this plant more than once or twice per month. Larger plants can easily go a month or more between waterings and tightly potted smaller plants should go two weeks without water. Water thoroughly but allow the plant's soil to dry out about three-quarters of the way down before watering again. Once a week will most likely be too often, but it will depend on light, moisture and temperature.

Not allowing the soil to dry out deep enough into the pot is the most common problem people have with his plant. Excessive moisture will cause stems to rot at the soil line and emit an obnoxious odor when pulled out.

Pot Size

Keeping your Snake Plant very potbound is the key to its longevity. A potbound Snake Plant is one that will dry out quickly and prevent inadvertent overwatering. If you move this plant to a larger pot, the excess soil will retain water for a time long enough to start rotting the roots. When you purchase a Snake Plant look for one that is *very* potbound.

New growth emerges from below the soil. Each leaf quickly grows to its maximum height and stays that way indefinitely. Eventually, the pot becomes filled with an abundance of leaves crowded together. This crowding will not harm the plant. When it becomes so crowded that the underground rhizomes (roots) are starting to distort the shape of the plastic pot, then is the time to consider moving it to a pot one size larger. At this point it may be necessary to crack or cut through the pot in order to remove the plant.

When you repot, use a potting mix that has extra sand or perlite. The aim is to provide more room for the roots but not a soil mix that retains water for a long time. For more information on repotting see Chapter 1.

Toughness

Not only does the Sansevieria thrive on neglectful watering, it is also very pest resistant, and is not bothered by heat or cold drafts, but do keep it above 45°F. It also does well in very dry air and requires little or no fertilizer. So in many ways this is not a fussy plant, although that hardly means it is indestructible.

Flowers

Surprisingly, the Snake Plant flowers quite readily when tightly potted and given lots of light. Although this plant is in the Lily family, its flowers are much smaller and don't make a great display. But these flowers are a sure sign of a healthy and happy plant.

Propagation

You can propagate your Sansevieria by division or by leaf cuttings. Don't attempt to divide the roots unless your plant is healthy and quite potbound. To divide your Snake Plant, get a sturdy, sharp knife and slice through the rootball from top to bottom. You will cut through some roots and rhizomes, but don't worry about that. This is a tough plant and can survive your slicing.

After doing a root division, move the sections into the smallest pots that they will fit into. Remember this is a plant that thrives when potbound, so keep it tight and use a porous potting mix with extra sand or perlite.

Healthy leaf sections can also be used to propagate Snake Plants. Insert several 2 to 3-inch leaf sections into a pot filled with a damp porous potting mix. Keep it warm (above 70°F) and in bright light. Try to keep the soil barely damp. In time, new shoots will emerge from the underground rhizomes.

Snake Plants in Low Light

Although I do not recommend the Snake Plant for use in low light, I recognize that many folks acquire this plant with the misunderstanding that it will do well in low light. Assuming you already have a Snake Plant and do not have good light for it, here are some suggestions for prolonging its life. First, do not repot or fertilize it. Second, water very sparingly. That means that you must allow the soil to dry out nearly all the way to the bottom of the pot. Then add just enough water so that it dries out again within about two weeks. Remember, Snake Plants use very little water when in low light.

Succulents

Succulents   Sedum

The term succulent is not the name of a particular plant. It is a descriptive term used to identify a wide range of plants that generally have soft, fleshy stems and leaves that store water. Cacti are succulents, but so are lots of other plant species. Most succulents come from arid regions of the world so they have small, root systems and the ability to withstand long periods of drought. In addition, most succulents tend to grow in open areas where there is lots of direct sunlight.

Although some succulents grow quite tall, most sold as indoor plants are quite small and can be used successfully in locations that have limited space.

Because there are so many varieties of succulents with unusual physical characteristics, I think of them as being like snowflakes — each one unique.

Many succulents are sold in small dish gardens with a variety of different species planted together in a shallow planter. These plants grow slowly and have small root systems so there is no good reason to separate these individual plants.

Identification

Many succulents are sold without proper identifying labels and retail clerks often do not know succulent plant names. Here is a list of broad categories of succulent species that are most commonly sold: Cactus, Aloe, Sansevieria, Sedum Echeveria, Kalanchoe, Euphorbia, Crassula (including the popular Jade Plant),

Sempervivum, Agave, Haworthia, Pachypodium, and Lithops. This is not a complete list, but a starting point in helping you identify the species name of your succulent.

Roots

Nearly all succulents have fine and somewhat fragile root networks. This root structure helps them absorb maximum moisture from short, infrequent rains in their native habitats. The roots absorb moisture quickly from the poor sandy soil they grow in and move the water to the fleshy stems and leaves where it is stored until the next rainfall. Succulent roots can withstand drought, but rot very easily.

Soil

Succulents grow in arid regions where the soil is thin and gritty or sandy. Cacti grow in deserts and many other succulents grow in tiny crevices of rock formations where a bit of soil or sand has accumulated. Succulents have adapted to survive on infrequent rain and in soil that has few nutrients. Standard potting soils that usually have a peat moss base to absorb and retain moisture are not appropriate for succulents. A Cactus potting mix works well for most succulents.

Repotting

Because of the nature of their root systems, succulents are almost always grown in small pots and almost never need to be repotted. Indeed, the less the fragile roots are disturbed, the healthier your succulent will be. If you don't like the appearance of the plastic nursery pot, insert that pot inside a more attractive planter that is large enough to accommodate the plant and its nursery pot. Avoid disturbing the roots. For more information on repotting see Chapter 1.

Water

Most succulents thrive on water neglect, but will not tolerate soil that stays constantly moist. Many succulents will go a month or even longer without water. Allow the soil to dry at least halfway deep into the pot before watering. If leaves start to shrivel a bit, that may be a sign that your succulent is ready for water. But, if in doubt, it is always best to wait. Succulents may shrivel and lose some leaves in extended periods of dryness, but they will revive when watered.

However, roots damaged by constantly damp soil will die and never recover. Succulents can also tolerate hard water better than most plant species. That is because they are from areas where the mineral content of soils is naturally quite high.

Light

Succulents thrive on sunny indoor windowsills. Although some can adapt to and survive for a long time in low light, it is always preferable to provide as much light as possible.

Temperature & Humidity

It is probably not surprising that succulents are adapted to desert dry air. However, it may surprise you to learn that most succulents can survive temperatures close to freezing and some can tolerate light frost. Many succulents grow in rocky areas high in the mountains where there is lots of sun, dry air and cool temperatures at night. If you have a cold or drafty windowsill, a succulent might be a good choice.

Fertilizer

Succulents are slow growers and use very little nutrients. A very dilute standard fertilizer applied no more than a couple of times each year is more than adequate. Make sure the fertilizer is not intended for acid-loving plants.

Pests

Mealybugs are the most common pest problem for succulents. They appear as tiny bits of white, cotton-like substance on leaf and stem surfaces. Spray the plant thoroughly with a solution of water, alcohol and dish soap to treat mealybugs. Scale insects are less common, but are treated similarly. Chapter 10 provides detailed information on identifying and treating these indoor plant pests.

Propagation

It is hard to generalize about propagating succulents. Some push out offsets or small baby plants at the base of the main plant (Sedum, Lithops). Other succulents with stems and branches (Jade, Kalanchoe, and Euporbia) can be propagated by stem cuttings. And still others (Aloe, Sedum, and Sansevieria) can be propagated by leaf cuttings. When taking a leaf or stem cuttings from a succulent plant, allow the cut section to heal over in open air for about 24 hours before inserting the cut end upright in a small pot filled with damp cactus mix potting soil.

Flowering

Most succulents will flower if given lot of sunlight, cool temps and kept in the same pot for a long time. However, most succulent flowers are not particularly attractive and can be cut off at any time.

Yucca
Yucca elephantipes

The Yucca cane is often mistaken for the more common Corn Plant or *Dracaena massangeana* cane. Both have the same sturdy canes or trunks and a tall, slender profile.

Unlike the low light Corn Plant, the Yucca is a sun lover and does best in front of a sunny window. Yucca leaves are stiff, very pointed and have serrated edges that are surprisingly sharp. This is not a good plant if there are rambunctious children or pets about as the leaf edges can cause nasty cuts and the leaf tips can easily poke an eye.

'Canes'

The Yucca is often sold in the cane form. This refers to the very thick, bark-covered trunks of staggered heights that are rooted in soil and have foliage only at their tops. In tropical regions, Yuccas grow as tall trees with bare trunks, much like Coconut Palms.

Nurseries cut these tall trees down and chop them into one, two, three and four-foot long sections. These leafless sections or canes are then rooted by positioning them upright in damp potting material. The top ends are sometimes sealed with wax to prevent fungal infections prevalent in very damp tropical environments. As the damp potting material triggers root growth, bright direct sunlight promotes secondary stems with leaves to sprout from the tops of the canes.

Although the canes can be rooted individually, it is customary to put multiple canes of staggered heights in the same pot. This creates a single potted plant with leaves at staggered heights. Although the individual canes can be separated, doing so would defeat this purpose. Separating them also stresses them and I don't recommend trying it, for any reason.

The thick canes never grow taller or thicker. All future growth is in the secondary stems that sprout from the tops of the canes. These secondary stems can grow much taller than the canes, however. If you want to shorten or propagate this plant, you cut the secondary stems, never the thick canes. (See section on Propagation below). Although it is possible to saw through the canes and root them as nurseries do, it is very difficult to do outside of a carefully controlled nursery or greenhouse environment. That is why I recommend using only stem, not cane, cuttings to propagate more plants.

Light

Yuccas require much more light than Corn Plants so if you do not have a bright window to locate your Yucca, then a Corn Plant would be a better choice for you. Yuccas grow weak and spindly when they are not exposed to moderately strong direct sunlight. That means they need to be located within a couple of feet of a completely uncovered window that is not shaded by a tree or tall building nearby. Artificial light can supplement a Yucca, but these plants need natural light as well. Whereas a Corn Plant will burn when exposed to direct sunlight, the Yucca will thrive in locations where the rays of the sun fall directly on its foliage. In direct sun, Yucca leaves will be thicker and angle upward. In reduced light, the foliage is softer and arches downward.

Water

Yuccas have stronger root systems than Corn Plants. That means they are more forgiving of improper watering. In good light, a Yucca should be watered thoroughly as soon as the surface of the soil feels very dry. In less than ideal light, allow the soil to dry about an inch or so deep into the pot before watering.

This is a plant that can withstand drought quite well, although brown leaf tips may develop when watered improperly.

Symptoms

Brown tips on leaves are common. If the tipping is minor and limited to the lower leaves, then it is not a cause for concern. If it is more extensive, then it is probably a water related problem. Dry brown tips usually indicate excessive drying of the soil or an abundance of minerals in the soil caused by using hard water or too much fertilizer. (Someone will advise you that low humidity is the cause, but that is not true.) If the tips are very dark — almost black in color — then keeping the soils too moist is the likely problem. Lack of good light can also cause this symptom. Inadequate light and keeping the soil too moist often go hand-in-hand. Discolored leaf tips can be trimmed off with sharp scissors at an angle so that the original outline of the leaf is maintained.

Leaning Canes

Yucca canes sometimes start to lean noticeably. If so, don't up-pot for support because that doesn't work. Simply push the leaning cane to a vertical position and tamp the soil down tightly around the base of the cane to hold it in place.

Pot Size

The Yucca rarely needs repotting. An unnecessarily large pot will keep the soil too moist for too long and rot the roots. That is fatal. If the soil dries a quarter of the way deep into the pot every 2- 3 days after a thorough watering, then it may need a pot one size larger. Otherwise, leave the pot size and the roots alone.

Fertilizer

Yuccas are not heavy feeders and excess fertilizers build up in the soil and cause leaf tip burn. If your Yucca has been in the same pot for several years and is healthy and growing vigorously, then fertilize it three or four times per year but at half the dilution rate listed on the label. (See Chapter 8 for more detail on fertilizing your potted plants).

Water Quality

Yuccas are vulnerable to foliage damage when irrigated with hard water. If your tap water is hard, use distilled, filtered or rainwater as an alternative. The normal amount of chlorine and fluoride added to tap water will cause no harm, but hard water and water treated with softening agents will.

Pruning

In time Yuccas can become leggy looking or too tall for their space. You can cut these too tall secondary stems back to a shorter length, but leave at least one to two inches of secondary stem above the cane from which they will grow. New growth will emerge on the cut stem just below where you make the cut and grow upwards from there.

Propagation

The pruned off stems (see above) can be rooted in plain water or in a small pot filled with damp, porous soil. Trim the lower portion of the stem cutting so that it is no more than 2 to 4 inches below the lowest leaves.

Pests

Yuccas are quite pest resistant. Occasionally, mealybugs or scale insects are attracted to Yuccas. Both of tense pets can be treated with a solution of 1 part rubbing alcohol, 5 parts of water and a squirt of liquid soap. Be sure to drench all leaf and stem surfaces of the entire plant to be sure you get all of the critters, including the ones you cannot see. More information is available in Chapter 10.

Removing Dead Canes

It sometimes happens that one or two of the shorter canes in a single pot gradually die back. This often occurs because the shorter canes are shaded by the taller canes and do not receive enough light. If all of the foliage dies on a cane, then it will not recover and it is best for appearance's sake to remove the dead cane. Grasp the dead cane firmly and twist it in place until it spins freely. Then pull it up and out of the pot. It will come out cleanly without spilling soil or disturbing the roots of the other canes. Fill in the vacated hole by pressing in the surrounding soil. Sometimes a new shoot will emerge right at the soil line and attached to a dying cane.

This is usually the last gasp of the dying cane and the new shoot rarely survives. You may want to try cutting it off from the cane and rooting it in a very small pot with a porous potting mix.

Conclusion

The Yucca is a good plant because it fits in tight spaces, especially corners. However, it must receive good natural sunlight and be located close to an uncovered window. Be careful to avoid contact with sharp leaf edges and pointed leaf tips.

ZZ Plant
(Zamioculcas zamiifolia)

ZZ Plants

The ZZ Plant is the closest thing to a foolproof indoor plant. It will survive in a wide range of light conditions and it thrives on neglect, so that makes it a very practical plant for beginners, for those who believe they don't have green thumbs and for those who don't want to spend much time caring for their plant. In addition to being hardy, the ZZ Plant has an unusual, sculptural look that makes it appealing to many people who are tired of looking at the same old common houseplants. The stems are thick and tapered and the individual leaves are a shiny green color. The stems are upright and arch slightly as they mature.

ZZ are a relatively new plant — not on the planet, but as a commercially available plant. Nurseries have been growing them for fewer than 15 years so that is why it is not likely that you have inherited a ZZ Plant from your grandmother's collection!

The ZZ Plant is sold in pot sizes ranging from 6-inches to 14-inches. The smaller ZZ's are about 8 inches tall and the largest ones are about two and a half feet tall.

WARNING: The ZZ Plant is not a good plant for those who like to nurture and fuss over their plants. Keeping the soil too moist and repotting this plant unnecessarily are the two things that will cause the ZZ to fail.

What's in a name?

The botanical or scientific name for the ZZ Plant is *Zamioculcas zamiifolia*. Clearly, that is a mouthful so it has become abbreviated in the common parlance to ZZ Plant.

The ZZ Plant is a member of the Aroid family that includes Philodendron, Pothos, Peace Lily, and Chinese Evergreen, among others. Like all members of the Aroid plant family, the ZZ Plant is toxic to people and pets if ingested or chewed.

Rule No. 1: Don't Repot this plant!

When you purchase this plant, the chances are it will look like the roots are overcrowded and it needs a larger pot. In many cases the roots are exposed at the surface. Despite this appearance, ZZ Plants are best left undisturbed in their seemingly too-small pots. Plants that are very rootbound do not retain water around their roots for very long and that is important for plants that do not tolerate constantly damp soil. Repotting a ZZ Plant is an invitation to inadvertently rotting the roots, so I advise against it.

Watering

This plant comes from East Africa where there are periods of drought so it is adapted to withstand very dry soil. On the other hand, its roots are not equipped to handle soil that is moist for extended periods of time except in unusually warm conditions with good air circulation.

As a houseplant, a ZZ Plant will rarely need water more than every two weeks and some will easily go a month or more without water. ZZ plants kept in sunny locations and those in small pots will need more frequent watering than those in reduced light or in large pots.

The important thing to remember is that keeping the soil too moist by watering too frequently is the one thing that will kill this plant. So if in doubt about watering, it is better to wait.

Light

One of the great virtues of this plant is that it tolerates a wide range of light levels. It will thrive on a sunny windowsill, but it will also manage quite well in a moderately low light environment.

However, like all plants, the ZZ Plant does need at least some light bright

ZZ Plant in a 6″ pot

enough to read in comfort. In general, that means it should be within 5–6 feet of the nearest window.

The ZZ Plant is a popular office plant because it does very well under overhead fluorescent lights that are on for 8 hours per day. ZZ's do not do well under standard incandescent lights that emit light in the wrong part of the spectrum for plants to use.

In bright light, your ZZ Plant will grow more rapidly and need to be watered every two weeks or so. In low light, the growth rate will slow and monthly watering is best.

Temperature and Humidity

ZZ Plants are best kept in temperatures that are above 50°F. Hot dry air up to 85°F. is not a problem for these plants, although more frequent watering will be necessary when the it is hot and/or dry.

If you move your ZZ Plant outdoors in the warmer months, then it is best to keep it in a shaded area because outdoor light is much more intense than indoor light. Be aware of nighttime temperatures so that your ZZ is not exposed to temps below 50°F.

Fertilizer

If you never fertilized this plant, it probably would not make much difference. If you choose to fertilize, use any standard fertilizer but dilute it to half strength and apply it no more than once every two months.

Pests

The ZZ Plant is as pest resistant as any plant I am familiar with. In fact, I have yet to see any pests on one of these plants. Of course, it is always a good idea to check your plants periodically for signs of mealybugs, scale insects, aphids and spider mites. See Chapter 10 for more information on plant pests and their treatment.

Flowering

As ZZ Plants get older, they do produce flowers that many folks don't even recognize as flowers.

The flower stem emerges from the base of the plant and has a small, elongated spadix about an inch long that tends to bend over toward the ground. The flower is similar to the Chinese evergreen flower.

Flowering on this plant is an indication of good health and care. If you don't like its appearance or after it has started to dry up, simply remove it by cutting it off at its base.

Propagation

It is quite easy to get more plants from your ZZ Plant, but it will take some time. Both stem and leaf cuttings can be used to propagate your ZZ Plant.

Healthy stems can be cut off near their base and placed in a vase of plain water. After several months, roots will form near the cut end of the stem. After the roots are an inch or more in length, the rooted cutting can be moved into a very small pot fill with a porous potting mix that is a half cactus mix. It is best if you put several stem cuttings together in a single pot.

NOTE: Placing several ZZ stem cuttings in a narrow vase makes a lovely alternative to cut flowers. Although not as colorful, they will last indefinitely in plain water.

You can root individual ZZ leaves by inserting the cut end into a porous potting mix that is kept barely moist. The rooting mix should be half standard potting mix and half Cactus soil. Provide warm temps and bright indirect light for best results. I recommend rooting several leaves together in a single small pot. The rooting process is a slow one and it may be several months or more before you see signs of new growth. As long as the leaves remain firm and healthy, then you can be sure you are on the right path.

Yellow leaves

It is quite normal for some yellow leaves to develop occasionally on older stems. Simply remove them and cut back the entire stem if it yellows or loses most of its leaves.

If you notice several stems developing yellow leaves simultaneously or one right after another, then the most likely cause is over watering. However, prolonged periods of dryness can also cause this symptom. In any case, adjusting your watering routine will usually correct the problem.

Pale, Weak New Growth

If new stems have trouble supporting themselves and are a pale green in color, then you are not providing enough light. Cut off the weak stems and move your plant to a brighter location.

Pruning

The stems of older ZZ Plants sometimes start to arch over the side of the pot. There is nothing wrong with this, but you may find the plant is getting too wide for the available space or you simply may not like the way the drooping stems look. These stems can be cut off near the base.

The cuttings may root in water, but new growth will not emerge from the remaining stub left in the pot. So be sure to cut the stem close to the soil.

Summary

So there you have it. An unusual plant that you can put almost anywhere; never needs repotting; allows you to skip watering for up to a month; tolerates low humidity; doesn't need fertilizer; is pest resistant; and propagates easily.

When it comes to houseplants, it doesn't get much better than the ZZ Plant!

Index

About the Author

Will Creed, has over 35 years of professional experience caring for indoor plants in New
York City homes and offices. He is a hands-on plant care expert who has listened
to, observed and answered tens of thousands of indoor plant questions giving
him a unique understanding of the common mistakes and misunderstandings
that everyday folks have with their indoor plants.

In his early years, Will struggled with his personal plants and struggled even
more to find reliable sources of information on the care of houseplants. He now
understands that much of what passes for conventional wisdom today still dom-
inates the internet and plant care books. He hopes to remedy that in this book.
Will's knowledge does not come from the ideal growing conditions of a greenhouse or native habitats; it comes from the less-than-ideal conditions of homes
and offices.

Will is a college graduate who has taught 4th grade and worked in higher
education administration. He subsequently spent seven years working for both
small and large indoor landscaping companies in the NYC area. He started his
own company, Horticultural Help, in 1989 where he continues to perform all
plant care services himself.

After learning many professional secrets, Will started sharing his knowledge
with others in person, via the internet and in his Indoor Plant Bulletins. Every
day he spends time answering individual plant questions via the internet, email
and by phone. He does this gratis because he remembers how years ago he struggled to find detailed and reliable answers to his plant questions. Fielding plant
care questions has also enhanced his knowledge, making him a leading expert
on indoor plant care in the often difficult environments of homes and offices.

Much of his plant care wisdom is also available on his website. He continues to
respond to individual indoor plant questions.

Email: wcreed@HorticulturalHelp.com
Website: www.horticulturalhelp.com